This Happy Land

This Happy Land

William Cobbett on America
1794-1835

Molly Townsend

New European Publications

Published in the United Kingdom in 2007 by

New European Publications Limited
14-16 Carroun Road
London SW8 1JT, England

All rights reserved. No part of this publication may be reproduced, stored in a retrieval system, or transmitted, in any form or by any means, electronic, mechanical, photocopying, recording or otherwise, without the prior permission of New European Publications Limited.

This book is sold subject to the condition that it shall not, by way of trade or otherwise, be lent, re-sold, hired out or otherwise circulated without the publisher's prior consent in any form of binding or cover other than that in which it is published and without a similar condition including this condition being imposed upon the subsequent purchase.

British Library Cataloguing in Publication Data

ISBN 978-1872410708

Copyright © 2007 Molly Townsend

Typesetting by KAD

Printed and bound in Great Britain by Imprint Academic, PO Box 200, Exeter EX5 5HE UK

Contents

Introduction 1
1   Ploughboy, Pedagogue and Pamphleteer 7
2   Violations of Neutrality 31
3   Cobbett's Ugly Questions 59
4   French Decrees and British Orders 80
5   Hawks and Doves 108
6   War 1812-1814 128
7   Peace 1814-1815 152
8   The American Political Register 175
9   Exile on Long Island 209
10 Spanish America: Thomas Paine 245
11 The Monroe Doctrine 269
12 Banking, Paper Money and the National Debt 297
13 America in the 1820s: a Reappraisal 318
14 Member of Parliament 342
15 Andrew Jackson, the Greatest Benefactor of Mankind 372
Retrospect 397
Cobbett's writings referred to in the book 404
Bibliography 405
Index 410

To the gentle, generous and affectionate people of America under whose roofs I have spent some of the happiest hours of my life.

Introduction

When after the War of Independence, the Thirteen Colonies in North America embarked on the daring experiment of setting up a republic based on the ideals of liberty and equality, Britain reacted uneasily. In its diplomatic contacts with the United States, the government found itself in the humiliating position of having to deal as equals with a people who had had the temerity to rebel against and the effrontery to defeat their mother country. Furthermore, the egalitarian sentiments expressed in the Declaration of Independence were not confined to the American continent. In Britain, too, and partly inspired by the success of the American rebellion, the 1780's saw mounting dissatisfaction with the heavy burden of taxation, the unrepresentative nature of Parliament, and what one group of protestors called "the gross abuses in the expenditure of public money" by the government. Of importance also was the latent hostility of British manufacturers and traders towards the United States: for them the ending of the restrictions imposed on the former colonies' manufacturing and shipping meant an end to their near monopoly of commerce across the Atlantic.

It was, therefore, not in the interests either of the British landed classes or of the British merchant classes that the American experiment should succeed; the former feared that the example of a republican government bringing prosperity to its citizens would give impetus to the indigenous movement for a reform of the monarchical and aristocratic system of government at home; the latter saw in the prospect of a prosperous independent nation across the Atlantic a serious rival in trade.

All these considerations affected Anglo-American relations in the early years of the Republic. Although George III was coached into receiving John Adams, the first American ambassador to Great Britain, with some degree of courtesy and cordiality, the Americans soon found that fine words were not matched by deeds when it came to the implementation of the terms of the Peace Treaty which ended the War of Independence. Protests were brushed aside, promises made and not fulfilled, and procrastination ruled the day.

Britain's entry into the war against republican France in 1793, just ten years after the Peace Treaty with America, brought in its train far more serious causes of friction. It had long been established under the so-called Law of Nations that neutral nations were free to trade in non-contraband goods with belligerents. In return belligerents maintained a right to stop and search neutral ships suspected of carrying arms and munitions to their enemies and to seize and condemn any found transgressing the rules. During the anti-Jacobin and Napoleonic Wars — which lasted with only two short intermissions from 1793 until Napoleon's final defeat in 1815 — Britain constantly violated America's rights as a neutral. In a series of Orders-in-Council, Britain found specious pretexts to condemn American vessels trading with France and her allies. Worse, in American eyes, was her practice, when searching ships for contraband, of impressing American seamen into the Royal Navy on the grounds that, having been born British subjects, they owed allegiance to Britain for life, and it was this above all that led the United States to declare war on Britain in 1812. Since 1793 the American government had protested in vain about impressment and the numerous violations of her rights as a neutral, but had invariably been met with vague promises of redress followed by ever more flagrant examples of indifference to her protests.

Britain's cavalier attitude towards the United States stemmed from a number of reasons. Most important was that the war with France took precedence over all other considerations. But it should not be overlooked that her pride, already hurt by her defeat in the War of Independence, suffered a further blow when the significance of that defeat was made manifest by the United States adopting a neutral stance in the war in Europe and trading with both sides in the conflict. Deeply resentful at finding her former colonies providing supplies to her enemy, Britain adopted an arrogant and dismissive attitude to all the complaints she received from the United States about her actions. A third factor, and by no means a negligible one, was the belief in Britain that the Thirteen Colonies, widely dispersed and disparate as they were, could not long survive as a united nation. Undue emphasis was given to the dissensions between Federalists and Democrats in the United States, and many British statesmen believed that the powerful New England States would break away from the union and renew their old ties with Britain. Hence there was little need to make concessions to a nation whose continuing existence was precarious.

By a quirk of fate, America's declaration of war against Britain in June 1812 coincided with Britain's obtaining a secure foothold in Europe for the first time since the outbreak of her war with France in 1793. Wellington's successes against the French in the Iberian peninsular from 1812 onwards, which culminated in the defeat of Napoleon by the allied armies and his banishment to Elba in April 1814, meant that in Britain the war with America was almost completely overshadowed by the Peninsular War. Fate intervened a second time when the British forces released from Europe after Napoleon's defeat were sent across the Atlantic to invade America from the south. By the time news of their overwhelming defeat by America at the battle of New Orleans in January 1815 reached England, Napoleon had escaped from Elba and all attention was focused on preparations for his final confrontation which resulted in his last defeat at Waterloo in June of that year. Once again, events across the Atlantic were eclipsed by events in Europe.

With the ending of the French and American wars, it might be thought that relations between Britain and the United States would run into smoother waters. Unhappily the transition from a war-time to a peace-time economy brought widespread distress throughout the United Kingdom, and the call for a radical reform of Parliament, effectively stifled during the war with France, resurfaced. Demonstrations, riots and rick burning frightened the government into severe acts of repression which further inflamed the people and caused the government to fear full-scale revolution. Although the old monarchical regimes had been reinstated in Europe, there remained for the British government the spectre of a republic still existing across the Atlantic, and every effort was made by the government and its press to denigrate all things American and to promote the belief that the United States was riddled with discontent and disaffection with its government.

Throughout this whole period there was one powerful voice which attempted to dispel the misrepresentations of the United States put out by the government and its supporters. The voice was that of the great English journalist William Cobbett. The eight years he spent in Philadelphia from 1792 to 1800 when he wrote under the name of Peter Porcupine have been extensively explored by his many biographers and critics. This was the period when pro-French and anti-British fervour was at its height in America. Because at that time he viciously attacked all those who were critical of Britain, it has been assumed that he was anti-American. Nothing could be further from the truth. Even in those early years of his career as a political journalist, he strove hard to persuade his readers that there was a natural affinity between the two nations, and his spirited defence of George Washington from the calumnies heaped upon him after he had signed a commercial treaty with Great Britain in 1794, have been passed over almost without comment. His writings on America after he returned home have received no attention at all.

When living in the United States, Cobbett had attempted to explain Britain to his American readers; when he returned to England in 1800 he attempted to explain America to his British readers. In his great weekly newspaper *The Political Register*, he wrote numerous articles condemning Britain's violations of American neutrality and warned of their leading to war. During the war itself, he courageously praised the gallantry and skill of the American forces and, believing the war to be futile and injurious to both nations, constantly pressed for an early peace. After the war he continued to inform his readers about events across the Atlantic and to contrast the prosperity enjoyed by American citizens with the sufferings of his own countrymen. By now a leading figure in the movement for a reform of the British Parliamentary system, he held up the United States as a model which Britain would do well to emulate. A second sojourn in the United States from 1817 to 1819, this time on Long Island, only served to heighten his admiration of the American form of government and his affection for its people.

Passionately partisan in his comments, Cobbett

nevertheless meticulously documented the arguments on both sides, reporting speeches made in debates in the British Parliament and the Congress of the United States, publishing the full texts of American complaints and the replies of the British government, and giving details of the various engagements during the War of 1812 taken from both American and British sources. His easy colloquial style, his patient expositions of the issues involved, and the vigour with which he expressed his opinions still retain their freshness and bring vividly to life this period when relations between Britain and the United States were sour and misconceptions rife. In his life-time strenuous efforts were made to keep the British public ignorant of events across the Atlantic. The silence that surrounded the War of 1812 still persists. Using the leading (though maverick) political journalist of the age as guide and interpreter, this book attempts to recreate a fascinating but sadly neglected period in the history of Anglo-American relationships.

1

Ploughboy, Pedagogue and Pamphleteer

"Dear Father", wrote Cobbett, "When you used to set me off to work in the morning, dressed in my blue smock-frock and woolen spatterdashes, little did you imagine that I should one day become so great a man as to have my picture stuck in the windows and have four whole books published about me in the course of one week"[1]. Whether this letter actually crossed the Atlantic from Philadelphia where Cobbett was living at the time, to the modest farmhouse on the outskirts of Farnham in England, is immaterial; what is undoubtedly true is that in 1796 when Cobbett published the pamphlet in which this letter appeared, the writings of Peter Porcupine, the pen-name he assumed in America, were creating little less than a furore.

Cobbett's rise from a little English boy sent out in a "blue smock-frock and woolen spatterdashes" to scare the birds off the growing crops, to a person of some importance in what was then the capital of the new Republic of the United States was hard won. After working on his father's farm in his youth, he painfully acquired the art of orthography by working for some eight or nine months in the gloomy offices of an attorney in Gray's Inn in London

---

[1] Remarks on the Pamphlets lately published against Peter Porcupine. *Political Censor,* September 1796.

"from five in the morning till eight or nine at night, and sometimes all night long".² He escaped from this drudgery by joining the army as a private soldier and while in barracks made up for his lack of schooling by joining a circulating library in Chatham "the greatest part of the books in which I read more than once over. Novels, plays, history, poetry, all were read and nearly all with equal avidity."³ Having in these ways acquired by about the age of twenty good handwriting and a nodding acquaintance with the works of literature, for, Cobbett admitted, his reading at that time was but skimming over the surface of everything, he had still to master the art of composition. This he did by copying out and learning by heart Lowth's Grammar. "I repeated it every morning and every evening, and, when on guard, I imposed on myself the task of saying it all over once every time I was posted sentinel".⁴

Such exceptional diligence met with its reward. When in 1785, a year after Cobbett had enlisted, his regiment was posted to Nova Scotia and then transferred to New Brunswick, just after the War of Independence had ended, he "passed through every rank from that of a private sentinel, to that of sergeant major, without ever being once disgraced, confined, or even reprimanded".⁵ After these eight years of exemplary conduct in the British army, Cobbett obtained an honourable discharge and returned to England in the autumn of 1791. He was then twenty eight years old.

How did it come about that this self-taught and somewhat self-righteous son of a small farmer was to find his name blazoned in the newspapers and his picture placarded in

---

² *Life and Adventures of Peter Porcupine,* August 1796.
³ *Ibid.*
⁴ *Ibid.*
⁵ *Ibid.*

the streets of Philadelphia only a few years after he had left the army? Taken up by his commanding officer in Canada as a promising young man (diligence and sobriety were rare virtues among the common soldiers at the time), Cobbett was made clerk to the regiment, responsible for dealing with correspondence from the War Office and for keeping the regimental account books. This last duty opened his eyes to the corrupt practices rampant in the army and indeed in nearly all branches of government in the late eighteenth century. Cobbett, brought up on a farm, and, except for a brief period in Gray's Inn, moving immediately into the closed society of the army was so naive as to be deeply shocked to find that his Quartermaster in Canada kept back a quarter of the stores and equipment for the regiment, for his own profit. It was mainly for this reason that Cobbett asked for his discharge.

When he returned to England he laid the matter before the Secretary of War in London, but found himself subjected to delays and equivocations: the documents he wanted to produce were not secured for him; the charges he wished to level against his officers were whittled down; and the chief witness he wished to produce had been refused his discharge from the army and was still subject to military discipline. Warned that he himself might be charged with sedition if he were to pursue his charges without access to the proofs he needed, Cobbett decided it was useless to proceed further, and embarked with his young wife for France.

In his own writings, Cobbett gave as his reason for going to France a desire to perfect himself in the French language with a view perhaps to setting up a school in England. His acquaintance with French Canadians in New Brunswick had, perhaps, given him a smattering of the language beforehand. His stay in France was short.

He arrived in Normandy in March 1792 and left in the following September, "the six happiest months of my life", he recalled later. "The people were honest, pious, and kind to excess. I met everywhere with civility, and even hospitality, in a degree I had never been accustomed to"[6] Cobbett wrote, echoing the sentiments expressed by Wordsworth who, visiting post-revolutionary France some two years earlier, had

> ... found benevolence and blessedness
> Spread like a fragrance everywhere, like spring
> That leaves no corner of the land untouched.[7]

Cobbett had intended to stay in France for a year. But the calm of the early years of the French Revolution was shattered with the massacre of the royal Swiss Guards and the arrest and imprisonment of the King, and Cobbett, foreseeing that these events were in all probability to lead to a war with England, and fearing for the safety of himself and his young wife, set off for Le Havre and there embarked for America.

Cobbett explained the reasons why he decided to go to the United States in the course of a pamphlet he published some three years after he landed.

> My determination to settle in the United States was formed before I went to France, and even before I quitted the army. A desire of seeing a country so long the theatre of a war of which I had heard and read so much; the flattering picture of it by Raynal; and, above all, an inclination for seeing the world, led me to this determination. I thought that men enjoyed here a greater degree of liberty than in England; and this, if not the principal reason, was at least one, for my coming to this country.[8]

---

[6] *Life and Adventures of Peter Porcupine*, August 1796.
[7] *The Prelude* William Wordsworth, bk 11.
[8] *Life and Adventures of Peter Porcupine*, August 1796..

The Abbé Raynal whose writings had so inspired Cobbett was an influential figure among the *philosophes* of the eighteenth century in Europe. He believed, with Rousseau, that governments were created by society, and that the legitimacy of governments rested on how far they served the needs of the societies which created them. He supported the rebellion of the Thirteen Colonies of America in their war against Britain, arguing that the British government, like all the monarchies in Europe, oppressed its subjects, wringing taxes from the people, which they "prodigally squandered in a fatuous show of grandeur". Raynal believed that the American people, if successful in their struggle for independence, were ideally placed to give an example to mankind.

> Dispersed throughout an immense continent; free as the wild nature which surrounds them, amidst their rocks, their mountains, the vast plains of their deserts, they seem to receive from every natural object a lesson of liberty and independence. Besides, these people given up almost all of them to agriculture or to commerce, to useful labours, cannot be yet corrupted either by the excess of luxury or by the excess of want.[9]

In America's Declaration of Independence of 1776, justifying the overthrow of governments which usurped the powers entrusted to them by society, Raynal saw a hope for all the peoples of the world, and addressed the new nation he hoped would soon be firmly established.

> Let the recital of your happiness call around all the unfortunate of the earth. Let the tyrants of all countries, let all oppressors political or sacred, know that there exists upon the earth a place where a deliverance from their chains is to be found; where afflicted, dejected humanity has lifted up her head; where harvests grow

---

[9] The Abbé Raynal, *The Revolution of America*, London 1781.

for the poor; where religion is free, and conscience has ceased to be a slave; where, in short, nature seems to put in her plea of justification for having created man; and government, for so long time guilty, over all the earth, makes at last the reparation of its crimes.[10]

With these words resounding in his mind, Cobbett set sail from Le Havre in 1792.

For a man with his genius for industry and application, the six months that Cobbett spent in France were sufficient for him to master the language, and settling in Wilmington, Delaware, some thirty miles up river from Philadelphia, he almost immediately found employment translating French works into English, and teaching English to the many Frenchmen who had emigrated there, both from France and from the island of St Dominique, after the massacre and bloodshed during the great slave uprising there in 1791. According to Cobbett he entered the political arena by chance. One of his French pupils selected a newspaper article to read aloud to him during a lesson, which reported on an enthusiastic reception given by the citizens of Philadelphia to the English scientist and philosopher, Joseph Priestley, who had recently fled from England to seek asylum in America. Priestley had fallen foul of the law in England for strongly supporting the principles of the French Revolution, and in his speech thanking the Americans for their kind reception he spoke of his "having flown from the ill treatment in my native country" and of his pleasure in arriving in the United States where he was able to find "that protection from violence which laws and governments promise in all countries but which I have not found in my own". Hearing his native country attacked, and from the mouth of his own

---

[10] *Ibid.*

pupil too, Cobbett sprang to its defence. "The dispute was as warm as might reasonably be expected between a Frenchman, uncommonly violent even for a Frenchman, and an Englishman not remarkable for sang-froid; and the result was a declared resolution on my part to write and publish a pamphlet in defence of my country"[11].

From this dispute was born Cobbett's first pamphlet, published anonymously under the title *Observations on the Emigration of Joseph Priestley*, the precursor of a stream of pamphlets and eventually a newspaper supporting England in its war with France, and lambasting those many Americans who supported their sister republic in Europe, France, in its war with England. Cobbett's entry into the maelstrom of political journalism came at a time when anti-monarchical passions ran particularly high. Anniversaries of the storming of the Bastille and of the execution of the French king and his queen brought crowds into the streets chanting revolutionary songs and wearing caps of liberty and tri-coloured cockades, to demonstrate support for their sister republic overseas.

> The delirium seized even the women and children. I have heard more than one woman, under the age of twenty, declare that they would willingly have dipped their hands in the blood of the Queen of France. A third part of the children, at least, were decorated, like their wise sires, in tri-coloured cockades. "Dansons la Carmognole" pronounced in a broken accent, was echoed through every street and every alley of Philadelphia, by both boys and girls. Some ingenious democratic poet had composed the following lines: "Englishman no bon for me/ Frenchmen fight for liberty". "Poor devils", I thought when I used to hear

---

[11] *Political Register*, 29 September 1804.

them, "little do you know about liberty".[12]

Not all Americans were so enthusiastic. The bloody phase of the French Revolution had confirmed the fears of the more conservative and established section that too much democracy would lead to anarchy and mob rule and strengthened their belief that it was the educated and propertied classes who were the best guardians of a nation's well-being. Whereas the pro-French section could cite England's war with republican France as yet another example of Britain's desire to repress all movements for liberty, and call loudly for America to aid France in her struggle against the combined monarchies of Europe, those opposed to the excesses of the French, the so-called Federalist party, could not, so soon after America had fought to throw off the British yoke, openly espouse Britain's cause. They could only call for strict neutrality in the European wars. When Cobbett said of his first pamphlet that "Such truths as I had published, no man had dared to utter since the rebellion", he was not exaggerating. Whether or not Cobbett had uttered truths which no man had dared to utter since the war against Britain had been won, it was without question that no man had, since then, dared to utter such opinions. Yet this was not the only reason why his pamphlet had caused such a stir, and led to his having his picture stuck in the windows and "four whole books published about him". Until his entry into the field, nearly all the articles written from the Federalist point of view were couched in measured terms and in language suited to the utterance of high principles. Cobbett's robust colloquial style, his ability to poke fun at Priestley's inconsistencies and pretensions, his racy,

---

[12] *Porcupine's Works* Vol I, Preface, p 13.

and, if one may borrow his own phrase, his "delightfully-disgusting" descriptions of what was going in France — the guillotinings, the massacres of nuns, priests, women and children, the parading of severed heads on the ends of pikes — and his barbed rhetorical questions aimed at the self-styled 'defenders of liberty' were quite new. He was, as it were, writing Federalist tracts in anti-Federalist language. As Bernard Fay, in his analysis of the revolutionary spirit in France and the United States said of Cobbett, "il est curieux de noter que le seul homme d'accent vraiment democratique que le federalisme americain fut trouver pour plaider sa cause fut un Anglais".[13]

Cobbett's spectacularly successful career as a pamphleteer and then as an editor of his own newspaper has been extensively covered by his many biographers. Two aspects of his life during this period however are worth mentioning here. The first is the zest and enjoyment with which he wrote. Successful as he had been in his career in the army, it was not until he took up his pen and found himself famous almost overnight, that he realised his true vocation — that of a writer. Here is how Cobbett himself, later in his life described his eight years in Philadelphia:

> When I went to reside in Philadelphia nothing was heard in the streets, but praises of the French and abuse of the English. Never very patient, or given to yield to a torrent, I soon became a pretty busy partisan, and sought occasions to engage in disputes. Thus I became an author, I soon became known to the public, and then I call to witness all those who lived in Philadelphia at that time, what torrents of abuse were poured on me. Young, strong, with good health, always buoyant spirits, careless of consequences, I was a match for all

---

[13] Bernard Fay, *L'Esprit Revolutionnaire en France et aux Etats-Unis*, EO Champion, Paris, 1925.

my antagonists. I have laughed a thousand times, and
I laugh at this moment, at the recollection of the wars
that we used to carry on. My opponents contended that
nothing was good that belonged to England. I contended
that nothing was good that *did not* belong to her. I was
quite sincere; and I solemnly declare that I believed that
even the poultry and the apples were not half so good
as those in England.[14]

It is understandable that throughout his life he looked back upon those eight years in the United States with affection, for the very ferocity of the attacks on him gave him enormous pleasure. With what joy did he throw out his pamphlet *A Bone to Gnaw for the Democrats* and then answer his critics with *A Kick for a Bite*. How he delighted in his *Remarks on the Pamphlets lately published against Peter Porcupine* in enumerating the titles of those pamphlets — *A Blue Shop for Peter Porcupine*, *A Pill for Peter Porcupine*, *Peter Porcupine Detected*, *A Roaster for Peter Porcupine*. And with what boyish glee did he, after publicly acknowledging his British nationality, spend a Sunday arranging the windows of his bookshop on Second Street, Philadelphia, with portraits of English Kings, statesmen, bishops, judges and admirals, and with what relish did he take down the shutters on the Monday and wait for the inevitable hostile reactions of the astonished citizens.

The second aspect concerns a more serious side of his writings. Ferocious as were his gibes at those who abused England and sided with the French, he had no quarrel with America as a nation, or with the Washington administration which was strictly neutral in its relations with both belligerents. As will be seen in the chapters that follow, the anti-British feeling among the Democrat

---

[14] American edition of *Political Register*, 6 January 1816, published in New York 21 May 1816.

party in the United States stemmed not only because she was at war with republican France but from a series of difficulties arising from the non-implementation by Britain of some of the terms of the peace treaty which ended the War of Independence, and her illegal seizure of American vessels on the high seas trading with France. When George Washington proposed a mission to be sent to England to sort out some of the differences between the two countries, there was an outcry from some of the more bellicose of the democrats at this attempt at reconciliation between the two nations. In an early pamphlet when, writing under the name of Peter Porcupine, and aware that if the author were known to be an Englishman his comments would be condemned out of hand, Cobbett assuming the identity of a citizen of the United States attempted to persuade his readers that their distrust of Britain was ill-founded.

> Because a war once existed between the two countries, is that a reason that they should hate one another? They had their battles out; let them follow the good old custom, drink and shake hands, and not suffer themselves to be set together by the ears by a parcel of outlandish butchers *(Cobbett here is, of course referring to the French)*. Britain might have some excuse; it is almost impossible for the disappointed party not to retain some tincture of revenge; but for him who boasts of his victory, to brood over his ill nature, is, to say the best of it, very unamiable.[15]

A little later he returns to his theme that Britain and America should be natural allies as their interests were not dissimilar. Referring to those opposed to any treaty between the two nations he writes:

> "What", say they, "make a treaty with Great Britain?". And why not, wiseacres? Who would you make a treaty

---

[15] *A Bone to Gnaw for the Democrats*, Part 1, February 1795.

with but those with whom you trade? You are afraid of giving umbrage to France, eh? What is France to us, that our destiny is to be linked to hers, that we are not to thrive because she is a bankrupt?[16]

A year later when the democrats were baying for war with Britain, Cobbett made a further appeal.

> War is at all times, and to all countries, dreadful in its effects, but to no country and at no time was it ever so dreadful as it would be now to America. This is not a warlike nation, nor has this nation a warlike government. In a war with any nation whatever, the country can gain nothing, and in a war with Great Britain it has everything to lose. The warriors do not pretend that we could go and take Great Britain, they do not pretend that we could take Jamaica, they do not pretend even that we could take Bermuda. What then can we take? Why, Canada. If you ask them *how* they would do this, they tell you that men are not wanting: that four hundred thousand would turn out volunteers against Great Britain. I believe that twice that number would turn out for a field day with sticks and staves and return very peaceably home to supper, but would they do this two days running? It has been supposed that the people would all unite in case of war. But how far would this be from the case! Almost all the rich, almost all the people of property, would be opposed to it. There is another and still more dangerous kind of division which would finally end in a dissolution of the Union: I mean the division of the North from the South.[17]

War between Britain and America would, of course, spell disaster for Cobbett. By the mid 1790's he was firmly established in the city of Philadelphia, happy in his home life, with three children born to him while he was there,

---

[16] *A Bone to Gnaw for the Democrats*, Part II, March 1795.
[17] *Political Censor*, April 1796.

financially secure and fulfilled. He had taken great pains as a soldier to acquire the art of composition and America had given him a heaven-sent opportunity to employ that art. All seemed set fair for the future, but it turned out it was not a war that put an end to his stay in the States but his own exuberance.

As Cobbett became more successful and more confident as a polemical journalist, he began to attack some of the leading personalities, and in reporting the debates in his paper *The Political Censor*, did not hesitate to caricature some of the congressmen, for instance, Livingston as "the long man from New York" as compared with Swanwick "the short man from Pennsylvania". Another he called "the rawboned knight of the woeful countenance" and more viciously as "a man famous for low cunning and associating in his manners and disposition the tyger and monkey-like qualities so conspicuous in the French". When Cobbett extended his comments mocking the Spanish Minister to the United States and accused the Spanish as being "the only nation on earth that can vie with the French in perfidy and cruelty", the Spanish Minister instigated a law suit against him. Cobbett defended his case by quoting many cases where even more abusive phrases had been used in other papers and the jury acquitted him on the grounds of Ignoramus. Triumphant, Cobbett continued to speak out against those whom he chose to single out to attack. The last, to his undoing, was an attack on the leading physician of the day, a Dr Rush. During the epidemic of Yellow Fever in 1793, Dr Rush had recommended the "wild and novel practice of bleeding patients five or six times a day, and plying him at the same time with doses of calomel or mercurial purges". His methods had been criticised at the time by eminent physicians, and when the fever broke out again in 1797, Cobbett published in his newspaper a long report accusing Rush of being in "a state bordering on frenzy" in his belief that he had found the only true remedy for the sickness. Cobbett whose down-to-earth common sense told him that to bleed and purge all patients, young and old, strong and weak, would result in making them weaker still, made mock of Rush's remedy.

> Blood, blood! More blood! In every sentence they menace our poor veins. Their language is as frightful to the ears of the alarmed multitude as is the raven's croak to those of the sickly flock.[18]

He was tried, found guilty, and fined five thousand dollars, and his effects in Philadelphia, including his printing presses, were seized and sold. In June 1800 Cobbett left for England and arranged for a Farewell Address (described by G K Chesterton as "one of the least friendly farewells to be found in literature") to be published in the newspapers after he had embarked. Its startling opening sentence "When people care not two straws for one another, ceremony at parting is a mere grimace", has been interpreted by some as an indication that Cobbett never liked America. Yet the Farewell Address, with all its denunciations of American institutions and of the treatment he had received, concedes that

> If no man ever had so many and such malignant foes, no man has had more friends, and those more kind, more sincere and more faithful. If I have been unjustly vilified by some, others have extolled me far above my merits; if the savages of the city have scared my children in the cradle, those children have, for their father's sake, been soothed and caressed by the affectionate, the gentle, the generous inhabitants of the country under whose hospitable roofs I have spent some of the happiest hours of my life.[19]

---

[18] *Porcupine's Gazette*, 19 September 1797.
[19] *Porcupine's Works*, Vol XII, p 108.

Before his case for libel against Dr Rush came up for trial, Cobbett had moved from Philadelphia to New York where he set up shop in the city as a bookseller. When news came through of his huge fine, and the seizure of his assets in Philadelphia, friends of Cobbett both English and American got up a subscription and paid Rush his damages. Cobbett managed to sell his shop and its stock to the editor of a Federalist newspaper, *The Gazette of the United States*. So he was not without funds when he arrived in England, though he was very much poorer than when he was living in Philadelphia.

He set sail on June 1st 1800 with his wife and two children, Anne nearly five and William still a toddler. (His first born had died in infancy — "the dearest, sweetest, beautifulest little fellow that ever was seen", he wrote to a friend in England, reporting his loss. "We adored him, everybody admired him. When we lived in Wilmington, people came on purpose to see him for his beauty. I am sure I shall never perfectly recover his loss".)[20]

Cobbett had arrived in the United States in 1792 when he was 29 years old unknown and uncertain of what calling he should pursue. He left when he was 37 with no doubts in his mind as to his calling. His biographer of those eight years, Mary Clark, said of him "The maelstrom of ideas into which he was plunged precipitated him into a position which he found himself preeminently qualified to fill. Fill it he did with all the strength and fervour he possessed".[21]

Except for the few months Cobbett spent in England during his abortive attempt to expose corruption in his regiment, when he returned in 1800 he had been absent for the best part of eighteen years. Yet his name was

---

[20] Letter to Rachel Smither, July 6, 1794 (Nuffield).
[21] Clark, Mary E *Peter Porcupine in America*, p 2, Philadelphia, 1939.

by no means unknown in England. During his time in Philadelphia (then the capital of the United States and the seat of Congress), the British Ministers in Philadelphia, George Hammond, followed by Sir Robert Liston, worked hard to keep America neutral in the European war and kept the government in Westminster fully informed of Porcupine's efforts to do the same. At one time Cobbett was offered a substantial sum to reward him for his efforts for his native country, but fiercely proud of his independence, he refused the offer. He arrived home with glowing reports of his skill as a journalist preceding him, and confident that he could continue to use those skills on his return.

Looking back in later life on his achievements as a political writer in the United States, Cobbett summed them up in these words:

> Everything seemed to indicate that the (American) government would be forced into a war with England in aid of the French; I took the English side; the force of my writings gave them effect; it prevented that which both governments greatly dreaded; peace between America and England was preserved.[22]

Boastful words. But the treatment Cobbett received when he returned to British soil showed that he was not alone in considering himself in such a light. He found himself not only famous — many of his pamphlets condemning the French Revolution had been reprinted in England as war propaganda — but fêted. When his ship bound from New York to Falmouth touched in at Halifax, Nova Scotia, in June 1800, the British Governor welcomed and entertained him, "the first ladies in the place" waited on Mrs. Cobbett and took her and the children out in their

---

[22] *Political Register*, Vol 69, April 10, 1830.

carriages, and Royalty, in the person of George III's fourth son, the Duke of Kent, then Commander of the British forces in North America, requested an interview with Cobbett and later, after a review of the troops, "rode up to me on the Grand Parade and asked me my opinion on his corps".[23] On his arrival in England, Cobbett was taken up by Windham, Secretary at War in Pitt's government, and through him was invited to dine with Pitt, Canning and others in the Cabinet. Such was their opinion of his powers as a political journalist that they offered him the proprietorship of one of the two government newspapers — a very lucrative proposition.

Such adulation might well have gone to the head of a young man, or to one who, coming of humble stock, found himself being treated as an equal by men of high birth and station. But Cobbett was now thirty-seven years old, wary of politicians, and fiercely independent. He refused the offer, rejected another offer of money in the form of part of a government scrip, and although later he accepted subscriptions to set up a paper of his own, he did so only after insisting on written confirmation that he was under no obligation to reflect the views of his patrons.

Cobbett was now entering a new world; one much changed since he had left it some twenty years before, and one very different from what he had expected it to be. Nepotism, bribery, financial skulduggery, all these he had encountered during his sojourn in Philadelphia. What was to surprise him about England was that, unlike the United States where these existed, as it were, as aberrations on the body politic, in England they existed as integral parts of the whole system of government. As much as one third of the seats in the House of Commons were 'owned' by

---

[23] *Letters from William Cobbett to Edward Thornton*, ed G D H Cole, 1937.

a handful of aristocratic landlords who, either because of a restricted franchise (some seats had hardly any electors at all), or because of their influence over the electors, could nominate whosoever they pleased to represent their borough. Some of these seats were bought and sold through advertisements in the public press. Many were 'bought' by the government of the day and 'paid for' by rewarding the owners with titles or sinecure posts (positions which carried lucrative salaries but involved little or no duties at all) or pensions for themselves and sometimes for their wives, brothers, sisters, and even, in some instances, for their infant children.

It took some time for Cobbett to plumb the depths of the intricate system which lay behind the façade of the British Constitution, and when he returned to England he was no advocate of republicanism and no advocate of democracy. He had lived under a republican government in the United States and found it wanting; he had observed from afar the workings of democracy in France and found it appalling. An admirer of Burke, he believed with him that the British system with its checks and balances — an aristocracy with a long tradition of service to the country, wealthy and established enough to be independent of bribes and favours, a squirearchy rooted in the land and in touch with the common people, and a King bound by his Coronation Oath to uphold the rights and safety of all his people — these three great estates of King, Lords and Commons were, for Cobbett, the proven institutions of government that had made the British Constitution the envy of the world. Yet Cobbett's immediate and almost instinctive refusal of the government's offer to establish him, and establish him very comfortably too, as the proprietor of a daily newspaper and his even more abrupt rejection of the offer of government scrip, shows that he was well enough versed in political affairs to distrust politicians, even those holding office under the British Crown. But his early suspicions that there might be some things rotten in his native country did not deflect him from the cause he had espoused so consistently in America and which he continued to espouse on his return to England — the destruction of Jacobinism and unqualified support for those who were fighting it.

When Cobbett returned in 1800, England had already been at war with the French Republic for seven years, seven years in which all British attempts to invade the continent and meet the enemy had ended in ignominious defeat. An expedition sent to land and support a contingent of French royalists in Brittany had been a disastrous failure. The Royal Navy's capture of Toulon and the establishment of French royalists and British troops on French soil ended when a young French lieutenant, Napoleon Bonaparte, successfully drove them away, and in such haste that only four of the nineteen British ships investing the harbour escaped. Fifteen were left behind intact to be seized and added to the French navy. Twice the King's second son, the Duke of York, had led an army in the Low Countries to subjugate the French, and twice he led a defeated and depleted army home again.

> Oh, the grand old Duke of York,
> He had ten thousand men,
> He marched them up to the top of the hill
> And he marched them down again

was a popular, if somewhat irreverent, appraisal of British exploits on the continent.

At sea, from the British point of view, the situation was less gloomy. At this time the Navy's victories over the Spanish fleet at Cape St Vincent and the Dutch at

Camperdown in 1797, and over the French at the Battle of the Nile in 1798, meant that in spite of the reverses on land, fears of an imminent invasion of England by the armies of the French Republic, which had been a real possibility in the early stages of the war, were temporarily allayed.

Such was the position of affairs when Cobbett began his career as a political writer in England. Years of war were beginning to tell. Food shortages, high prices, heavy taxes, and unemployment due to the closure of European markets had led to occasional outbreaks of rioting, strikes and demonstrations against Pitt, the King and the war. With the spectacle of mob-rule in France before them, and the memory of the Gordon Riots in London as recently as the 1780's, the government passed repressive laws to curb any murmurings of discontent among the common people, although more recent research has shown that the incidents of violence arose more from real hardships than from any leanings towards abstract principles of liberty, equality and fraternity.

Cobbett came back to England with no doubts in his mind of the course he intended to pursue. He knew he was an influential writer with the ability to make people from all walks of life listen to him, and he was convinced without a shadow of doubt that France, under its present rulers, was an evil, bloodthirsty, atheistical, insatiable power which must be combated and destroyed. His refusal to take over a government paper was due to his belief that he could be more effective if he was, and was known to be, independent of any bribes or favours from any source whatever. The government was naturally somewhat discomfited at Cobbett's refusal of its offer and all the financial rewards attached to it, but he was potentially too valuable a supporter of the war to be ignored, (and potentially too formidable an opponent to be spurned), and Windham, the Secretary at War and almost as committed a Francophobe as Cobbett himself, continued to cultivate his friendship.

Before setting up an independent newspaper of his own, Cobbett needed to secure for himself and his family some financial stability. He had only a small capital sum left over after his losses in the States, but with this he set up in partnership with an old Philadelphian friend, John Morgan, a booksellers and publishers business in Pall Mall. Before he left America he had begun work on preparing a collected edition of his writings in the United States, but because his impending trial had forced him to leave Philadelphia for New York, the project had had to be abandoned. Cobbett now decided to issue this work in London. He knew his many connections in the States would ensure a sale there and with Windham's encouragement he began to compile what was to become a twelve-volume work, part of the title page of which read as follows:

PORCUPINE'S WORKS

> containing various Writings and Selections exhibiting a Faithful Picture of the United States of America from the End of the War in 1783 to the Election of the President in 1801.

By the autumn of 1800, Cobbett had compiled the first part of his *Porcupine's Works*, and with its sales guaranteed, he could turn his attention to his second project, the establishment of a daily newspaper. The first issue of *The Porcupine* appeared at the end of October. It was not a financial success. Cobbett refused to allow any quack medicine advertisements — a ready source of revenue to most newspaper proprietors at the time.

> Not a single *quack* advertisement will on any account

be admitted into the *Porcupine*. Our newspapers have been too long disgraced by this species of falsehood, filfth, and obscenity.[24]

(An echo of Cobbett's old feud against Rush? He refused, too, to indulge in the social gossip paragraphs which so helped the sales of most papers at that time.)

These were not the only obstacles to the *Porcupine's* success, for this stridently anti-Jacobin and pro-war newspaper was launched just at the time when hopes of success in the war were at their lowest ebb. Napoleon's coup d'état, making him First Consul for life and virtual dictator, had extinguished the prospect of France becoming weakened by the internecine quarrels which had characterised the previous rule of the Directory. Napoleon's success against the allied armies in June 1800 were repeated in December at Hohenlinden, and in February 1801 a peace treaty was signed at Luneville in which Austria recognised all French conquests in Europe. Prussia had earlier withdrawn from the coalition against France. Denmark, Sweden and Russia retired into a league of neutrality. Pitt's ruinously expensive policy of forming coalitions had failed and England alone remained at war with France.

By this time both England and France needed a respite from the war. Napoleon needed to consolidate his position inside France and externally in the conquered countries in Europe. He needed time, too, to build up a fleet if France was to become a great colonial power. On her side, England needed to quieten the discontent which the succession of failures in the prosecution of the war had brought dangerously near to the surface, and to replenish her coffers by re-establishing her overseas trade, devastated

---

[24] Quoted in Lewis Melville *The Life and Letters of William Cobbett*, pp 123-4, (Bodley Head, 1923.)

by the long conflict. Negotiations for peace were opened in March 1801 and a preliminary treaty, later to be confirmed at Amiens, was signed in October 1801. Throughout this period, the *Porcupine* continued its crusade against the French and decried any moves towards peace.

After the Peace of Amiens, Cobbett's daily newspaper closed. It had strongly supported the government while it was prosecuting the war against France, but with the cessation of hostilities Cobbett was at once freed from any restraints he may have imposed on himself in criticisms of the government. In June 1802, with Windham's support he founded a weekly newspaper the *Political Register* and from this time onwards until his death in 1835, he devoted himself to exposing the corruption, the maladministration, and above all, the criminal neglect shown by Whigs and Tories alike of the pressing need to alleviate the steadily deteriorating conditions of the working people. However, neither his disillusion with the governing classes, nor his increasing awareness of the sorry state of the labouring classes, diminished in any way his determination to protect his country from the French. Events seemed to confirm all he had said in opposition to the Peace Treaty. Napoleon was clearly planning fresh conquests in the East His designs on the West were apparent in his sending an expedition to San Domingo and there were rumours that he was planning to take over Louisiana from Spain, thus obtaining a foothold on the American continent and threatening Canada. The peace lasted only fourteen months, and in May 1803 hostilities between Britain and France were renewed. For the last time in his life, Cobbett lent his support to the government. He wrote perhaps his most powerful pamphlet of all — *Important Considerations for the People of the Kingdom* — in which he called on his countrymen to defeat the tyrant Bonaparte who:

with the word *Liberty* continually on his lips, erected a despotism the most oppressive, the most capricious, and the most cruel that the Almighty, in his wrath, ever suffered to exist... Shall we yield up this dear and happy land, together with all the liberties and honours, to preserve which our fathers so often dyed the land and the sea with their blood; shall we thus at once dishonour their graves, and stamp disgrace and infamy on the brows of our children? Mighty, indeed, must be our efforts, but mighty also is the need. Britain now attracts the eyes and the hearts of mankind; groaning nations look to her for deliverance; justice, liberty and religion are inscribed on her banners; her success will be hailed with the shouts of the universe, while tears of admiration and gratitude will bedew the heads of her sons who fall in the glorious contest.

The pamphlet, published anonymously under the Royal Seal, was distributed to every parish in the kingdom.

Cobbett wrote his clarion call to arms in his pamphlet *Important Considerations* because even though he was aware that an invasion of England by France would no longer bring Jacobinism in its wake, the experiences of the countries Napoleon had invaded offered a terrifying prospect. Britain's only sure bulwark against invasion was the Royal Navy. But across the Atlantic was a rival, steadily growing in wealth and population and profiting from the wars in Europe. Thomas Jefferson's election to the Presidency of the United States — a known francophile — posed new problems. How Cobbett assessed the likely effects on Britain's fortunes of the change of administration in America is the subject of the next chapter. To understand his attitude, it is necessary to retrace our steps and examine the relations between America and France from the time Cobbett left the States in 1800.

2

Violations of Neutrality

In 1796, four years before Cobbett left America for England, President Washington resigned after his two terms in office, and in the ensuing election, greatly to Cobbett's relief, John Adams, the Federalist candidate, won by a small margin of votes against the Democrat candidate, Thomas Jefferson. At that time Cobbett had considered Jefferson to be a dangerous Francophile, sympathetic to the atheistical principles of the French republic and an enemy to any rapprochement with Great Britain. When there had been a possibility that Jefferson might win the election of 1796 after Washington's retirement, Cobbett had written in his Philadelphia paper *The Political Censor*, this assessment of Jefferson's character.

> A man who is a deist by profession, a philosopher by trade, and a Frenchman in politics and morality; a man who has written a passport for Tom Paine's Rights of Man; a man, in short, who is at the head of the prostituted party by whose intrigues he has been brought forward and is supported. If this man is elected President, the country is sold to the French; and as plantations are generally sold with the live stock on them, I shall remove my carcass, for I am resolved never to become their property. I do not wish my family vault to be in the guts of cannibals.[1]

In his term of office as President, John Adams took a firm stand against the very serious depredations of American shipping by the French and authorised the United States

---

[1] *Porcupine's Works*, Vol 4, p 267.

navy to seize French armed vessels in retaliation. In this, he was strongly supported and praised by Cobbett. But towards the end of his term of office, Adams sent a mission over to France to end this state of quasi-war with France which resulted in the Convention of 1800 under which France renounced her right to seize and condemn American vessels carrying goods and persons belonging to the enemy, but deferred the question of paying indemnity for all those she had captured previously "until a convenient time". Cobbett considered this a miserable capitulation on the part of the United States which had earlier professed that the object of the mission to France was to obtain "satisfaction for insults and reparation for injury".

> …. this immense claim has been quietly laid on the shelf, and all the insults, the scourgings, the thumb-screwings, the shootings, the saberings and the hangings of the poor American citizen sailors have been laid on the shelf along with it.[2]

Had the election of Jefferson occurred during the quasi-war with France Cobbett would, no doubt, have been greatly alarmed at the change of administration. But coming as it did when the quarrel between France and America had been ended by the Convention, the election of a man known to be friendly to France was of lesser significance, since a rapprochement between France and the United States had already taken place. Cobbett had hoped that France's seizures of American ships and the confiscation of their cargoes and imprisonment of their crews might have drawn America into an alliance with Britain, but his hope had ended with the Convention.

So, some five years after he had expressed his opinion of Jefferson, and with his carcass safely removed and

---

[2] *Porcupine's Works*, Vol 12, p 238.

no longer in danger of ending up in the guts of French cannibals, and perhaps five years wiser, Cobbett seemed to suspend judgement on Jefferson as President. It is possible that Jefferson's inaugural speech caused him to be cautious in any immediate condemnation of the new administration in the United States. Its conciliatory tone — "We are all republicans, we are all federalists", its call to the American people to distance themselves from "the throes and convulsions of the ancient world" and to rejoice in the fact that America was "kindly separated by nature, and a wide ocean, from the exterminating havoc of one quarter of the globe", and its ending with the prayer "may that infinite Power, which rules the destiny of the Universe, lead our councils to what is best, and give them a favourable issue for your peace and prosperity"; all these sentiments were a far cry from the shrill, revolutionary sentiments which Cobbett associated with the pro-French Democrats and which he might have expected to hear from the leader of the Democrat party.

The first years of Jefferson's Presidency gave promise that his prayer might be answered. The Convention between America and France was followed by the Peace Treaty between Britain and France drawn in May 1801. For a short period between May 1801 and May 1803 American ships and their cargoes could sail unmolested on the high seas. (It was estimated that cargoes worth over twenty million dollars had been confiscated by the French during the quasi-war of the late 1790's.) But the renewal of the war between England and France in May 1803 meant that once again America's rights as a neutral country were grossly violated.

The position of a neutral during a major war is never an easy one, and during the anti-Jacobin and Napoleonic wars both Britain and France accused the United States of favouring the other. When this was compounded with the fact that America was separated from the two great belligerents by three thousand miles of ocean, and protests from the New World to the Old or from the Old World to the New could take as long as eight weeks to arrive, and explanations or justifications another eight weeks to reach the protestor, the situation of America as a neutral became fraught with misunderstandings. Furthermore, the fact that the Americans had so recently been British subjects and had so recently rebelled against the British Crown, caused the British government to view the declared neutrality of the United States with some suspicion; the known sympathy of a large number of American citizens for their sister republic in France deepened the mistrust and led Britain to act with a combination of insolence and arbitrariness towards her former colonists which was eventually to lead to war.

Most of the problems were apparent during the first phase of the Franco-British war (1793-1801), but the flagrant violations of America's rights by the French which led to the quasi-war between France and the United States in the late 1790s had pushed British violations into the background. In the second phase (1803-1815), they were quickly to come to the fore.

The most intractable and emotive source of friction in Anglo-American relations arose from the British practice of recruiting sailors to the Royal Navy by impressment. Unable to man her wartime fleet by volunteers, the British government sent out press gangs to ports throughout the kingdom to seize by force able bodied seamen serving in merchant vessels and fishing fleets and impress them into service. In *Sylvia's Lovers* set in England in the 1790s, the nineteenth century novelist, Mrs. Gaskell, describes how the press gang system worked:

> The servants of the admiralty lay in wait for all merchantmen and traders; there were many instances of vessels returning home after long absence, and laden with rich cargo, being boarded within a day's distance of land, and so many men pressed and carried off, that the ship with her cargo became unmanageable from the loss of her crew, and drifted out again into the wild wide ocean; sometimes such vessels were never heard of more. The men thus pressed were taken from the near grasp of parents and wives, and were often deprived of the hard earnings of years... We read of the military being called in to assist the civil power in backing up the press-gangs, of parties of soldiers patrolling the streets, and sentries with screwed bayonets placed at every door which the press-gang entered and searched each hole and corner of the dwelling; we hear of churches being surrounded during divine service by troops while the press-gang stood ready at the door to seize men as they came out from attending public worship.[3]

Even without pressed men on board, discipline in the crowded ships, sometimes at sea and on station for as long as two years at a stretch, had to be very strictly enforced. With a portion of the crew forced into service against their will and often sullen, resentful and looking for an opportunity to jump ship to escape, the ships became little less than floating hells; the two great mutinies at Spithead and the Nore in 1797 and 1798 brought attention to the intolerable conditions, and some efforts were made to alleviate them. But throughout the wars a large number of men on board His Majesty's ships were serving against their will. With United States shipowners offering sometimes as much as a hundred per cent higher wages than the Royal Navy, desertions from British to American ships were frequent. America, as was customary for a neutral nation,

---

[3] Mrs Gaskell *Sylvia's Lovers*, 1863 (Everyman's Library, 1964).

allowed warships to enter her harbours for victualling and repairs and although sailors were confined on board when ships entered foreign ports, parties had to be sent ashore to obtain water, provisions and equipment. In 1799 a British consul in America wrote:

> His Majesty's Packet Boats invariably lose a part of their crew every time they enter this port by desertion... The enormous pay offered by Americans to Seamen is too great a temptation to our Sailors to resist.[4]

The British government's reaction to the loss of so many men from the Royal Navy was to order her naval officers to search American merchantmen not only for contraband of war, but to seize and impress into the navy any British subjects found on board. Immediately the question arose as to what made a man a British subject. The United States granted naturalisation to those who had been resident in the country for five years. Great Britain herself granted naturalisation to foreigners who had served two years on British ships, either merchantmen or ships of war. Yet, at the beginning of the anti-Jacobin war she peremptorily declared that only those who had been resident in the United States on or before the separation of the colonies from Britain, ie on or before 1783, would be considered exempt from impressment. For the rest, the British government would apply the doctrine of indefeasible allegiance: subjects could not divest themselves of citizenship without the consent of the nation of their birth. Cobbett, when still in America, stoutly supported this doctrine, writing in his Philadelphia paper *The Political Censor* of November 1796:

> And is it not just that the state which has bred, nourished and protected you, should have a title to your allegiance?

---

[4] Bradford Perkins, *The First Rapprochement: England and the US, 1795-1805,* p 61 University of Pennsylvania Press 1955.

> To say that you "never asked for protection" is the same thing as to say that you never asked to be born. Should the state now withdraw its protection from you or drive you out of its boundaries, would you not exclaim against such a step as an act of brutal injustice? And yet this is no more unjust than for you to withdraw your allegiance, cast the state from you, and leave it to the mercy of its foes.[5]

Such arguments were not likely to appeal to those young men, many of whom had come to the United States as children, who found themselves torn from their families and forced to fight in a war with a country which was at peace with the nation they considered as their own. In American eyes the doctrine of indefeasible allegiance was an insult to the sovereignty of the United States. Should Britain, who granted naturalisation after two years in her merchant navy, deny the right of America to grant citizenship? There were practical difficulties too, for how were the officers of the Royal Navy to distinguish a British subject from a citizen of the United States when they boarded an American merchantman? Naturalisation papers were known often to be forged, even to be openly on sale in some ports. The arrogance of many British naval officers was a byword in the States. In a much publicised incident in the West Indies in 1796, one of them was heard to say that he would "strip the whole of the American vessels that night of their men".[6] With officers such as these, far from home and answerable at the time to no-one but themselves, hundreds of American citizens found themselves pressed into the Royal Navy, and anti-British feelings were succintly expressed by Madison (later to become President of the United States) in 1799.

---

[5] *Porcupine's Works,* Vol 4, pp 234-5.
[6] J F Zimmerman, *The Impressment of American Seamen,* p 27, Columbia University, 1925.

> She takes by force her own subjects voluntarily serving in our vessels. She keeps by force American citizens involuntarily serving in hers! More flagrant inconsistencies cannot be imagined.[7]

In the ten years between 1793 and the Peace of Amiens, over two thousand seamen were taken from American ships by the Royal Navy, and while Cobbett was in America impressment was the issue above all else that inflamed the people of America against Britain. In spite of repeated protests from the United States government, and the appointment of agents to negotiate with the British for the release of wrongly impressed American citizens, Lord Grenville, the British Foreign Secretary, insisted on Britain's right to impress and maintained that very few American citizens had been taken. During the short peace between Britain and France from 1801 to 1803, over one thousand American seamen were discharged from the Royal Navy.

When war broke out again in 1803, England, facing the build-up of Napoleon's armies and flotilla only twenty miles across the Channel, needed every man she could get to serve in the Navy. This was not the time to take into account the refinements of who was or was not a British subject when searching American vessels or to listen to American complaints about the practice of impressment. In this second stage of the Franco-British war the number of seamen taken from American ships multiplied (between 1803 and 1810 some eight to ten thousand were estimated to have been seized), and in 1807 the American Agent for Seamen sent to negotiate for the release of American citizens declared: "There is not, at this time, I believe, a single ship of war in the British navy whose crew does not consist partly, and in some instances

---

[7] Quoted in *Zimmerman, op cit*, p 99.

on distant stations, principally of American seamen".[8] If in England impressment into their own navy to defend their own country excited such feelings as Elizabeth Gaskell describes in the extract below, what must have been the feelings of Americans when they found their husbands, sons and lovers impressed into the service of a foreign power? Here, again from *Sylvia's Lovers*, Elizabeth Gaskell portrays the agony of Englishwomen waiting on the quays to welcome their menfolk home from the sea, only to witness them being seized by the press gang and rowed out to a man-of-war as their ships touched shore.

> Their wild, famished eyes were strained on faces they might not kiss, their cheeks were flushed to purple with anger or else livid with impotent craving for revenge. Some of them looked scarce human: and yet an hour ago those lips, now tightly drawn back so as to show the teeth with the unconscious action of an enraged wild animal, had been soft and gracious with the smile of hope; eyes, that were fiery and bloodshot now, had been loving and bright; hearts, never to recover from the sense of injustice and cruelty, had been trustful and glad only one short hour ago.[9]

No comparable American can be found to describe what must have been even more heartrending scenes when news reached American homes of men snatched from their ships, though newspapers reported harrowing incidents of impressment with comments such as:

> Thus does the British power and barbarity daily rend asunder those who are connected by the tenderest ties of nature and affection. (*Boston Independent Chronicle*)

> Some of these unfortunate people are American born, and have wives and children whose existence, perhaps,

---

[8] Quoted in Zimmerman, *op cit*, p 26.
[9] Mrs Gaskell, *op cit*.

depends on the welfare of a husband in slavery, a father in chains. (*New York Argus*)

Looking back in later life, another President, John Quincy Adams, summed up the reactions to the practice of impressment.

> This authorized system of kidnapping upon the ocean was practised under the odious pretence of a *right* in the king of Great Britain to force his own subjects into his naval service in time of war. To the execution of this law, no judge, no jury, no writ of habeas corpus, affords to British seamen the protection of liberty or of life... The *pretence* of the king was to take his own subjects only; the practice was to presume every man a British subject who was wanted. Whenever an American merchant ship met a British armed vessel at sea, she was visited by a midshipman or lieutenant from the man-of-war, at whose command her whole crew was summoned upon her deck; and there every man of them passed into review before this often beardless boy, who compared their persons with their certificates, and finished by taking or leaving the man, just as his temper or fancy decided his choice.[10]

The problems created by the widespread desertion of British sailors both to American merchant vessels and, though less frequently, to American ships of war, came to a head in 1807. In that year a boat load of seamen from a British warship escaped, some of whom were known to have subsequently enlisted in the American warship *USS Chesapeake*. When news of the desertions reached Vice-Admiral Berkeley, the British officer in command of the North American station at Halifax, Nova Scotia, he ordered the navy to watch for and detain the *Chesapeake* and bring off the deserters for trial. In

---

[10] Quoted in Dumas Malone, *Jefferson and his Time*, Vol 5, p 401, Little Brown & Co, Boston, 1970.

doing so he violated the accepted law of nations which, though allowing neutral merchant ships to be searched for contraband, had always respected the sovereignty of the armed vessels of neutral powers. *HMS Leopard*, acting upon the admiral's instructions, found *USS Chesapeake* and ordered it to heave to and allow its officers to come on board to retrieve the deserters. The American commander of the *Chesapeake*, rightly believing his warship to be inviolate under international law, refused. *HMS Leopard* responded by firing two broadsides into the *Chesapeake*, killing three of the crew, wounding eighteen, and inflicting serious damage on the American ship The *Chesapeake*, unprepared for action, was forced to surrender and British officers boarded the ship and took off four men.

> When the bloody bulk that was the *Chesapeake* limped back to Norfolk (Virginia) with a tale of humiliation, a wave of indignation swept over all America... "Never since the battle of Lexington", wrote President Jefferson, "have I seen this country in such a state of exasperation as at present, and even that did not produce such unanimity". "I have only to open my hand", he further said, "and let havoc loose".[11]

At this point, when Great Britain and the United States were on the brink of war, the *Chesapeake* incident must be set in the wider context of the Napoleonic wars. Though the attack on the *Chesapeake* was the grossest violation of America's neutrality, both Britain and France had consistently been guilty of equally serious, though less dramatic, infringements of America's rights as a neutral.

Throughout the anti-Jacobin and Napoleonic wars both belligerents needed and obtained provisions from the United States. It had long been established that neutrals

---

[11] Thomas A Bailey, *A Diplomatic History of the American People*, p 123, Appleton-Century Crafts, NY, 1964.

were free to trade with both sides during wars between nations, but certain shipments were forbidden and classed as contraband. These included all arms and munitions and certain other articles obviously destined for use in war. To ensure that neutrals were carrying only permitted goods, belligerents assumed the right to stop ships suspected of carrying contraband and bring them into a port belonging to the captor for adjudication. If contraband was found, the ship was seized and condemned. If the suspicion was found to be groundless, the ship was released. Definitions of what constituted contraband were the source of endless debate, and the delays incurred in waiting for clearance could spell ruin for shipowners.

There were two further restrictions during the Napoleonic wars. The first was a British ruling that forbade neutrals to act as carriers for the belligerents. Under this ruling, Britain claimed the right to seize and condemn neutral ships carrying goods directly to and from an enemy country and its colonies, or between one enemy colony and another. The second was that if a port was blockaded, any neutral ship attempting to penetrate the blockade was liable to seizure and confiscation.

With ships of war and privateers operating at the mouths of harbours and on the high seas to search for contraband — they infested the English Channel and the coasts of Europe as well as along the North America seaboard and in the West Indies — the difficulties of transporting goods by sea resulted in very high prices being paid for cargoes that successfully completed the hazardous voyage. Inevitably, therefore, American shippers were tempted to undertake both 'legitimate' and 'illegitimate' trading. Their merchant fleet greatly expanded and British shipping interests watched the growth of a rival mercantile fleet with alarm. It was greatly in Britain's interests to cut off supplies to the enemy because by doing so she could both weaken France and simultaneously curb the growth of the American merchant marine. After the great victory of Trafalgar, British ships of the line outnumbered the combined fleets of France, Spain and Holland, and, no longer fearing invasion, Britain was free to concentrate her attention on a war of attrition by wearing down the enemy by cutting off his supplies. The year of 1805, however, saw not only Trafalgar, but a sweeping victory by Napoleon at Austerlitz in which he crushed Britain's only effective ally in Europe, Russia, and now complete master of the continent, he could turn his attention once again to England. The United States, a major source of supply to both belligerents, was caught in the crossfire.

The first shot in the war of attrition was fired by the appearance in England of a pamphlet "War in Disguise: or the Frauds of Neutral Flags" by James Stephens. As was seen earlier, Britain maintained she had a right to seize and condemn ships carrying the property of the enemy to or from its colonies. American shippers had circumvented this prohibition by the so-called "broken voyage" process, whereby ships carrying goods to and from Europe and her colonies, touched in at American ports and paid duties. The cargo now technically "American cargo" could then be sent to its real destination. This process allowed France and her allies to ship goods to and from their colonies under the guise of trading with a neutral country; had the goods been carried in French or her allies' ships they could, of course, be attacked by Britain in the course of war. Stephen's thesis was that this "broken voyage" practice was, in effect, a violation of the law, and in 1805 the British government upheld this view in the *Essex* case, which was to have far reaching repercussions. The US merchant ship the *Essex* had briefly landed its goods in an American port on a voyage from Barcelona to the Spanish colony of Cuba. The ship was seized by the British on the grounds that the cargo had never, in reality, been imported into the United States, and that the *Essex* had made a continuous voyage from Spain (then allied to France and so an enemy to Britain) to one of her colonies and was, therefore, lawful prize.

As an immediate result of this decision, the Royal Navy and privateers, always alert for opportunities to win prize money, hovered outside the harbours of Europe, the United States and the Caribbean, searched merchantmen entering the ports, and on the slightest suspicion seized the ships and sent them for examination to Admiralty Courts. The anger aroused by the *Essex* decision and by these wholesale seizures which followed it was immense. The fact that no formal notification had been given to the United States that the longstanding practice of "broken voyage" was no longer allowable; the ignorance of the masters of the ships seized of any change in British policy; the delays in adjudication in the Admiralty Courts; the seeming impossibility of obtaining redress if the American owner questioned the Court's decisions; and the widespread belief that the *Essex* decision was made because of Britain's desire to ruin its rival in mercantile trading; all these added fuel to the flames. Indignation reached boiling point in 1806, a year before the *Chesapeake* incident, when a shot from a British ship *HMS Leander*, ordering an American merchantman off New York to heave to, broke a spar which struck and killed the mate. His mangled body was paraded through the streets of New York as an example of British perfidy.

From January to June 1800, Cobbett had lived in New York before returning to England from America, and had found the city noisy, unruly, and a hotch-potch of recent immigrants from Europe. Hence his comment on the scenes in New York:

> The ferment, we are told, which has been excited in New York and other towns, on the death of an American seaman, was beyond anything the reader can conceive... No Englishman could appear in the streets but at the hazard of his life. All this I, who know them, can easily believe of the mongrel rabble at New York, who call themselves Americans, but who, for the far greater part, perhaps, have escaped from their creditors or the persons they have robbed in Europe. Very different will, I am certain, have been the feelings of the *people of America* properly so-called; and agreeably with their better feelings, the President seems to have acted.[12]

Jefferson's reaction to the clamour for reprisals to be taken against Britain was to send Thomas Pinckney, a Maryland lawyer, to join James Monroe the American Minister to England, to press for a reversal of the *Essex* decision, to continue to allow the former practice of "broken voyage", and to demand indemnity for the numerous seizures which had resulted from that decision. The mission was also to insist on a renunciation by Britain of the right to impress seamen on the high seas. As an earnest of her resolution to uphold her rights as a neutral, the American government also passed a non-importation act restricting the importation of certain goods into the United States, but the implementation of the Act was to be deferred pending the result of the Monroe-Pinckney mission. "The conduct of the President has, in this case, been moderate and dignified", Cobbett wrote. "He is too wise to plunge the country into war for the purpose of gratifying the hatred of the dominant party at New York".[13]

---

[12] *Political Register,* Vol 9, June 14 1806.
[13] *Ibid.*

Jefferson's hopes that the Monroe-Pinckney mission might succeed were partly based on the fact that after the Prime Minister Pitt's death early in 1806, the new Prime Minister had appointed Charles Fox as Foreign Secretary. Fox had supported America in the War of Independence and was known to be friendly to the United States. "In Mr Fox personally, I have more confidence than in any man in England", Jefferson wrote to Monroe in England. His hopes were short lived for by the time Pinckney arrived in London, Fox was seriously ill and in September 1806 he died. With him died the prospect of accommodation with Britain, and the Monroe-Pinckney mission obtained no more than a vague promise to refrain from molesting bona-fide American citizens when searching merchantmen.

Cobbett's attitude to impressment was based on the premise that so long as American shipowners continued to inveigle British sailors into their service, the British government had no option but to impress men from American ships in order to keep her ships manned. He was not unsympathetic to American complaints of the cavalier attitude of the naval officers on board His Majesty's ships, many of them, he declared, "seeming to think that they inherit from nature all the power that their king and country have placed in their hands".[14] In February 1806, he commented on the new administration formed after Pitt's death:

> With the United States of America, Mr Pitt has left us with a dispute not easily settled without an abandonment on our part of much of that which we have heretofore contended for and maintained. A pretty mixture of arrogance and imbecility in our ministers had produced the dispute; but it is by no means certain that contrary

---

[14] *Ibid.*

qualities in their successors will issue a favourable termination of it.[15]

The failure of the Monroe-Pinckney mission was not the only disappointment for the American government in 1806. Britain's wholesale seizure of American ships after the Essex decision, threatening as it did supplies of much needed goods from the New World to France and her allies, led Napoleon to retaliate. In his Berlin Decree of November 1806, he declared the whole of the British Isles to be in a state of blockade and all vessels sailing from British ports to be lawful prize. In doing this, he was following the British practice which for some years had been a source of complaint by the United States against Britain. To prevent supplies from reaching European ports, Britain had, from time to time, declared certain ports to be in a state of blockade when, in fact, no ships were actually present around the harbours, and had seized ships bound to or coming from such fictionally blockaded ports. Napoleon's Decree was an even more flagrant example of this so-called "paper blockade" inasmuch as the immense superiority of the Royal Navy made it impossible for France to institute an effective blockade of a single British port. Britain responded by a series of Orders in Council forbidding any neutral ship to trade between any ports belonging to France unless it first entered a British port and paid fees to Britain. Napoleon counter attacked by a further Decree in 1807 which stated that all ships which submitted to these British Orders in Council, or allowed British ships to search them, were in collusion with the enemy and were therefore lawful prize.

Such then was the unhappy position of the United States facing the contradictory orders of the two great belligerents. If she accepted the British Orders in Council

---

[15] *Political Register*, Vol 9, February 8 1806.

and touched in at British ports on the way to Europe, her ships were liable to be seized and condemned when they arrived in French or her allies' ports. If she failed to obey the Orders in Council and her ships sailed direct to Europe, they were liable to be seized and condemned by the British. Although both parties were culpable, and both seized and condemned her ships, Britain was seen as the worse offender. Only Britain impressed her citizens; it was Britain that had initiated the paper blockade system; with the final indignity of the attack on the *Chesapeake*, one can understand the significance of Jefferson's remark: "I have only to open my hand and let havoc loose". A President dedicated to peace faced a country clamouring for war.

Jefferson's immediate action after the *Chesapeake* incident was to command all armed vessels of Great Britain within American waters to depart, and to prohibit by law the furnishing of any supplies to the Royal Navy. His next move was to demand from England a repudiation of the *Leopard's* attack on the *Chesapeake*, punishment of Admiral Berkeley who had ordered the attack, restoration of the four seamen taken and reparation for the injuries inflicted. To these demands he added one other: that Britain should abolish the practice of impressment from American vessels — a demand that was greatly to complicate the issue, but one that, if not included, would have failed to dampen the clamour for war.

Although Jefferson was not sanguine in his expectations of a favourable reply from Britain, he had, by sending a strongly worded protest, gained two important objectives. The long delay before a reply could reach America allowed time for tempers to cool, and preparations could be put in hand for the defence of the country. He authorised the call-up of militia in the States and the construction of gun boats to defend the harbours. In the four months that elapsed before Britain's reply was received, Jefferson strove to win over Congress to his deeply-held belief that commercial restrictions were preferable to war. It was, he said, for Congress to decide whether "war is the most efficacious mode of redress in our case, or whether, having taught so many other useful lessons to Europe, we may not add that of showing them that there are peaceable means of redressing injustice by making it the interest of the aggressor to do what is just, and abstain from future wrong".[16]

In November 1807, the long awaited reply arrived in Washington. In a note from Canning, the British Foreign Secretary, the British government disavowed the action against the *Chesapeake* and offered reparation, but only on the condition that the United States renounced in turn its practice of harbouring deserters from the Royal Navy, and reopened its harbours to British armed vessels. Over the question of impressment it refused to negotiate at all. Congress reacted by immediately putting in force the non-importation act against certain British goods which had been on the statute book since 1806 but held in abeyance in the hope that the threat might make Britain relax her obnoxious Orders in Council.

In the *Political Register*, Cobbett faithfully reported the actions of the President, publishing in full Jefferson's Proclamation forbidding British warships to enter or remain in American waters, his call-up of the militia, and his speech to Congress in October 1807 justifying the measures he had taken. In commenting on the *Chesapeake* incident, Cobbett reiterated his belief that by harbouring and enlisting deserters, the United States was aiding the French.

---

[16] Quoted in R Horsman, *The Causes of the War of 1812*, p 104, University of Pennsylvania Press 1962.

> Mind, I do not pretend to say that we may not, in this instance, have been in the wrong because there is nothing authentic upon the subject; nor am I prepared to say that our right of search, in all cases, extends to ships of war; but of this I am certain, that if the law of nations do not allow you to search for deserters in a friend's territory, neither do they allow that friend to inveigle away your troops or your seamen, to do which is an act of hostility; and I ask for no better proof of inveigling than the enlisting and refusing to give up such troops or seamen.[17]

As for the call-up of the militia, Cobbett assured his readers that they had nothing to fear.

> Every man, capable of bearing arms, is a militia man in the American states. I belonged to that respectable body for several years; but never did I join for one moment in my life; and what is more, I never personally happened to know any man that did. I never saw that militia out at parade, or drill, nor any portion of it; and though I was told that some few men, unable to pay half-a-crown fine, sometimes did attend, with sticks or staves for arms, I cannot say that I believed the fact.[18]

But it was in his report of the debate in Congress on the implementation of the non-importation act that he was most scornful.

> And what is this Act? What is this thing, which is to awe England into submission? A non-importation act. An act to prohibit the importation of all English goods? No: not an act to prohibit the importation of coats, waistcoats, breeches, shirts, cravats, stockings, caps, handkerchiefs, petticoats, blankets, sheets, swaddling clothes and shrouds; not an act to prohibit the importation of knives, locks, scissors, razors, buttons,

---

[17] *Political Register,* Vol 12, January 8 1807.
[18] *Political Register,* Vol 12, September 5 1807.

keys and candlesticks; all these things must be had from us, therefore, the Congress, in its wisdom, has thought it advisable not to include them (making in amount four-fifths of all the goods imported) in the articles prohibited. Well done "King Cong". And does Your Majesty really imagine that we are to be frightened by an Act like this?[19]

No sooner had the non-importation act been put into effect, than the final insult to the American government arrived in the form of a Proclamation issued by George III recalling all British seamen serving in foreign vessels back home, and ordering the navy to search for and impress all British subjects found on board foreign vessels and denying the validity of naturalisation papers. John Adams, the former President, commented that "not all the murders on board the *Chesapeake* nor all the other injuries and insults we have received from foreign nations, atrocious as they have been, can be of such lasting and pernicious consequence to this country, as this proclamation, if we have servility enough to submit to it".[20] Such an unequivocal rebuttal of Jefferson's demands for an end to impressment from American ships called for sterner measures than non-importation, and the United States embarked upon the experiment of an Embargo. An act confining all American ships to port passed both houses of Congress in December 1807.

Jefferson's choice of an Embargo in preference to war was dictated by many factors. L M Sears considered it to be "the projection into foreign affairs of the peace ideals of a democracy, the contribution to international polity of one of the world's greatest democrats".[21] That

---

[19] *Political Register*, Vol 13, January 9 1808.
[20] Quoted in Zimmerman, *op cit*, p 178.
[21] *L M Sears, Jefferson and the Embargo*, p 4, Duke University Press, 1927.

Jefferson, the author of the Declaration of Independence, sincerely believed that the republic of the United States was a precious experiment in creating a new form of government under which men would be free to exercise their inalienable rights to life, liberty and the pursuit of happiness, there can be no doubt; nor that he considered it to be his mission when called to the Presidency to preserve the republic as a shining example for all peoples suffering from oppression and injustice. His idealism is expressed in a speech he made in New York in 1808 justifying his preference for an Embargo as opposed to war.

> There can be no question in a mind truly American, whether it is best to send our citizens and property into certain captivity and then wage war for their recovery, or keep them at home, and to turn seriously to that policy which will plant the manufacturer and the husbandman side by side, and so establish at the doors of every man that exchange of mutual labor and comforts which we have hitherto sought in distant regions, and under perpetual risk of broils with them.[22]

As well as his aversion to war and his hopes that by keeping America independent of foreign nations a new unity would be forged throughout the country, other factors must be taken into account to explain both Jefferson's decision and Congress's endorsement of it. Foremost amongst them was the unpreparedness of the nation for war, and closely allied to this, and indeed one of the causes of the poor state of the defences, was the Republican party's rooted objection to high taxation and government borrowing without which war could not be waged. Although most historians are agreed that had Jefferson persuaded Congress to declare war immediately after the *Chesapeake* incident, he would have had the bulk of Congress and the nation behind him,

---

[22] Quoted in Sears, op cit, p 65.

as the months went by awaiting Britain's reply to his protest, the powerful New England States, whose prosperity was based on commercial ties with Britain, began openly to voice their opposition to a break with England. To complicate matters further, it was precisely during the waiting period that Napoleon issued his Decree stating that all neutral vessels which submitted to the British Orders in Council were lawful prize. If America had declared war on Britain after Canning's insolent reply to Jefferson, it would have been hard for her to justify not declaring war on France too, after Napoleon's equally insolent Decree stating that if America complied with any of Britain's demands, she would be considered an enemy to France.

The Embargo, forbidding all trade with foreign powers, was a bold attempt to coerce both Britain and France to "do what is just and abstain from future wrongs". Jefferson hoped that the complete stoppage of all supplies to both belligerents would result in their returning "to some sense of moral duty". What he failed to take into account was that a sense of moral duty was absent amongst a large section of his own countrymen.

> Most fundamental of the obstacles to success (of the Embargo) were the facts of human nature. Jefferson was asking his countrymen to play a passive role. They were pitted against Europe, but the struggle was negative — a test not of aggression but of endurance... The rich merchant who would willingly have given his son for his country, scorned a country which asked only for his moneybags.[23]

Cobbett put it more crudely:

> Mr Jefferson's hatred may be great, and his party may be strong: but he will have two most formidable enemies

---

[23] L M Sears, *op cit*, p 73.

to cope with at home; namely the *back* and the *belly*. Coffee, molasses and rum are, in that country, nearly necessaries of life and they come only in ships. Of the absolute necessity of woolens I spoke before.[24]

The Embargo necessarily involved tremendous sacrifices from all those whose livelihood depended on mercantile trade, and the effects within the United States were little less than catastrophic. Ships on pretext of coast-wise trading, slipped out from the harbours to trade with Europe and the West Indies; smuggling across the Canadian borders and through the Great Lakes proliferated with smugglers sometimes resisting arrest by force of arms, and the draconian measures of the United States government to ensure compliance with the order heightened hostility. One Congressman, John Randolph went so far as to say: "An experiment, such as is now making, was never before — I will not say tried — it never before entered into the human imagination. There is nothing like it in the narrations of history or in the tales of fiction".[25]

Petitions for the ending of the Embargo poured in from New England States where shipowners faced insolvency and shipwrights and seamen were thrown out of employment. "Ships rotted at their moorings; forests of bare masts sprang up in many harbours; grass grew on once bustling wharves; soup kitchens opened their doors; bankruptcies, suicides and crimes increased".[26] By December 1808 the State of Massachusetts proclaimed a day of mourning on the anniversary of the passing of the Embargo Act, and an editorial in a Washington newspaper commemorated the anniversary by stating:

This ill-shapen brat of backstairs intrigue has now

---

[24] *Political Register*, Vol 12, December 12, 1807.
[25] Quoted in Dumas Malone *op cit* Vol 5, p 579.
[26] Quoted in Thomas A Bailey, *op cit*, p 125.

lived a year. And Mr Jefferson is the only potentate that ever lived who had either will or power to keep such a monster alive for such a length of time.[27]

Jefferson, by now nearing the end of his second term as President, was forced to accept defeat. With the threat of the secession of the north-eastern states from the Union, a bill was rushed through Congress in March 1809 and the grand experiment was over. The President, handing over the reins of government to his successor, James Madison, commented sadly:

I feel extreme regret that an effort, made on motives which all mankind must approve, has failed in an object so much desired.[28]

The Embargo was not without its effects on the belligerents. France and her allies, and their dependencies in the New World suffered a shortage of provisions, though Napoleon gained some eight million dollars' worth of ships and cargoes by confiscating all American ships in French harbours on the grounds that he was helping America by enforcing Jefferson's edict which had forbidden all American vessels to leave the United States! In England the effects were most severely felt in the cotton industry, and during 1808 numerous petitions were presented to Parliament asking for the repeal of the Orders in Council which had led to the Embargo. But throughout the country as a whole, the effects were greatly mitigated by the opening of new markets in the Spanish and Portuguese colonies in South America. Revolts in Spain and Portugal at this time against Napoleon's occupation resulted in these countries allying themselves with England, and this alliance resulted in a rush of trade between Britain and their colonies in

---

[27] Quoted in Dumas Malone, *op cit* Vol 5, p 642.
[28] Quoted in Dumas Malone, *op cit* Vol 5, p 657.

the New World. In many ways the Tory administration in England welcomed the Embargo, as it effected the very same objectives that its own Orders in Council were designed to achieve. It cut off supplies to the enemy and severely crippled America's mercantile marine. Canning could afford to adopt an arrogant attitude towards the United States, knowing that the growing opposition to the Embargo within America meant that it was unlikely to last long enough to create very serious shortages in Britain, and with the opening of new markets in South America he was able to ignore protests from those British merchants who felt the Embargo's effects.

Cobbett's reaction throughout this period was one of uncompromising hostility to the United States. He clung to his conviction that America was at fault in inveigling British seamen into her service, and that Jefferson and the Democrat Party hated England and wished success to France.

> They care not who rules us, or how we are ruled, so that we do but suffer; so that misery alight upon our persons and disgrace upon our name. And is there one of English birth, a wretch so unnatural as to love them? Is there one so criminal as to wish success to their endeavours.[29]

And again a month later, Cobbett castigates the Americans:

> The fact is, that with all their hypocritical cant about the blood of their citizens flowing in the Chesapeake, they were glad of the event; and eagerly seized hold of it as a ground whereon to urge demands which we had theretofore rejected, and in which they hoped now to

---

[29] *Political Register*, Vol 12, December 19, 1807.
[30] *Political Register*, *Vol 13, January 9 1808*.

succeed by coupling them with this recent case.[30]

In Cobbett's eyes Jefferson had insulted England by issuing her with an ultimatum.

> "You shall yield to me", he says, "your right of searching for seamen, or I will pass a non-importation act and lay an embargo". Would you, reader, had you been a minister of England, have advised the King of England to enter upon a negotiation with Thomas?[31]

And he resurrected for his readers the story of the treatment he had received in the United States in 1800.

> The Americans, under pretences the most false, by means the most base that ever were employed, by the vilest mockery of judicial proceedings, by openly-avowed and boasted-of perjury, robbed me of the earnings of my life up to that time, left me to begin anew with a family dependent solely on my exertions, and have since cruelly persecuted several of my friends.[32]

Aware that many of his readers might remember his earlier praises of the American people, Cobbett justified himself by saying that with the exception of a number of individuals he had known in Pennsylvania and the pro-British Federalists, the fact that

> I hate the United States and all their mean and hypocritical system of rule, I have a thousand times declared in print as well as in conversation; and I have further frequently declared that if I, or any one dear to me, were destined to lose my or his life in a *just* war, I know of no case in which that life would be lost with so little regret, as in demolishing the towns of America and in burying their unprincipled inhabitants under the rubbish.[33]

---

[31] Political Register, Vol 13, April 9 1808.
[32] *Political Register*, Vol 13, March 26 1808.
[33] *Political Register, Vol 13, March 26, 1808.*

What can have caused such venom and such vindictiveness in a man who, not so long before, had attempted to reconcile the differences between the two countries? To seek an answer, we must turn our attention away from the United States and examine Cobbett's involvement in the domestic politics of his own country.

3

Cobbett's Ugly Questions

Cobbett's bellicose stance against America stemmed from his conviction that England should stand firm against France. But whereas in 1803 he was calling on the British nation to rally behind the government in its renewal of the war with France, his anti-American writings in 1807 and 1808 were a call to the nation to insist that the government, which he believed to be wavering, should stand firm against American demands which, if conceded, he believed would result in a weakening of Britain's dominion of the seas and thereby her defence against Napoleon.

Between 1803 and 1807 Cobbett had become increasingly distrustful of the government and had in his *Political Register* exposed and attacked the numerous abuses in domestic politics — the maladministration, particularly in the armed forces, the corruption manifest in the wholesale granting of pensions and posts to friends of the parties in power, and the financial policies which had led to the growth of rich fundholders and bankers, and to the worsening condition of the labouring classes, all of which he originally attributed to the policies of "Pitt and his crew". (Pitt had been Prime Minister since 1804.) When, after Pitt's death in 1806, a new coalition was formed, with Fox, the Whig Foreign Secretary, Cobbett naturally looked to the new administration to address itself immediately to rooting out these crying abuses. It did not take long for Cobbett to realise that the new ministry from which he had hoped so much, had no intention to change the system, and that the evils he had attributed to Pitt were indulged in by Whigs and Tories alike. He now broke the link with the new government and dramatically flaunted the break by offering in his *Political Register* to stand for Parliament himself, if no one else came forward, in a by-election in Honiton, Devon, on the single issue of putting an end to the endemic corruption in high places. In the event the colourful Lord Cochrane took up the offer. Cobbett went down to Honiton to support him and witnessed at first hand the bribery that attended Parliamentary elections, and from that time forward he consistently castigated Whigs and Tories alike and lent his support only to radical candidates pledged to root out abuses. By the end of 1806

> The anti-Jacobin pamphleteer had become the democratic leader, the associate of Cabinet Ministers, the leader of an extra-parliamentary campaign for the abolition of abuses. The prodigal son had come back to his own people.[1]

So ended Cobbett's association with and support for the Tory party. It had throughout been based on his naive belief that those who opposed the principles of the French Revolution were men above corruption and dedicated to the welfare of their country. Just as he had found the workings of the republican government of the United States far from the picture drawn of it by the Abbé Raynal (whose description was quoted in the opening chapter) so he found the much vaunted British Constitution far from the Burkean ideal he had imagined it to be when living in the United States.

A government riddled through with corruption, an idle parasitic class of nouveaux riches profiting from the war,

---

[1] G D H Cole, *The Life of William Cobbett*, p109, W Collins & Sons, 1924.

and a growing number of labourers dependent on the parish for relief; this was how Cobbett saw England when Jefferson challenged her Orders in Council by imposing the Embargo in December 1807. Fears had been expressed in England that her trade would be ruined by America's non-importation acts passed earlier. To these Cobbett had responded by belittling its effects in his 'King Cong' article quoted in the last chapter. When news reached England early in 1808 of the much more severe Embargo Act, petitions poured in to Parliament for the repeal of the Orders in Council which had provoked it. Meetings were held arguing that the Orders in Council, issued to counteract Napoleon's Decrees, unjustly punished America which not only had had no hand in making the Decrees, but had protested to France against them.

The possibility that Parliament might give in to these demands and revoke her Orders in Council aroused in Cobbett a fierce determination to defend his country's interests. This time, just as earlier, he saw her most pressing need to be in an impregnable position with regard to France. Although after Trafalgar there was no immediate fear of invasion, Napoleon had in a series of brilliant campaigns crushed Britain's allies, Austria, Prussia and Russia, and by 1807 these countries were leagued with France against Britain.

With Jacobinism dead, and France now ruled by Napoleon, Cobbett had drawn closer to the Foxite attitude of leaving Europe to fight its own battles, and he had poked fun at the few disastrously mismanaged sorties which Britain had made on the continent in 1805 and 1806. But although he was against any renewal of the policies of forming and financing coalitions of European powers to check Napoleon's designs on Europe or of attempting to aid them militarily, he was adamant that Britain should enter into no new negotiations for peace with France. Peace, he argued, would enable Napoleon, now master of so many ports and arsenals in Europe, to create a navy sufficient to overpower the British and once again England would be in danger of invasion.

It was Cobbett's opinion that absolute dominion of the seas was essential to Britain's survival as an independent nation. To maintain dominion she must resist all demands which might weaken the Royal Navy, and he saw the revocation of the Orders in Council as the first step to such a weakening. Already, to his dismay, Britain had capitulated to American demands by disavowing Admiral Berkeley's order to attack the *Chesapeake* and undertaking not in future to search American ships of war. If further concessions were made, America would next renew her demand that Britain should renounce her right to search merchant vessels and remove seamen from them. If this were conceded, any British sailor could go to any American ship and be safe for ever, and the Royal Navy would be seriously depleted of crews. The Jeffersonian administration was fully aware that if England renounced her practice of impressment on the high seas, the Royal and merchant navies would suffer and "It was precisely because they knew it would have this effect, that the Americans demanded it at our hands".[2]

The reasons why Cobbett so strenuously endeavoured to arouse in his readers' minds a determination to hold out against the Embargo, even to the point of war, were, therefore, based on a number of factors. Paramount was his belief that Napoleon, having conquered Britain's former allies and forced them into a league against her, would once again attempt to subjugate his oldest and most persistent

---

[2] *Political Register*, Vol 13, January 23 1808.

enemy, England. Cobbett saw, with some justification, that the new Decrees forbidding neutrals any intercourse with Britain were a sign that he now felt strong enough to begin preparations to that end. Secondly, Cobbett foresaw correctly that the Embargo would create great dissension in the United States and could not be enforced for any length of time without a break up of the Union. Aware of the unpreparedness of the United States for war, Cobbett was convinced that if England adopted a belligerent attitude and made it clear that she would not respond to American demands, the Embargo would die of itself.

Of almost equal importance was Cobbett's detestation of the current doctrine that Britain's prosperity depended on commerce, "exports of every sort, generally speaking, only tend to enrich a few persons and to cause the labouring parts of the people to live harder than they otherwise would do".[3] Many of the objections to the Embargo came from British merchants who had interests in trading with Britain's overseas colonies and from plantation owners in the colonies themselves. Cobbett was at this time very much a "little Englander", believing that the possession of colonies far from enriching the nation caused enormous expense in maintaining military and diplomatic posts, and were a rich source for corruption in that lucrative positions as governors, secretaries and officials were among the perquisites that the government could hand out to their supporters. The fact that objections came also from cotton merchants "opulent manufacturers who keep thousands of English workers to 'work and weep' for their own profit and for the clothing of Americans"[4] while so many Englishmen in town and country were clothed in

---

[3] *Political Register*, Decmber 6 1806.
[4] *Political Register*, August 1 1807.

rags, added to his mistrust of the doctrine that England's prosperity depended on the export trade.

One last factor should not, perhaps, be overlooked — Cobbett's own personal pride. Had England made concessions to America in response to Jefferson's Embargo, it would have submitted to the very party in America that had been responsible for his persecution and losses in 1800. Surrender would have involved not only England's humiliation but his own.

When it became apparent that opposition to and evasions of the Embargo within the United States made it almost a certainty that it was doomed to failure, Cobbett ceased his attacks on America. Only when news arrived of the ending of the Embargo do we find him once more returning to the theme and pugnaciously justifying his conduct, but this time with a lightness of tone reflecting his sense of relief that the danger was over and that his predictions had been correct.

> Did I not say that if our ministers held firm, they would be compelled to repeal the Embargo Law? What are now become of all the predictions and alarms? All the threats of starvation and ruin? America had her Embargo and Bonaparte has shut up all the ports of the Continent; and how do you feel yourself, my honest, duped John Bull. Are you starved yet? Do the oxen fat in Devonshire? Do the sheep breed in Dorsetshire? Do hogs breed and fat in Hampshire and the bees still collect honey there? This nation is never to be so duped again. The time for that gross duplicity is past. We now have proof that our own resources are quite sufficient for us, and of this valuable knowledge we shall, I trust, make proper use.[5]

---

[5] *Political Register*, April 8 1808.

For Cobbett, for England and for many Americans in the New England states the ending of the Embargo was a cause for rejoicing. But for America as a nation, its failure was a bitter humiliation. The weapon forged to assert America's right as an independent nation had proved to be a broken reed. After fourteen months of great hardship, impressment continued unabated, no reparations had been made for the *Chesapeake* outrage, and French Decrees, British Orders in Council and paper blockades still exposed American ships and crews to seizure by both belligerents. Although the Presidential Election at the end of 1808 had returned the Jefferson party to power, the new President James Madison, Jefferson's former Secretary of State and close colleague, "inspired little affection and no enthusiasm."[6] Cobbett had written a vivid and cruel description of his physical appearance in an article in his *Political Censor* describing the Proceedings of Congress in 1794.

> Madison is a little bow-legged man, at once stiff and slender. His countenance has that sour aspect, that conceited screw, which pride would willingly mould into an expression of disdain, if it did not find the features too skinny and too scanty for its purposes. His thin sleek hair, and the niceness of his garments are indicative of that economical cleanliness which expostulates with the shoe-boy and the washerwoman, which flees from the dangers of a gutter, and which boasts of wearing a shirt for three days without rumpling the ruffle. In short, take him altogether, precisely the prim, mean, prig-like look of a corporeal mechanic,* and, were he ushered in to your parlour, you would wonder why he came without his measures and his shears.[7]

---

[6] S E Morison, *The Oxford History of the American People*, p 377, OUP 1965.
[7] *Porcupines Works*, Vol 2, p 7.
*A somewhat heavy-handed term for a tailor.

In March 1809, twenty-five years after Cobbett had penned this picture, Madison was inaugurated President of the United States. After the ending of the Embargo, Congress replaced it by a non-importation Act against the belligerents. The cargoes of any British or French vessels entering American ports were to be subject to forfeiture, and all American harbours were closed to both French and British ships of war. If one or the other belligerent revoked its decrees against American shipping, restrictions would be lifted for that country, but remain in force for the other until it, too, revoked its decrees.

The failure of the Embargo and the election of a new President seemed to the British Government a favourable time to renew negotiations with the United States with a view to reopening trade between the two countries. Canning, the British Foreign Secretary, instructed Erskine, the British Minister to the United States, to sound out prospects for resolving the differences, and he was ordered to convey to the American government an intimation that the British would consider making reparations for the *Chesapeake* incident and repealing her Orders in Council if the United States removed her non-importation Acts against British goods, and the interdiction of her harbours to British warships, while continuing to keep both Acts in force against France. Furthermore, to ensure non-intercourse with France and her allies, the United States was to allow the British Navy to capture any American ship which attempted to trade with France or her allies. The question of impressment was not to be raised.

Erskine, more friendly to the United States than his predecessors, and anxious for accommodation, entered into discussions with Robert Smith, Madison's Secretary of State, and began by hammering out a draft agreement on the *Chesapeake* affair. Britain would restore the seamen taken and pay compensation to the victims of the incident. Agreement over the rescinding of the American non-importation Act against Britain, but keeping it in force against France presented no difficulties, for in passing the act, Congress had stipulated that non-importation would end if the Orders in Council were revoked, and June 1809 was agreed as the date when the British Orders and the American non-importation Acts would be revoked. On the last issue, that the United States should allow a foreign power to enforce an American law, by giving that nation permission to seize any vessel infringing it, the American Secretary of State was adamant. To have allowed the Royal Navy to stop and search American ships suspected of trading with France would have been a gross violation of its sovereignty and aroused all the hostility surrounding impressment. Erskine, aware that this was an impossible demand to make of the United States, and not willing to jeopardise the great progress made so far, took upon himself the responsibility of ignoring this part of his instructions and proposed a draft treaty omitting this requirement. In April 1809, only six weeks after his inauguration as President, Madison accepted the treaty and proclaimed that in response to Britain's offer to revoke her Orders in Council, the non-intercourse against her would be lifted as from June 1809.

The news was received with jubilation in the United States and scores of American merchantmen left harbour, in anticipation of the formal ratification of the treaty, loaded with foodstuffs and raw material for Great Britain. The euphoria was short-lived, for when the draft treaty reached England, Canning repudiated it on the grounds that Erskine had exceeded his instructions.

> At one stroke Canning threw away a settlement of the *Chesapeake* affair, made impossible the withdrawal of

the non-intercourse act by America and the Orders in Council, and repelled a hopeful move to reach an agreement on impressment.[8]

Erskine was recalled from his post in the United States and Canning appointed Francis Jackson as his successor in Washington.

When Jackson arrived in Washington in September 1809, his manner and behaviour were not conducive to better relations between the two governments. He appeared to be contemptuous of the people and customs of the Americans he met and he not only condemned Erskine's conduct in proposing the aborted treaty, but insinuated that when Madison signed the treaty he was aware that Erskine was exceeding his instructions. Jackson's condemnation of one of the few British Ministers to the United States who had shown some respect for and understanding of the Americans, coupled with his insinuations against the President, made him *persona non grata* in Washington. Official communications between him and the American government ceased after only a few weeks and he returned to England. No Minister was appointed to succeed him.

When Congress met at the end of 1809, there was little cheer in the President's message. The non-importation Act which had replaced the Embargo was due to expire early in 1810. It had failed to persuade either belligerent to rescind their orders and decrees against American shipping. Without a Minister in Washington, the American government could carry on negotiations with Britain only through the American Minister in London, William Pickney. He found himself continually frustrated by the courteous but dilatory new Foreign Secretary, Marquis

---

[8] Patrick C T White, *A Nation on Trial: America and the War of 1812*, p 61, John Wiley & Sons, 1965.

Wellesley, who had replaced Canning in October 1809. Wellesley promised much but repeatedly failed to match his words with his actions. Over the affair of the *Chesapeake* Pickney wrote of Wellesley

> Nothing could be fairer than his conversations on that case. He settles it with me verbally over and over again. He promises his written overture in a few more days and I hear no more of the matter.[9]

Similarly, in spite of repeated requests by Pickney for a new Minister to be appointed to Washington, months went by while Wellesley put off a decision on the grounds that he was still searching for a suitable candidate for the post.

Faced with humiliation, obstruction and frustration in all their attempts to uphold America's rights as a neutral and to exact reparations for the numerous wrongs inflicted upon the country, Congress was divided as to what action to take. Many began openly to declare for war with Britain as the only answer, and the so-called War Hawks, led by Henry Clay, pointed to the possibility of invading Canada as one way to force the British into meaningful negotiations. But the lack of military preparedness, exacerbated by the unwillingness of many Congressmen to vote funds to provide adequate forces, led to one further attempt to use economic measures, but this time by offering bribes rather than intimidation, to the offending powers. In May 1810 an Act was passed repealing all the commercial restrictions and opening trade to both France and Britain on an equal footing, but stating that if either of the belligerents revoked its decrees against American shipping, restrictions would be reimposed on the other within three months. Madison, who had hoped for sterner measures, was not sanguine. "However feeble it may appear", he said, "it is possible that

---

[9] Patrick C T White, *op cit*, p 71/2.

one or other of those powers may allow it more effect than was produced by the overtures heretofore tried".[10]

When news of the American act opening trade between all countries and the ending of the non-importation Acts reached Europe, the reactions of the two belligerents were very different. Britain, now at last actively prosecuting the war against Napoleon in the Spanish peninsula with some signs of success under the Duke of Wellington, continued to turn a deaf ear to any propositions from the United States.

> If anything the British government had become even more scornful towards the United States in the years from 1807 to 1811. As time progressed, the government became increasingly confident that the United States had neither the power to injure nor to wage war against Britain.[11]

France, on the other hand, suffered severely from the freeing of trade because the overwhelming superiority of the Royal Navy on the seas resulted in Britain being able to enforce her blockades of European ports and French ships were frequently captured and condemned if found trading with the United States. It was, therefore, to Napoleon's advantage to accept America's offer and he agreed to rescind her Decrees against neutral shipping as from November 1810, on the understanding that the American government would reimpose non-intercourse against Britain.

With events crowding one upon another during 1809 and 1810 — the Erskine treaty and its repudiation by Canning, the disastrous appointment of Francis Jackson; the non-importation Acts, and America's threat to invade Canada,

---

[10] Patrick C T White, *op cit*, p 68.
[11] R Horsman, *The Causes of the War of 1812,* p 190, University of Pennsylvania Press, 1962.

one would expect and hope to find in the pages of the *Political Register* Cobbett's probably startling and certainly idiosyncratic comments on all these happenings. Such expectations, however, are doomed to disappointment, for from July 1809 onwards Cobbett was living under the threat of prosecution and was destined for a two-year prison sentence in Newgate gaol in London.

In the summer of 1809 a mutiny had broken amongst some militia men in Ely in Cambridgeshire, over what they considered an intolerable reduction in their pay. A party of German mercenaries stationed nearby was called in, the mutiny suppressed, and the ringleaders sentenced to five hundred lashes each. Cobbett threw caution to the winds and wrote an article condemning the sentences "What, shall the rascals mutiny, and that, too, when the German Legion is so near at hand? Lash them, lash them. Oh yes, they merit a double tailed cat".[12] His fury at the injustice and severity with which the protest had been squashed led him to end the article by pointing out that the severe punishments imposed in the French army had often been used to prove that Napoleon was unpopular and was forced to adopt draconian measures to keep his soldiers in subordination. If German soldiers were necessary to keep English soldiers in order, was there not an obvious parallel to be drawn? To suggest, in wartime, that one's own government might be as hated as that of its arch enemy, Napoleon, was a fatal blunder and the government was quick to pounce. In July 1810 the case was heard, Cobbett found guilty of criminal libel, sentenced to two years in prison and fined one thousand pounds. What neither the government nor Cobbett could foresee was that Newgate gaol was to be for him not a prison but

---

[12] *Political Register*, July 1 1809.

a heaven-sent opportunity for study. Newgate became Cobbett's University.

To be confined for two whole years within the walls of a prison was a revolutionary change in Cobbett's pattern of life. His friends rallied round and raised enough money and he was enabled to rent the use of a sitting room and two bedrooms in the prison keeper's house for twenty guineas a week. So he was well-housed, well fed (food could be brought in from outside and hampers were regularly sent up from Botley), and able to keep fit by exercising each morning on the roof of the prison. Though not free of worries (his fine and the rent made his financial position extremely parlous and throughout his confinement he was constantly writing orders as how to run his farm), within a month of his arrival in prison he produced not one but two issues of his *Political Register* each week, taunting the government by appending at the foot of every article he wrote, Wm. Cobbett, State Prison, Newgate. Yet for a man accustomed to so many and such varied activities, two Registers a week by no means exhausted his energies.

Before Newgate, Cobbett's activities as a family man, an active farmer, and editor of a political journal were prodigious. To his house in Botley came a stream of visitors "The house had room for all", wrote Miss Mitford the somewhat gushing author of *Our Village*, "Everything was excellent, everything abundant, all served with the greatest nicety; and everything went on with such quiet regularity, that of the large circle of guests not one could find himself in the way."[13] Another visitor said of Botley House, "I never saw a finer baron of beef at any nobleman's county ball at Christmas time than I have seen at Cobbett's table,

---

[13] Lewis Melville, *The Life & Letters of William Cobbett*, Vol 1, p 247, John Lane, The Bodley Press, 1913.

and he seemed to have a peculiar pleasure and pride in standing up before it, a large carving-knife and fork in his hand, ready to give a prime cut."[14]

In prison, life was very different. Cobbett now had time, and opportunity to study. In his Botley days he had not confined his reading to British papers and reports. The *Political Register* had from the start published articles and reports from foreign journals, but more often than not, they were inserted without comment. Cobbett's distance from London, the need to produce one or two long articles every week to a deadline, and his immersion in his duties to his family, his farm, his employees and his guests meant that unless he felt the matter to be of pressing importance his perusal of foreign papers was necessarily cursory. Another factor of importance was that spending so much of his time at Botley, he had not been in close touch with other reformers and critics of the government. The publicity surrounding his sentence (the popularity of his paper made Cobbett's name a household word), the sympathy it aroused, and his now permanent availability in the centre of London, resulted in his being visited by many of the leading radicals of the day. Sir Francis Burdett, whose generosity in lending Cobbett a large sum of money relieved him from the harshness of prison life, Major Cartwright, Alderman Wood, Henry Hunt, were among the many who made the pilgrimage to Newgate, and through discussions with them, Cobbett's horizons were widened. Cobbett himself wrote that during his two years in Newgate deputies of societies and clubs came from one hundred and ninety-seven cities and towns of England, Scotland and Ireland to visit him. The University of Newgate provided seminars as well as a well-stocked reading-room.

---

[14] *Ibid*, Vol 1, p 246-7.

When Cobbett entered prison, Sir Francis Burdett, MP, one of the tiny handful of radicals in the House of Commons, had taken up the cause of a British sailor, Robert Jeffery, who had been punished for a minor breach of discipline on board the sloop *HMS Recruit* by being put ashore and marooned on a barren island without clothing or provisions. His case had come to light after he had been found by chance by an American vessel and brought to the United States where his story received wide publicity. In Newgate Cobbett pursued the matter relentlessly in issue after issue of the *Register*, not only exposing the severity and savagery of the punishment, but also the very suspect efforts of the government to hush up the scandal. Burdett's attempt to raise the question in Parliament had been criticised as being likely to excite discontent in the navy, but Cobbett sprang to his defence.

> What could possibly be better calculated to inspire the seaman with confidence in the justice of this country than this vote for an address to the king in behalf of a common sailor? How much more likely are such exposures (especially if proper steps are taken by the government in consequence of them) to prevent discontents from swelling into open mutiny, by showing the seamen that however distant from home, they will, when their treatment be made known, not fail to meet with protection in England.[15]

In August 1810, a month after Cobbett began his sentence, news reached England that Napoleon was consolidating his grip on Europe, having taken direct rule of Holland, and had replaced the Swedish Crown Prince with Bernadotte, one of his greatest generals. As a result Napoleon now had command of all the ports, the arsenals and the seamen of the two great maritime powers of Northern Europe,

---

[15] *Political Register*, Vol 18, August 18 1810.

Holland and Sweden. Throughout that autumn Cobbett wrote article after article warning his readers that France was preparing a fleet and armaments only four or five hours' sail from the east coast of England. And yet, he wrote:

> instead of preparing the minds of the people for this danger, our ministerial writers seemed to have formed a deliberate plan for making the people of England believe that so far from Napoleon's being able to *attack* us from Holland, he is likely to be attacked himself by Holland. Shocking infatuation. If this information continue, what must be the consequences.[16]

From his own study of the news from the Continent, Cobbett drew a very different picture from that portrayed by the 'ministerial writers'.

> If what our public prints tell us is true, Napoleon is hated by every soul on the continent of Europe. The Dutch hate him, the Spaniards hate him, the Swiss hate him, the Germans hate him, the French hate him. All his generals hate him. Every living creature wishes him dead. But in the middle of this universal hatred, we see him quitting his capital and his kingdom for weeks and months together, and we see him in battle after battle without any hurt to his person.[17]

What, then, had caused the government so to misrepresent the state of affairs in Europe and to belittle Napoleon's increasing domination so fraught with danger to England? In October Cobbett spelt out the answer.

> The reason why these efforts are made is plain enough. If the people were to see the thing in its true light at once, the effect on their minds would be great. They would see the danger to their country and, of course,

---

[16] *Ibid*, Vol 18, September 1 1812.
[17] *Ibid*, Vol 18, August 25, 1810.

to themselves, from the event. They would then, as men generally do in such cases, begin to enquire whence that danger had arisen. They would find the immediate cause to be the *irresistible power of France*. But they would not stop there; for recollecting that England was *once* as powerful as France, that England had *once* the power of preventing France from tyrannising over the smaller states of Europe; recollecting this, the people of England would be very apt to ask, how it has happened that England does not possess this power *now*; how she came to *lose* this power; *since when* she lost it; what was the *cause* of her losing it, and *who* are the persons who have managed her affairs, who have had the command of her resources, since the time when she possessed this power? These would be ugly questions. To answer them would not be a pleasant task. Therefore all manner of endeavours are used to prevent the questions being put.[18]

Cobbett asked other awkward questions too. How was it, he asked, that in spite of all the talk of the ruin Napoleon's system had brought to Europe, England had just proposed to Napoleon that France should send grain to England in return for sugar from the British colonies?

If Napoleon has more corn than he wants and we more sugar than we want, it is very natural that we should wish to make the exchange proposed. I commend the ministers for making the proposal. But, *at a time when they are making such a proposal*, let not the prints devoted to them speak of the French as a people steeped in misery, owing to the "folly" and "cruelty" of him to whom this proposal is addressed.[19]

Cobbett's close study of news from the continent led him to question more openly than before the objectives of

---

[18] *Ibid*, October 13 1810.
[19] *Ibid*, Vol 18, August 11 1812.

England's war with France. Not for one moment did he waver from his conviction that England must preserve her independence and repel Napoleon's designs to subjugate her; but he became ever more strongly critical of the government's declared aim to restore the old dynasties in Europe. Now, more aware than before, of the repressive nature of the old regimes in Europe and beginning to realise that Napoleon was welcomed by many of the common people in Europe as a liberator from serfdom and oppression, he believed that England should leave the continent to its fate and allow it to be "new-modelled in the way its new master may choose".

> We *deplore* the fate of Holland and Sweden and Naples and Switzerland and Prussia and Genoa and Piedmont and Austria; but what is the use of this, when we have not the power to render the smallest assistance to any one of them? What is the use of deploring the fate of Holland and of giving such a frightful picture of its situation, if we cannot do any thing to better that situation?
>
> What wisdom dictates to us is this: *to look at home*; to look well into our means of preserving ourselves; to diminish our expenditure; to reform all abuses and tear up corruption by the roots. These are, in my opinion, the things which wisdom dictates to us; and if we listen to her voice, though we must still look with anxiety at the dreadful power of our enemy, we need look at it without fear.[20]

In the first six months of Cobbett's incarceration in Newgate, his concern with the marooned sailor, the Jeffrey affair, and the alarming news of Napoleon's successes on the Continent, meant that he devoted little space for the news from America. But at the end of the year, Britain

---

[20] *Ibid*, Vol 18, October 6 1810.

was faced with a very difficult problem.

Towards the end of 1810 when Cobbett had been six months in prison, Britain was faced with a very serious problem in its relations with America. France agreed to lift all her Decrees against American shipping and in return America agreed to reimpose her non-importation Acts against British shipping, unless Britain also revoked all her Orders in Council against American shipping. Britain was faced with a dilemma. To have acquiesced in America's decision to break her commercial ties with Britain unless she revoked her Orders in Council would have indicated weakness; to have revoked her Orders in Council in response to America's threat would have seemed little short of surrender. In December 1810 Cobbett highlighted this dilemma facing the government in a long article entitled "Look before you Leap".

Convinced that dominion of the seas was essential to Britain's survival as an independent nation, Cobbett continued to believe that any American demands which might weaken this dominion should be resisted. But, as we have seen, his attitude to the war with France was changing. It was becoming apparent, too, that the severity of the punishment imposed on him by his own government was lessening the resentment he harboured against the Americans for their treatment of him ten years earlier, and during his period in Newgate we begin to see him taking a more sympathetic attitude towards the United States. The dubious practices he had attributed to the Democrat party in America and against which he had fulminated as Peter Porcupine, began to pale into insignificance besides those of all the parties, Pittites, Whigs and Tories alike which governed Britain. In "Look before you Leap", the indications of this more sympathetic attitude are evident, and for this reason the article deserves close attention.

Having for some time devoted little space in his paper to American affairs, Cobbett felt it necessary, in order to explain the present crisis in Anglo-American relations, to refresh his readers' minds with a history of the French Decrees and the British Orders in Council, which had provoked it. In view of the digression exploring in some detail the hardening of Cobbett's attitude to his government and his reappraisal of Britain's role in her war with France, it is not out of place to refresh our own minds, too, by briefly retracing with him the long chain of events which was to reach its tragic climax eighteen months later in the Anglo-American War of 1812.

4

French Decrees and British Orders

In January 1810, six months before he went to prison, Cobbett had published in his *Political Register* some of the correspondence between Francis (Copenhagen) Jackson, the British Minister in Washington, and Robert Smith, the American Secretary of State, dealing with various matters of dispute between the two governments, with the comment: "you cannot for your life tell what is, or what is not, the subject-matter of it", and went on to say:

> The eldest of my children was unborn, when this dispute began, and I should not be without hopes of being a great grandfather before the dispute would end. We have had six envoys (and retinues) and permanently three and sometimes five commissioners; there have been from six to ten able bodied writers and (what makes the thing more serious), most of them lawyers, too, hard at work for the last sixteen years. Mercy on us! What bales, what waggon-loads of tautology!![1]

But by December of the same year Madison's acceptance of the Cadore Letter put a different complexion on the matter. Britain could no longer prevaricate. The government had been told that as France had revoked her Decrees, non-intercourse would be put into effect against Great Britain unless she followed France's example and revoked hers too. So, with this new situation, Cobbett declared that the time

---

[1] *Political Register* Vol 17, January 13 1810.

had now come to cut through "the prodigious volumes which the lawyer-like statesmen on both sides of the water have piled together on the subject"[2] and to examine the history of the events which had led to America's ultimatum. His article "Look before you Leap" did just that.

Beginning with Britain's "paper blockade" of European ports, he described Napoleon's counter measure in his Berlin Decree of November 1806 declaring the whole of the British Isles to be in a state of blockade; he then detailed how Britain had retaliated with a series of Orders in Council forbidding all trade between the United States and Europe unless the goods were first brought to British ports and paid duties; and how this in turn had led to Napoleon's Milan Decree of December 1807 calling on the United States either to resist these British Orders or to be considered as an enemy to France.

> Both the nations made an appeal to America (for she was the only Neutral in fact) in this way: *Each* said to her, it is *your* fault for suffering our enemy to enforce such restrictions; it is for *you* to compel our enemy to respect your flag, and *until you do that*, I will enforce against you my measures of retaliation as my only means of self-defence against the tyrannical measures of my enemy.
>
> America, as was very natural in her situation, complained of both: after having tried negociation in vain, she fell upon this expedient. She protested against the grounds of justification by both parties; she declared that both had violated her rights; but she, at last, determined to submit, for the present, while she endeavoured to prevail upon one party or the other to give way first and revoke their Orders or Decrees.[3]

---

[2] *Political Register* Vol 18, December 15 1810.
[3] *Political Register* Vol 18, December 15 1810.

She did this in the Macon Act by lifting all the restrictions she had imposed on both the belligerents in protest at their violations of her rights as a neutral, but also declared that if one of the belligerents revoked its edicts, she would reimpose non-importation and close her harbours against the other until it, too, rescinded its edicts. France had responded by revoking her edicts, but at the time Cobbett was writing, Britain had not rescinded her Orders in Council.

Having thus traced the history down to this point, Cobbett then addressed himself to the question as to whether Britain should follow France and revoke her Orders in Council. His answer was unequivocal. "My opinion is that they ought to be revoked, and, indeed, that they ought to have been revoked in August last, upon the notification of the revocation of the Berlin and Milan Decrees being made to our government".[4] In twenty dense columns of small print, Cobbett appended to his article the texts of the Berlin and Milan Decrees issued by Napoleon, the texts of the British Orders in Council, Madison's Proclamation accepting France's revocation of her edicts, and the official letter of the American Minister to London to the British government informing it of France's revocation.

The reason Cobbett gave for his opinion was that it was abundantly clear from the documents he appended that Britain had stated that her edicts were imposed only as a means of defence against her enemy.

> The Orders were, from first to last, declared to be acts of retaliation; they express the *regret* of the King of England at being obliged to adopt measures so injurious to the commerce of neutrals; they clearly convey the idea that they are to continue in force no longer than the Decrees of the enemy, whence they have arisen.[5]

---

[4] *Ibid.*
[5] *Political Register* Vol 18, December 15 1810.

A reading of the documents, Cobbett stated, showed that it was impossible to escape the fact that Britain had declared that as soon as America had prevailed on France to revoke her edicts, Britain would revoke hers. The American government clearly understood this to be the case, for when informing the British government in August 1810 that France had offered to revoke her Decrees, the American Minister to Britain, William Pinkney, had ended his letter to Wellesley, the British Foreign Secretary, in these words: "I take it for granted that the revocation of the British Orders in Council will follow of course; and I shall hope to be enabled by your lordship, with as little delay as possible, to announce to my government that such revocation has taken place".[6]

Wellesley's reply to Pinkney's letter was, however, not encouraging. Although he assured him that it was the earnest desire of His Majesty's government to see commerce between Britain and the United States "restored to that freedom which is necessary to its prosperity", he stated that the British Orders would be revoked only when the repeal of the French Decrees "should have actually taken effect, and the commerce of neutral nations should have been restored to the condition in which it stood previous to the promulgation of these Decrees". Cobbett considered such prevarication unwarranted.

> The French Minister said in his letter to America "the Decrees are revoked". What was he to say more? In what way was an actual revocation to take place if not in this way? And how was the fact to be communicated to us, except in the way in which it was communicated — that is to say officially through the American Minister? Really, I cannot, for my part, form any notion of what we could require further.[7]

---

[6] *Ibid.*
[7] *Ibid.*

Britain had expressly stated to the United States that she would act "pari passu" with France in relaxing her edicts against neutral shipping. But had she acted up to this declaration? "'Pari passu' (a term which the learned make use of to show, I suppose, the *utility* of Latin) means here 'with equal pace' or 'to keep pace with', and the declaration clearly meant that we would keep pace with her in softening the rigour of our measures".[8]

Towards the end of his article, Cobbett reiterated his conviction that Britain needed to retain sovereignty of the seas and said that if it were merely a matter of expediency, it might be preferable to keep the Orders in Council in force. But, he argued, over and over again Britain had maintained that she had issued her Orders only as a necessary measure of defence against Napoleon's Decrees, and would revoke them whenever the French Decrees were lifted. "It is a question of justice, demanded by a particular compact, clearly understood between the parties".[9] In Cobbett's eyes, the British government had reneged on its promises, and the government stood condemned.

It is interesting to note that throughout the article Cobbett constantly criticised Wellesley's statement that Britain would revoke her Orders only when France's revocation "should have actually taken effect". Yet Wellesley's distrust of Napoleon was not unfounded: between the time of his announcement of the intention to revoke (August 1810) and the date when the revocation was to be put into effect (November 1810), American ships in French ports continued to be seized. Even after November, when the Decrees were officially ended, "Almost every mail (arriving in the United States) for the next two years, brought news

---

[8] *Political Register* Vol 18, December 15 1810.
[9] *Ibid.*

of fresh seizures and scuttlings of American vessels by French port authorities, warships and privateers".[10]

Cobbett's condemnation of Britain's failure to act 'pari passu' with France, in spite of well-attested examples over the years of Napoleon's failure to keep his promises, must be attributed to his determination to expose the shortcomings of the government. He could hold up Britain's continuing refusal to repeal her Orders as a striking example of the cant and hypocrisy of which he had been accusing the government for many years past. What had become of her professions that her Orders in Council were imposed unwillingly, her statements that she had been forced to adopt them only as a means of defence against Napoleon's Decrees? Here were sticks ready to hand with which to beat the government, and Cobbett did not scruple to use them.

The British government, not trusting Napoleon, kept her Orders in force, and in February 1811 the United States, acting on the terms of her Macon Act, put into effect her non-importation of British goods, and closed her waters and harbours to British shipping. Cobbett warned that the dispute was coming to open rupture though not, he hoped, to war. He supported the stand taken by America. He had, as was mentioned earlier, for some years been attacking the doctrine that a country's prosperity was enhanced by a large export trade, and the United States was, in his eyes, to be commended for its efforts to become self-sufficient. "They have seen what Banks, and East India Companies, and Meetings of Merchants and Bankers have produced in England; and they seem to have resolved that the same shall not happen to their country".[11] He explained to his

---

[10] Morison, S E, *The Oxford History of the American People*, p 378 OUP, 1965.
[11] *Political Register* Vol 19, March 6 1811.

readers that before the Embargo of 1807-09, America had been dependent on foreign trade for many of the necessities of life, but when all imports were forbidden during Jefferson's Embargo, they were forced to become manufacturers themselves, and had made astonishing progress in setting up industries to supply their needs. Furthermore, their absolute dependence on Europe, and Britain in particular, for wool had been overcome by the introduction of a breed of sheep into the New World which could be kept in sheds in winter and fed on hay, straw and root vegetables and so survive the severe winters. In 1807 Cobbett had correctly predicted that America could not long endure the Embargo, but by 1811 her position had changed radically and he applauded the change.

The position in England, too, was now very different from the time when Jefferson had imposed his Embargo. Then, it will be remembered, the hardships it might have imposed on merchants had been largely mitigated by the unforeseen opening of markets in South America. But the opening of these markets to British goods had precipitated wild speculation and in 1810 the boom had collapsed, a number of banks had failed, and manufacturers found themselves heavily overstocked with goods for export. When the American markets were closed to them in February 1811 the effect was little less than catastrophic.

> In Birmingham, where it was estimated that almost half the total volume of the city's output was produced for the American market, there were 9000 people in receipt of poor relief in the summer of 1811, and 'every manufacturer is overloaded with stock'. 'Never in any former instance, or upon any other subject, were the genuine feelings of by far the greater majority of the inhabitants of the town so strongly excited, or so unequivocally expressed'. Urban demonstrations in many other British cities provided a sharp reminder to

Perceval's government that business opinion could no longer be overlooked.[12]

Distress was not confined to the industrial section of the country. A bad harvest in 1811 spread misery and disaffection to the countryside, and the year 1811 was marked by a formidable outbreak of rioting by hand-loom weavers, thrown out of work by the introduction of frame machines, who banding together under the name of Luddites, went about the country smashing the frames which had deprived them of their livelihood. The government, confronted by these demonstrations of discontent in town and country, and fearing full-scale revolution, reacted by sending troops to quell the disturbances, introducing spies among the working people to scent out the hotbeds of rebellion, and promulgating laws to terrify the people into submission, including making frame-breaking a capital offence. Lord Byron, whose sympathies lay with the starving people, defended the desperate labourers and protested against the proposed legislation to make frame-breaking an offence subject to the death penalty. In a speech to the House of Lords, he said:

> Is there not blood enough upon your penal code, that more must be poured forth to ascend to Heaven and testify against you? Are these the remedies for a starving and desperate populace? But suppose it passed; suppose one of these men, as I have seen them — meagre with famine, sullen with despair, careless of a life which your Lordships are perhaps about to value at something less than the price of a stocking-frame; — suppose this man surrounded by the children for whom he is unable to procure bread at the hazard of his existence, about to be torn for ever from a family which he lately

---

[12] Asa Briggs, *The Age of Improvement*, p 165 Longmans, 1959.

supported in peaceful industry, and which it is not his fault that he can no longer so support; — suppose this man, and there are ten thousand such from whom you may select your victims, dragged into court, to be tried for this new offence, by this new law; still there are two things wanting to convict and condemn him; and these are, in my opinion, — twelve butchers for jury and a Jeffreys for a judge.[13]

And yet, to England's shame, the Bill was passed and butchers and hanging judges were found to hang or transport the frame-breakers.

From prison, Cobbett noted the growing distress, and though never condoning the violence he, like Byron, attacked the repressive measures imposed by the government. "Measures ought to be adopted, not so much for putting an end to the riots, as to prevent the misery out of which they arise".[14] His researches into the growth of banking and borrowing made him ever more conscious that the government consistently put its own interests and those of the financiers to whom it was indebted for its borrowings above those of the country as a whole.

Deaf to the growing demands throughout the country for a repeal of the Orders in Council, seemingly utterly indifferent to the hardships which the closure of American markets had imposed, Spencer Perceval's administration continued to keep them in effect, and American merchantmen trading with France and her allies were subject to seizure and condemnation. American anger over Britain's refusal to rescind her Orders was exacerbated by repeated violations of American territorial waters by the Royal Navy and by impressment from American ships continuing unabated, sometimes actually within sight of

---

[13] Ed, Christopher Hampton, *A Radical Reader*, pp 394-5, Penguin Books, 1984.
[14] *Political Register* Vol 20, November 23 1811.

the coast. In May 1811 an incident occurred reminiscent of the *Chesapeake* affair, but this time it was a British ship that suffered and surrendered. HMS *Guerriere* stopped and searched a coastal vessel sailing within American territorial waters, and impressed some seamen from it. An American frigate, USS *President,* was ordered to stop and search the *Guerriere* and retrieve the impressed seamen. USS *President*, under her commander John Rodgers, sighted and overhauled a ship thought to be the *Guerriere*, and shots were exchanged in which nine British sailors were killed and twenty-three wounded. The British ship was in fact not HMS *Guerriere* but HMS *Little Belt*, a smaller corvette of twenty guns as opposed to the *President's* forty-four. She surrendered and was brought captive into an American port, and in the subsequent enquiry both commanders maintained that the other had fired the first shot. Cobbett published in his *Political Register* the text of the enquiry, and believing it impossible to ascertain for certain which vessel had fired first, made the common sense suggestion that rather than an appeal to arms, "there is a much better way of settling the matter; and that is, to say no more about it which may be done without any stain on the honour of either party".[15]

In the United States the crippling and surrender of a British ship of war was greeted with jubilation. At last the humiliation engendered by the surrender of the USS *Chesapeake* could be set against the surrender of the *Little Belt*, and the Royal Navy had been shown to be vulnerable. In England much play was made of the fact that the *Little Belt* had been attacked by a ship greatly outnumbering her in guns, but the humiliation rankled. On both sides of the Atlantic, war was in the air.

---

[15] *Political Register* Vol 20, September 14 1811.

On August 2nd, 1811, Cobbett had published the twenty-ninth and last of his series of articles *Paper Against Gold* which had filled so many pages of his *Political Register* while he was in prison, and was free to devote a large section of his paper to the crisis facing the country — the prospect of war with the United States. He had now been in prison for over a year and his wide reading and his contacts with a large cross-section of the public had confirmed and strengthened his conviction that the war with France, now in its nineteenth year, was achieving nothing except increasing hardship and misery for the labouring people. Napoleon had long since abandoned his plans for an invasion of England, and Cobbett believed that the war was now being waged solely in order the reinstate the old regimes in France and her satellite countries in Europe. And he attributed the government's stubborn refusal to rescind the Orders in Council to its desire to cause dissension in the United States and, if possible, to break up the union of the United States. The widespread riots and the mass demonstrations against government policies caused the administration to fear revolution and to see "Jacobins" and "levellers" behind every disturbance. In its eyes, France and the United States, both of which had overthrown their established governments, were, by their very existence, an example to the disaffected and a threat to the established order in Great Britain. It was the intention of the government to do all in its power to destroy both.

Earlier in the year, expectations had been raised that the Opposition Whigs (always critical of the French war) might be asked to form a government when the Prince of Wales was appointed Regent after his father, George III, had been become insane. In his youth the Prince had consorted with the Whigs, had been a close friend of Charles Fox, always a supporter of both France and the United States, and he was believed to favour a more liberal government than that of Spencer Perceval. The expected change never materialised; after flirting with the Whigs, the Prince Regent declared in favour of retaining his father's Ministry, excusing himself on the grounds that if he were to change his father's Ministers, he might retard the King's recovery. His decision to retain the hated, repressive Perceval administration and his excuse for doing so — many believed his debaucheries and extravagances had been one of the causes of his father's illness — brought him even further into public detestation and contempt. Already his quarrels with his father, his bigamous marriage to Caroline and his subsequent estrangement from her, his neglect of their daughter the Princess Charlotte, and his flaunting of his mistress Lady Hertford, had been the subjects of vicious caricatures. His extravagances (he had recently had built the exotic new palace on the coast, the Brighton Pavilion, at enormous cost to the nation) at a time when so many of his subjects were starving, were luridly illustrated by his holding a party for two thousand guests at his London residence, Carlton House, in June 1811 where

> the long table was set for two hundred of his most honoured guests beneath ornate lanterns fixed to the fan-vaulted ceiling of the Gothic conservatory. On the table in front of him was a miniature fountain whose waters flowed in a silver-bedded stream to right and left of him. The stream was bounded by mossy banks, water plants, and flowers; tiny gold and silver fish swam through the arches of miniature bridges, or sadly, lay dead, floating on top of the water. A model lake was surrounded by miniature urns from which rose the breath of fragrant smoke.[16]

The poet Shelley commented; "It is said that this

---

[16] Christopher Hibbert, *George IV Regent and King*, p 3, Allen Lane, 1973.

entertainment will cost £120,000. Nor will it be the last bauble which the nation must buy for this overgrown bantling of Regency".[17]

Seen against this background, Cobbett's decision to embark on his next project — an analysis of the crisis that was facing Britain in her relations with the United States — in the form of a series of Open Letters to the Prince Regent, was a master-stroke. With so large a portion of his countrymen behind him, Cobbett could present himself as a spokesman for the Regent's suffering subjects and could appeal to him as their lawful Protector against a callous Ministry. The tone he adopted was always respectful; nowhere in the Letters can one find a hint of the Prince's extravagances, his infidelities, his riotous living, his treatment of his wife or his callous behaviour to his old, blind, mad father. Throughout he addressed him as a man sensible of his obligations to his people and concerned for their welfare. In so doing, Cobbett was able subtly to contrast the man as he was known to be, with the Sovereign Prince he should have been, without once stepping outside the limits of what might have been written by a loyal subject petitioning his sovereign for redress. It should be noted too that Cobbett was not only fined and imprisoned, but was also bound over in the sum of £5000 to keep the peace for a further seven years after his release. It was therefore imperative for him to couch all his writings in terms that could not be open to charges of treason or of inciting discontent.

Cobbett opened his first Letter to the Prince Regent by suggesting that had the country in 1792 and 1793 listened to Fox who had counselled peace with the French Republic in the early days of its existence, Europe would never

---

[17] *Ibid* p 6.

have had her kings overthrown. Fox had believed that the coalition of European powers, heavily subsidised by Britain, had, by their attempts to invade the young Republic and overthrow its regime, been instrumental in causing the Republic to instigate its Reign of Terror. Remembering the calamities which had arisen by our undertaking this earlier war,

> it is natural for us, when threatened with a new war (while smarting and writhing under the effects of the war with France) to enquire betimes what are the grounds of such war; whether it would be *just*; if just, whether it would be *necessary*; and be the cause what it may, whether the *consequences* are likely to be good or evil.[18]

He then briefly outlined the longstanding dispute between Britain and the United States which had existed ever since America gained her independence in 1783. He deplored the fact that the British government took ten years before it sent a Minister to reside in America, and then when at last it did, interminable squabbles ensued about claims for debts owed by Americans to British merchants before the War of Independence. Even though Commissioners had been sitting and wrestling with these claims ever since 1794, the debts remained unsettled and the Commissioners had "swallowed up in expenses to this nation, a great part of what would have sufficed to satisfy our own claimants without any application for money for that purpose to the United States".[19]

Having thus castigated successive British governments for maladroitness in their dealings with the United States, he turned his attention to the non-intercourse Act against Britain which Madison had imposed in February. This, he

---

[18] *Political Register* Vol 20, August 31 1811.
[19] *Ibid.*

admitted, was undoubtedly a hostile act, but was it not, as America protested it to be, justified by provocative acts of Great Britain? "We may find, perhaps, that she is not only not blameable for what she has now done, but is entitled to praise for her forbearance and moderation".[20] In detailing for the Prince Regent the history of the French Decrees and the British Orders in Council, Cobbett went further in justifying America's retaliatory measure against Britain than he had done in his article "Look before you Leap" written eight months earlier. This time he explored the doctrine of the right of belligerents to search neutral ships. Even those writers who maintained that belligerents had a right to search for contraband or enemy goods had never, he argued, claimed that a belligerent had a right to seize in a neutral ship the goods of a neutral country. Yet the British Orders in Council, against which America was now protesting, did just this. The government had justified these seizures of non-contraband goods in neutral ships on the grounds of the law of retaliation. France, by her Decrees, was doing so, therefore, Britain must do the same. "It is a singular species of law", Cobbett wrote, "which, because a weak nation has been injured by one powerful nation, subjects it to be injured by another." He illustrated the point by an analogy with two leading prize fighters of the day, Belcher and Crib (representing France and Britain) attacking the Prime Minister and his Secretary of War (representing America).

> If Belcher were to beat Mr Perceval and Lord Liverpool in the street, Crib would not, for that reason, be justified in beating them too.[21]

A particularly happy illustration, for many of his readers would have relished the notion of these two popular prize

---

[20] *Ibid.*
[21] *Political Register* Vol 20, August 31 1811.

fighters giving those hated Ministers a sound thrashing in public.

In his second Letter to the Prince Regent published a week later, Cobbett brought up the matter which he had raised in his earlier article "Look before you Leap" of Britain's refusal to rescind her Orders until it was proved that the French Decrees had actually been revoked. On being informed that France had revoked her Decrees, the British government replied, in effect, that it did not believe it.

> This, may it please your Royal Highness, was, it appears to me, a very strange kind of language to use towards other powers. It was treating the American government as a sort of political ideot. It was telling it that it did not understand the interests of America, and that it was unworthy to be entrusted with power. And it was saying to the Emperor of France that he was to be shut out of the pale of sovereigns; that he was on no account to be believed. Thus, then, the door against peace, against the exchange of prisoners, against the softening of the rigours of war in any way or in any degree, was for ever barred.[22]

Britain was now bringing forward another reason for continuing the Orders in Council. Recently she had declared that until Napoleon lifted his restrictions on American ships bringing English goods into the continent (the so-called Continental System), she would continue her Orders in Council. Yet Napoleon's orders prohibiting the importation of English goods into Europe were an exact counterpart of the long-standing British practice of forbidding French goods to enter Britain.

> This being the case, it does seem to require an uncommon portion of impudence or of self-conceit for

---

[22] *Political Register* Vol 20, September 7 1811.

us to demand of the Americans to cause the Continental System to be abandoned as a condition upon which we are willing to cease violating their rights.[23]

In his third Letter Cobbett dealt with the *Little Belt* incident. Here he criticised the press for their strictures against the American people for expressing exultation at the killing of British sailors and the capture of the ship He asked the Prince Regent to see the incident in its context. The *Little Belt*, he explained, was part of a British squadron stationed near the American coast which "stopped, rummaged, and insulted their merchantmen; and in many cases seized and carried away their own people out of their own ships within sight of their own shores".[24] To understand the feelings of the Americans, one had only to imagine what the feelings of the British people would be if the position were reversed and American ships impressed British sailors into their ships.

> For an American vessel to meet a packet between Cork and Bristol and to take out some of her sailors and carry them away to the East or West Indies to die or be killed, is something so monstrous that one cannot bring oneself to feel as if it were real. Yet that is no more than what the Americans complain of; and if there be good ground, or only slight ground; if there be any ground at all for such complaint, the affair between the American frigate and the Little Belt is by no means a matter to be wondered at. I beg your Royal Highness to consider how many families in the American States have been made unhappy by the impressment of American seamen; how many parents have thus been deprived of their sons, wives of their husbands, and children of their fathers, and when you have so considered you will not, I am sure, be surprised at the exultation that

---

[23] *Political Register* Vol 20, September 7 1811.
[24] *Political Register* Vol 20, September 14 1811.

appears to have been felt at the result of the affair with the Little Belt.[25]

The irony of Cobbett's appeal to the finer feelings of the Regent who, in Leigh Hunt's words in the Examiner was "a violator of his word, a libertine over head and ears in debt and disgrace, a despiser of domestic ties, the companion of gamblers and demireps, a man who has just closed a half century without one single claim on the gratitude of his country or the respect of posterity" would not have been lost on his readers. For writing the article from which these words have been taken, Leigh Hunt, like Cobbett before him, was fined and sentenced to two years' imprisonment. Cobbett had good reason to be cautious and the subtlety he displayed in criticising the government in the form of Open Letters to the Prince Regent acquires deeper significance seen in the light of the Regent's unpopularity at this time.

For the next five months, Cobbett dropped his Letters to the Regent and commented on America in the "Summary of Politics" section of the *Political Register*. With the prospect of war drawing ever nearer, the ministerial newspapers used every effort to persuade their readers that Madison was unpopular, and most Americans were opposed to war with Britain, and they reprinted articles from the pro-British American papers criticising Madison's administration. Great emphasis was placed on the writings of Timothy Pickering and the former Secretary of State, Robert Smith, (whom Madison had replaced with James Monroe), who were urging accommodation with Britain. Cobbett believed that the majority of the people in America clearly understood that Madison had just cause of complaint against Britain, and the fact that Pickering had recently lost

---

[25] *Ibid.*

his seat in the Senate showed how unrepresentative he was of the temper of the people. Indeed, Cobbett went so far as to say that if Pickering knew how his words were being used to deceive the British public, he would desist from his attacks on the President.

> Mr Pickering is an honest man; a man who, I believe, sincerely loves his country and would, as he has done before, stake his life in defence of her liberties. I knew him very well: I always saw in his actions proof of great public spirit and of the strongest attachment to his native country and to public liberty; and as I am convinced that he is still the same excellent man, I beg him (if this should happen to have the honour to meet his eye) to observe that his present writings are applauded and fostered in England by those, and those only, who are the bitterest enemies of public liberty all over the world, and who hate America chiefly because her institutions and the happiness of her people are living and permanent evidences against their intolerant and tyrannical principles.[26]

Cobbett was right in his diagnosis of the temper of the American people, for throughout 1811 the so-called War Hawks in Congress were steadily gaining ascendance. Although impressment and the seizure and condemnation of ships were paramount in arousing support for war with Britain, they were not the only causes for antipathy. "The Indian" question was another source of contention (throughout this book, the word "Indian" is used to describe Native Americans, since that was the word used during the period). After the British evacuated their posts in the North West territories of the United States under the Jay Treaty of 1794, the lands alongside the frontier with Canada attracted more and more pioneer settlers,

---

[26] *Political Register* Vol 20, September 28 1811.

and these American frontiersmen had over the years and often by dubious means, bribed or cajoled the Indians into yielding up some 48 million acres of their lands. Bloody clashes between white settlers and dispossessed Indians were frequent, and it was widely believed that the British administration in Canada fostered discontent among the Indians and supplied them with arms. The suspicion was reinforced in 1811 when the United States sent an army to disperse a coalition of Indian tribes who had mustered on the Wabash River in what is now Indiana, and were threatening to raid the settlements. In the subsequent battle of Tippicanoe, the Indians were found to have been using newly marked British arms. With the threat of war between the United States and Britain and the possibility that if hostilities broke out the Americans might attempt to invade Canada, the British Governor of Canada had undoubtedly cultivated friendship with the Indians on both sides of the border, seeing them as invaluable allies should Canada be invaded, but the accusation that he incited the Indians against American settlers or was in any way instrumental in encouraging them to form a coalition is not substantiated. The ever increasing encroachment on their lands by American settlers was amply sufficient to explain their hostility. An American historian goes so far as to say that most Americans "knew in their hearts that the unrest among the Indians did not spring from British actions. But it is easier to ascribe your trouble to villainy from abroad than to admit that it stems from your own conduct".[27] Another, examining the causes of the war of 1812 writes:

> Feeling against Britain as instigators of the Indians was growing at this period, but it was growing because the British were becoming further and further enmeshed in activity among the Indians in order to meet the threat

---

[27] White, Patrick C T, *A Nation on Trial*, p 101, John Wiley & Sons, 1965.

to Canada that was inherent in America's reaction to England's maritime policy. The root of the problems pushing England and America toward war was at sea, not on the Northwest frontier.[28]

Nevertheless, the opportunity to invade Canada which would open up from a declaration of war was of especial appeal to the Northwesterners because they could thereby destroy the safe harbours to which the Indians could retreat after their marauding expeditions on the American settlements.

Support for the War Hawks came not only from the Northwestern settlers but was paralleled in the southwest. Bloody clashes between Indians and American settlers occurred along the borders between the United States and the Floridas, then still under the Spanish. The line of demarcation between the United States and West Florida had not been clearly drawn at the time of the Louisiana Purchase in 1803, and from the start the American government had questioned whether it should not lie further east along the Pearl or even the Perdito rivers. In 1810, Spanish maladministration in her colonies in Florida had caused unrest among her colonists, and they had revolted against the governor and put themselves under the protection of the United States. America responded by incorporating part of West Florida up to the Pearl river into the United States Territory of New Orleans. Two years later, friction between settlers and Indians resulted in an excuse for the United States to push her frontier further east still and for annexing the area of West Florida up to the Perdito river. Spain, then allied with Britain in the Napoleonic Wars, called on Britain to aid her in protecting her borders, and the prospect of British troops reinforcing

---

[28] Horsman, Reginald, *Causes of the War of 1812*, p 171, University of Pennsylvania Press, 1962.

the Spanish garrisons there aroused violent anti-British feelings among the Americans in the area.

One source of friction, though, had at last been removed. Nearly two years after the British Minister to Washington, Francis Jackson, had become *persona non grata* with the American administration, Marquis Wellesley had finally appointed Sir Augustus Foster as Minister, with instructions to settle the *Chesapeake* affair. Foster, like Erskine, his predecessor but one, had already served in America when he had been Secretary to the Legation under Merry. Perhaps due to Merry's influence, he had at that time tended to adopt his superior's haughty and condescending attitude to the Americans, but when he took up his post in Washington in the summer of 1810 he was pleasantly surprised to find himself being courteously received and he established good relations with James Monroe, Madison's Secretary of State. The *Chesapeake* affair was settled on the same lines as Erskine's repudiated agreement of 1809: the British government agreed to restore the three surviving seamen taken from the *Chesapeake* (the fourth had died in captivity) and to make reparations to the families of the killed and wounded. Monroe, though regretting the long delay and protesting against the failure to reprimand and punish Admiral Berkeley who had ordered the attack, accepted the agreement. Most of the British press, always ready to denigrate the American government, condemned what they considered Monroe's grudging acceptance of a generous offer, but Cobbett saw it as a sign that "The Americans take higher ground than ever. They talk more boldly. They evidently feel a degree of confidence that they never felt before. The truth is that they know they are safe".[29]

---

[29] *Political Register* Vol 20, December 28 1811.

Foster was also instructed to protest, on behalf of Britain's ally Spain, against America's annexation of part of West Florida, and Cobbett published in the *Political Register* the texts of the correspondence between Foster and Monroe between July and November 1811. He explained to his readers the belief of the American government that the Louisiana Purchase included territory in West Florida, and expressed his surprise that they "did not proceed to take possession of the territory as soon as the treaty was ratified".[30] Instead they agreed to enter into negotiations with Spain for a settlement of the boundary, and it was not until the area fell into disorder under Spanish maladministration that the Americans intervened. His support for American action in West Florida was expressed even more forcefully when he published the correspondence on the same issue between Wellesley and the American Minister in London, William Pinkney. Referring his readers to Pinkney's letter to the Foreign Secretary justifying America's annexation, he begged his readers to study it closely. "I have read a great many diplomatic letters in my time, but such a letter as Mr Pinkney's I certainly never read. It is a masterpiece of reasoning and the style and manner are equal to the argumentative powers displayed".[31]

Cobbett had returned to the subject of the failure of the British to repeal her Orders, when he published in full Madison's speech to Congress of November 5th in which he informed Congress that Britain had now stipulated that the Orders would remain in force until France allowed American ships to carry British goods to Continental ports. Cobbett had already made his views on this subject abundantly clear, but this time he pointed out the difference between Britain's treatment of America

---

[30] *Ibid.*
[31] *Political Register* Vol 21, January 11 1812.

and that of France. "Napoleon leaves the trade between America and England perfectly free, but we will not suffer any trade, in any ships, between America and France".[32] That Napoleon allowed American ships to carry goods to Britain unwillingly; that if he had the ships and troops to prevent it he would undoubtedly do so — both of these Cobbett was prepared to admit. But to expect America, a neutral, to force France to allow her to take British goods into the Continent was surely unreasonable. Yet this was what the government expected, and an article in *The Times* went so far as to call the President's speech in which he had complained of Britain's unreasonable demands, "barbarous beyond all conception" and written "in jargon such as was never before put together, except, perhaps, by the Wabash and Swanee savages". Was this the kind of language, Cobbett asked, that should be used in speaking of America? "When the Americans see, if ever they should see, this criticism of their President's speech, what must be their contempt for the critic and for the public that would seem to tolerate him?"[33]

Yet for all the high tone adopted by the ministerial papers, Cobbett believed the government could not hold out much longer. The reports of the debates in Congress showed that the Americans were not prepared to allow the Orders in Council to remain in force. In England, suffering severely from depression, the demands for their repeal were mounting insistently, and even the press began to climb down and were beginning to deny that England had ever insisted that the Orders would be repealed only when France allowed American ships to bring British goods into the continent. In January of the new year, Cobbett wrote of the Orders:

---

[32] *Political Register* Vol 20, December 7 1811.
[33] *Political Register* Vol 20, December 14 1811.

Shall we repeal them or shall we not? My opinion is *that we shall*. Aye, hard as the thing may be to get down, my opinion is that we shall swallow it. It will mortify some people but it will be done. It will make the Jacobins and Levellers in America laugh, and Mr Madison more, perhaps, than anybody else; but I say it will be done. Bonaparte will laugh too, but it will be done; and perhaps not the least mortifying circumstance will be, that it is what I recommended fifteen months ago.[34]

In February, with preparations for war being carried out in the United States, Cobbett began on a second series of Letters to the Prince Regent. Once again he warned him of the misrepresentations of the British press in portraying the American government as unpopular. Once again he listed the just grievances of the Americans: the seizure of their ships bound for France, the impressment of their sailors when the British officer boarding the ship "is at once accuser, witness, judge and captor",[35] the reports reaching America from released impressed seamen of their ill-treatment on board British ships and of the deaths and injuries suffered by their fellows forced into action. He listed too, for the Prince Regent, the formidable preparations now in hand in the States: the offer of 160 acres of land to those enlisting in the army, the preparations for building a navy and the arming of merchant vessels, the high rewards being offered to those bringing British ships of war into American ports, the high rate of desertions from British ships which this would entail, and the call up of the militia which meant that every American citizen would be armed to defend his country. Cobbett was not sanguine about the results of the war. He foresaw the possible loss of Canada and the severing of Britain's mercantile connections with the United States.

---

[34] *Political Register* Vol 21, January 18 1812.
[35] *Political Register* Vol 21, February 1 1812.

He warned of the possibility of France and America forming a coalition and combining their navies. Unless Britain repealed her Orders in Council and abandoned impressment, Cobbett thought war inevitable.

In the early months of 1812 events in England conspired to bring the government round to Cobbett's point of view. Mass unemployment and distress, widely believed to be the result of the continuation of the Orders in Council, brought further outbreaks of rioting. In May, the Prime Minister, Spencer Perceval, was assassinated in the lobby of the House of Commons. Although the assassination was committed for non-political motives by a man who had a personal grievance against the government, so great was the hatred in which the government was held that the news was greeted with jubilation. In one city, church bells were rung to celebrate his demise; in others, feasts were organised in celebration, and in Westminster "the most savage expressions of joy and exultation were heard, accompanied with regret that others, and particularly the Attorney-General, had not shared the same fate".[36] When the culprit was led out from Newgate gaol for public execution (Cobbett's windows overlooked the gallows and he kept the blinds permanently drawn on that side) he was greeted by cries of "God bless you, God Almighty bless you".

Spencer Perceval was succeeded by his Secretary of War, the Earl of Liverpool who retained most of the members of Perceval's administration. However, in view of the temper of the country which had been so violently and luridly demonstrated at the time of Perceval's murder, within a month of its inauguration it capitulated, and on June 16th, 1812, the Orders in Council were repealed.

---

[36] Quoted from Romilly's *Memoirs in G Spater*, William Cobbett: *The Poor Man's Friend*, Cambridge University Press 1982.

Cobbett, as might be expected, used another Open Letter to the Regent to report that what he had been saying must come to pass, had come to pass. There is triumph, but there is sadness too. Sadness that all the sufferings which British stubbornness in refusing to repeal her Orders in Council had brought upon the people had been in vain. Quoting his earlier Letter in which he had said that in spite of all their protestations to the contrary, the government would eventually have to swallow its words, he went on:

> These passages, Sir, were published on the 18th of January last; so that it would seem that, though shut up in one of "His Majesty's Jails", I knew what I was doing better than "His Majesty's Ministers" did. How much better if my advice, so urgently and so respectfully tendered to your Royal Highness, had been followed. What national shame, what humiliation, what misery, what melancholy scenes, would have been avoided.[37]

For, as he pointed out, nothing had changed. If the Orders had been necessary in 1811, they were still necessary now. The only change was that since they were promulgated, America had begun to threaten war in earnest. "It must, with your Royal Highness, be a subject of deep sorrow and mortification, to see your ministers now lowering their tone, and taking a cowering attitude, without any new reason being afforded in the conduct of either France or America".[38] He expressed his fears that the repeal had come too late to avert war and ended the Letter with a warning about America's feelings about impressment:

> I implore you to resist the advice of those who would fain make you believe that we ought to persist in these impressments. I implore your Royal Highness to reflect on the manifold miseries that may arise from this cause;

---

[37] *Political Register,* Vol 21, June 21 1812.
[38] *Ibid.*

and to be pleased to bear in mind that to yield hereafter, to yield upon force or menace will be disgrace; whereas to yield now would indicate a sentiment of justice.[39]

On the 18th of June, two days after Parliament had repealed the Orders, and as the ship bearing the olive branch of peace to America was leaving port, the United States declared war on Great Britain. When the news of the declaration of war reached England towards the end of July, Cobbett had completed his sentence in Newgate, and was back home in Botley.

---

[39] *Ibid.*

5

Hawks and Doves

The decision of Congress to declare war on Great Britain was by no means unanimous. In the House of Representatives it was passed by a vote of 79 to 49; in the Senate by just four votes — 19 to 13. Opposition to the war, strongest in the New England States and the commercial centres of New York and New Jersey was not confined only to those areas which were dependent on connections with England for their prosperity. The old Federalist ethos, so stridently proclaimed by Cobbett in the 1790s, lingered on. There were Americans who still subscribed to Peter Porcupine's sentiments that the United States were tied by kinship and common institutions to Britain and who looked back with dread to the demonstrations of those pro-French Democratic mobs who had rejoiced at the execution of Louis XVI and Marie-Antoinette, who had pulled down statues of Kings and nobles and had burned Jay's effigy in 1794 — those events which Porcupine had so vividly described when he was living in Philadelphia. For these, opposition to the war sprang from a genuine respect for the common inheritance of the British and American peoples, and an admiration of Britain for the stand she had taken against Jacobinism and all it stood for. Cobbett's former opinion that the Republican party hated Britain and wished success to France was still held in 1812 by the old guard of the Federalists. When war seemed imminent, the *Boston Gazette*, a leading Federalist paper, thundered:

> Is there a Federalist, a patriot, in America, who conceives it his duty to shed his blood for Bonaparte, for Madison or Jefferson, or that Host of Ruffians in Congress who have set their faces against the United States for years, and have spirited up the brutal part of the population to destroy us?[1]

Although few, perhaps, would have gone so far as to condone Britain's violations of America's rights as a neutral, many were prepared to excuse her actions as necessary weapons in her fight against France. Nor was this faction slow to expose France's continuing seizures and confiscations of American shipping or the brutal treatment meted out to American sailors captured in French ports who had been:

> marched without shoes to their feet or clothes to their backs in the most inclement weather some hundreds of miles into the interior of France, lashed along the highways like slaves, treated with every possible indignity, and then immured in the infernal dungeons of Arras or Verdun.[2]

Other sections were opposed to war for different reasons. There were the American financiers, merchants, shipowners, shipwrights and sailors whose livelihood depended on overseas trading. Amongst these opposition to the war did not spring from a feeling of friendship for a country which seized and condemned their ships and cargoes and forcibly removed the seamen from them. The roots of their aversion to war lay in the belief that a bad situation would be made worse, that some trade was better than no trade, and that France's seizures made the singling out of Great Britain as the enemy unjustifiable.

---

[1] Quoted in Updike, Frank A, *The Diplomacy of the War of 1812*, John Hopkins Press, 1915.
[2] From the *New York Evening Post*, 12.7.1809. Quoted in Bailey, *op cit*, p 142.

Even many of the Republican party's bellicose speeches were uttered more in the hope that they might frighten the British government into repealing her Orders in Council and abandoning her practice of impressment than from an active desire for war. Henry Clay, the Speaker of the House of Representatives and the leading War Hawk, felt it necessary to emphasise that war was being considered only as a last resort.

> Not a man in the nation could really doubt the sincerity in which those in power have sought, by all honorable pacific means, to protect the interests of the country.[3]

A statement later confirmed by Augustus Foster, the British Minister to America, during the years immediately before the declaration of war, who wrote in his memoirs;

> Even the late war was not determined on until the most earnest secret struggles to avoid it on the part of the American government, who were pushed into it by the faction which supported them, but not before they had endured for many years what they were pleased to call the wrongs and insults which at last occasioned their determination.[4]

However, the failure of the non-intercourse Act which had been imposed in 1811 to coerce Britain to respect American neutrality, the belief that the British administration in Canada was aiding the Indians along the Northwest frontier in their attacks on American settlers, and perhaps above all the humiliation engendered by the constant rebuttal of all American demands for redress made the situation in 1812 well nigh unendurable. Monroe, the Secretary of State, summed up the prevailing feeling.

> War, dreadful as the alternative is, could not do us

---

[3] Quoted in Roger H Brown, *The Republic in Peril*, p 65, Columbia Univ Press, 1964.
[4] Sir Augustus Foster, *Jeffersonian America*, p 4, Huntingdon Library, 1954.

more injury than the present state of things, and it would certainly be more honorable to the Nation, and gratifying to the publick feeling.[5]

Nor should it be overlooked that Jefferson's belief that the republican form of government must be preserved was shared by his successor. Madison justified the necessity for war by declaring that, had the nation shrunk from it, it would have "betrayed the magnificent legacy which we hold in trust for future generations",[6] and his words were echoed by another Republican, Richard Rush. "Being the only republick, the destinies of that sort of government are in our keeping. Should we stand by and see it longer debased by submission, or sordid avarice, its cause is gone forever".[7]

Before war was declared in June, one last effort had been made to convince Britain that the United States would no longer tolerate the wrongs inflicted on her. The non-importation Act of February 1811, though forbidding the importation of British goods and closing American harbours to the British navy, allowed American shipowners to trade with whom they pleased, and throughout this period large supplies of food and raw materials were shipped to Britain and to Wellington's armies in the Peninsular. In April 1812, as an earnest of her determination to uphold her rights, America proclaimed an Embargo to last for ninety days. By confining all her vessels to port, the American government demonstrated that it was preparing for war by protecting her merchantmen from seizure on the high seas if hostilities broke out, and hoped, too, that the stoppage of raw materials to Britain might swell the discontent in Britain which the Orders in Council had provoked and

---

[5] Quoted in Caffrey, Kate, *The Lion and the Union*, p 126, Andrew Deutsch, 1978.
[6] Quoted in Brown, Roger, *The Republic in Peril*, p 84, Columbia Univ Press, 1964.
[7] *Ibid*, p 84.

force the British government to revoke them.

In the event, this ninety day Embargo failed in its intent. Petitions chiefly from the New England States for the ending of the Embargo poured in to Congress, and the British Minister in Washington, Sir Augustus Foster, anxious as always for peace between the two countries, and consorting in his private capacity mainly with Federalists, saw the opposition to the Embargo as a sign that the American people were not behind the War Hawks in Congress in their demand for war. Partly misled by Foster's reports into thinking that there was stronger opposition to war than really existed, and believing that if war were to be declared there was every likelihood that the New England States would secede from the Union and continue to supply Britain with the goods she needed, the Perceval administration in England stood firm. With continuing unrest and rioting throughout the kingdom, the British government was fearful of showing any signs of weakness: had it given in to the mass demands for the ending of the Orders in Council, the ugly question of a reform of Parliament might be next on the list As was seen earlier, it needed a truly dramatic incident, the assassination of Spencer Perceval, to shake it from its obstinate adherence to policies which spelt ruin for merchants and starvation for labourers, and when it was so shaken in May 1812, it did too little, too late.

America's imposition of an Embargo in April of that year was in effect an ultimatum to Britain. If, at the expiry of the ninety days, Britain did not respond, the United States could not in honour have stood idly by and allowed the situation to continue. Matters were, however, brought to a head earlier. In March, the publication of cor-respondence between John Henry, an Irishman resident in Boston, and the Governor of Lower Canada, Sir James Craig, indicated that the British government through its administration in Canada had been active in subverting the Federalists in the New England States and encouraging them to secede from the Union of the United States. The hostile feelings this news aroused were further deepened when at the end of May a despatch from the British Foreign Secretary to his American counterpart, James Monroe reached Washington. It dashed any hopes of any concessions from Britain. Written before the assassination of Perceval, it responded to the Embargo by repeating the government's argument that France had not in reality repealed her Decrees (French depredations on American ships in French ports had sharply increased in the early months of 1812), and stating that France had deliberately deceived the American government in order to foment discord between Britain and America. "America", Castlereagh wrote, "can never be justified in continuing to resent against us that failure of Relief, which is alone attributable to the insidious Policy of the Enemy. We are entitled to claim at Her Hands, as an act not less of Policy than of Justice, that she should cease to treat Great Britain as an Enemy".[8] Such was Britain's reply to America's hopes that the imposition of an Embargo might wring concessions. Once again, the lofty tone, the humiliating accusation that the American government had been duped by Napoleon, and the brushing aside of America's grievances as ones that she had brought upon herself by her acceptance of Napoleon's untrustworthy declarations, seemed, in American eyes, a calculated insult. Madison had now no choice but to set forth in a message to Congress a catalogue of all the wrongs under which the nation was suffering.

In reading the extracts from Madison's 'Message to Congress' below, one is immediately aware of how

---

[8] Quoted in Caffrey, Kate, *op cit,* p 145.

accurately Cobbett had, in his Letters to the Prince Regent, reflected the mood of the Americans at this time. Though it was now twelve years since he had lived in the United States, and though his knowledge of American affairs since then had been gleaned almost solely from a perusal of their newspapers and journals, his eight year sojourn in Philadelphia had given him an insight shared by no other comparable English writer of the period. Madison's 'Message', delivered on June 1st, 1812, began with the question of impressment and declared that under her pretended practice of searching for her own subjects,

> thousands of American citizens, under the safeguard of public law and of their national flag, have been torn from their country and everything dear to them; have been dragged on board ships of war of a foreign nation and exposed, under the severities of their discipline, to be exiled to the most distant and deadly climes, to risk their lives in the battles of their oppressors, and to be the melancholy instruments of taking away those of their own brethren.

*****

> British cruisers have been in the practice also of violating the rights and peace of our coasts. They hover over and harrass our entering and departing commerce. To the most insulting pretensions they have added the most lawless proceedings in our very harbours, and have wantonly spilt American blood within the sanctuary of our territorial jurisdiction.

*****

> Under pretended blockades, without the presence of an adequate force and sometimes without the practicability of applying one, our commerce has been plundered in every sea, the great staples of our country have been cut off from their legitimate markets, and a destructive blow

aimed at our agricultural and maritime interests.

*****

In reviewing the conduct of Great Britain toward the United States our attention is necessarily drawn to the warfare just renewed by the savages on one of our extensive frontiers — a warfare which is known to spare neither age nor sex and to be distinguished by features peculiarly shocking to humanity. It is difficult to account for the activity and combinations which have for some time been developing themselves among tribes in constant intercourse with British traders and garrisons without connecting their hostility with that influence and without recollecting the authenticated examples of such interpositions heretofore furnished by the officers and agents of that Government.

*****

Our moderation and conciliation have had no other effect than to encourage perseverance and to enlarge pretensions.... Whether the United States shall continue passive under these progressive usurpations and these accumulating wrongs, or opposing force to force in defense of their natural rights, shall commit a just cause into the hands of the Almighty Disposer of Events, is a solemn question which the Constitution wisely confides to the legislative department of the Government. In recommending it to their early deliberations I am happy in the assurance that the decision will be worthy the enlightened and patriotic councils of a virtuous, a free and a powerful nation.

The solemn question was debated; the decision made. And in the words of an American historian:

> Deeply and bitterly divided we went to war in 1812. Public demonstrations across the nation showed the split in opinion. Illuminations, parades, and cannon-firing welcomed the decision; tolling church bells, flags

at half-mast and empty shops and counting houses bore witness to condemnation.[9]

For a nation to embark on war with the country "deeply and bitterly divided" does not augur well; when the anti-war faction is also the moneyed section of the nation, it augurs ill indeed. In the War of 1812, lack of finances played as important a part in America's initial defeats at the hands of the British as did the reluctance of many of its citizens to take the offensive. When in April 1812 Congress took the decisive step towards war by imposing the ninety day Embargo, it was fully aware that preparations for providing men and the money to pay them were woefully inadequate. In the previous session of Congress of 1811, when the War Hawks were gaining the ascendancy, bellicose words were never matched by bellicose acts. It was true, as Cobbett had written in one of his Letters to the Prince Regent, that Congress had authorised the call up of the militia, had offered generous terms to those volunteering to serve in the regular army and had commissioned the building of gun boats, the refitting of warships and the arming of privateers. But by June 1812, the hoped for recruitment of twenty five thousand volunteers to swell the existing standing army had produced a mere five thousand. As for the militia who were recruited by the individual States, no agreement had been reached as to whether they could be used outside the territory of the United States, and when war was declared, the Governors of Massachusetts and Connecticut refused to allow their militia to take part in the invasion of Canada on the grounds that the President had authority to call for their use only to suppress insurrection or repel invasion.

Under the Constitution, the Federal army was limited

---

[9] Brown, Roger H, *op cit*, p 177.

to ten thousand men, and when war was declared even this number was three thousand under strength. In June 1812, the additional five thousand recruited brought the number up to a mere twelve thousand, as against the thirty-five thousand which had been confidently predicted and thought to be necessary when Congress began seriously to consider war preferable to repeated rebuffs and humiliations.

To understand how it came about that the United States was so unprepared, almost to the extent of criminal negligence, a number of factors must be taken into account. One of them, and perhaps the most difficult to comprehend for modern readers, was the deep-rooted abhorrence of the Republican Party to a standing army in peace time under the control of the central government. The War of Independence had been fought for its name. In the eyes of the Republican Party, independence meant not just independence from colonial rule, but the independence of each State of the Union to pursue its own interests and the independence of each individual citizen to pursue his with the absolute minimum of interference from either Federal or State governments. For any colonial, in any part of the world, it is above all else the presence of the army of the colonial power that symbolises its subordination to the mother country. After the several separate British colonies in North America had united to free themselves from colonial rule in 1776, the newly independent nation, and the Republican Party in particular, were determined that British rule should not be replaced by a central authority wielding the power and aping the trappings of their erstwhile masters. Hence the insistence on individual State Rights and the desire to curb the powers and trappings even of the revered first President of the United States which had so shocked Cobbett when George

Washington entered his second term in office.

Until the actual outbreak of war in June 1812, therefore, any growth in the strength of Federal forces was looked upon with suspicion. For a free self-governing nation it was considered enough to rely on a small army and navy which could, when necessary, be augmented by enlisting volunteers to serve only during the emergency and then to be discharged. It is worth noting that Cobbett, alone among English writers, understood this antipathy to a standing army. Whereas the British press seized upon the lack of preparation as yet another sign that the Americans were a poorly organised and contemptible enemy, Cobbett tried to explain to his readers why the Americans disliked the concept of a large standing army in peace time. Here he is writing later on in the war after the Americans had suffered a number of raids on their coastal towns by the British. Still cautious, because still under bonds of £5000 for good behaviour, he uses wit and irony to get over his message and cleverly exposes the nepotism and corruption rampant in the British standing army without laying himself open to prosecution.

> They prefer a few towns sacked or beaten down, now and then, to the paying for a standing army, for barracks, depots and military colleges. Their taste may be bad. They may prove themselves very stupid in not liking to see their streets crowded with beautiful, tall, straight gentlemen, with pretty hats and caps, with furs and whiskers, with cloaks and glittering swords and boots that shine like japan mugs. But stupidity is no crime, and if they do not like these things, we, who have so much more refinement among us, should view them with pity rather than with scorn; should speak of them with compassion, rather than reproach.[10]

---

[10] *Political Register* Vol 26, 8 October 1814.

Another factor which caused the American army to be so seriously under-manned was the unwillingness of Congress to vote adequate funds to arm and clothe the volunteers it had agreed should be recruited. After the President had been authorised to recruit twenty five thousand volunteers, Congress refused to vote the necessary imposition of taxes and duties to pay for the enlarged army until war had actually been declared. The result was that

> Throughout 1812, officers constantly complained that the shortage of clothing gave the recruits a grievance, which, once it became widely known, proved to be an obstacle to continuing enlistments. The spectacle of ragged, barefoot, and destitute soldiers, or soldiers with trousers but no coats, brought the army, the United States government, and ultimately the war into public disrepute.[11]

Lack of funds was matched by a lack of an experienced corps of officers. By 1812 even the youngest veterans of the War of Independence were men nearing their sixties. Given the shortage of officers due to the small size of the Federal army, to whom were the government to look for men of the right calibre to recruit and train an effective force? James Monroe, the Secretary of State's answer to the problem shows a naiveté almost bordering on the ludicrous when one considers that the United States was embarking on a war against the experienced, well drilled and accoutred, and highly disciplined forces of the British army stationed along the Canadian borders. He proposed that officers should be selected from "prominent men, who by virtuous conduct had acquired the confidence of their fellow men". These men, he suggested, "would go to their homes, look around the country where they were known, and seek volunteers". Monroe was confident that

---

[11] Stagg, J C A, *Mr Madison's War*, p 173, Princeton Univ Press, 1983.

many patriots would be found to come forward and offer their services to the nation, and the corps so formed would have the great advantage of consisting of "neighbours, friends and brothers."[12]

An illustration of the composition of one of the armies so formed can be found in a contingent of men sent to the Canadian frontier at Detroit to be ready for invasion or defence should hostilities break out. The Governor of Michigan Territory, William Hull, a veteran of the War of Independence, had reluctantly accepted the post of brigadier some months before war was declared, and in May he was ordered to proceed to Dayton, Ohio, to take command of three regiments of militia recruited there and march them to Detroit. His volunteers were to be joined en route by an infantry regiment from the Federal army. The volunteer regiments were commanded respectively by a rich speculator, a former Mayor of Cincinnati, and an attorney — all three doubtless men of "virtuous conduct", but not one of whom had had any previous military experience. The men they had recruited were "armed with a mixed collection of muskets and sporting rifles and dressed in homespun jackets and breeches, and felt hats". Fortunately for Brigadier Hull, when these volunteers after marching for some weeks towards Detroit refused to go any further until they had been paid, the regiment of regulars had already joined up with them, and "quelled the incipient mutiny by advancing on the volunteers with levelled muskets and arresting three of their ringleaders".[13] The intimidation was successful and the mixed army of regulars and volunteers, some 1200 in all, marched on to Detroit.

Across the border, in Upper and Lower Canada, New

---
[12] Quoted in Stagg, *op cit*, p 148.
[13] Caffrey, Kate, *op cit*, pp 154-5.

Brunswick and Nova Scotia, there were at the outbreak of war some five thousand regular soldiers. The enormous length of the border, some twelve hundred miles, and the difficulties of communication and transport along its length; the knowledge that with the Peninsular War raging in Europe no troops could be spared from Britain to reinforce the army in Canada; and the huge discrepancy between the populations of the United States and British North America, the former totalling nearly eight million and the latter less than half a million, caused the British administration to hope for no more than to defend and hold the main centres of the Province — Quebec, Montreal and Kingston in Upper Canada, and York (now Toronto) the capital of Lower Canada. And just as the Americans were doubtful of the loyalty of militia men recruited in Federalist centres, so were the British doubtful of the loyalty of militia men recruited from the French speaking population of Canada, or the many recent American settlers in the Province. Whether the Indians would be prepared to assist the British was always unpredictable.

Such then is the briefest sketch of the strengths and weaknesses of the two combatants at the outbreak of war. In Great Britain itself there were no reasons for welcoming the war. Heavily dependent on the United States for provisions for its army in Spain and Portugal, unable to send reinforcements to its colonies in North America if Canada were invaded, England reacted to the news of America's declaration with dismay tempered with disbelief. The grievances were almost entirely on the side of the United States, and because one of the main reasons for America's hostility were the Orders in Council — almost as unpopular in Britain as they were in the States — there could not be the usual clarion call to arms or appeals to patriotism in this new war. Even if the British government had had on its side a writer of the calibre of William Cobbett, he would have been hard put to produce a document comparable in any way with Cobbett's "Important Considerations" in which he called on the nation to support the government in its war with France in 1803.

The ministerial papers, therefore, adopted a dismissive tone, emphasising the unpreparedness of the United States, Madison's unpopularity in the country, and allaying any fears by assuring their readers that once the news of the repeal of the Orders in Council reached the American government, it would quickly come to its senses. As was mentioned earlier, the British press seized upon speeches and articles published in American papers opposing the war, and the belief in its unpopularity was dramatically confirmed by the fact that an enormous quantity of goods from the United States had recently arrived both in Britain and the Spanish Peninsular. When the War Hawks persuaded Congress to impose an Embargo in April 1812, news of the impending Bill was deliberately leaked to the major ports by the Opposition Federalists. It was estimated that in the few weeks between the leakage of the news and the actual imposition of the Embargo, some two months worth of supplies reached the British army in Spain, and some $15 million worth of goods in all left the States for Great Britain. Such a response could only encourage the British government to believe that the war was not just unpopular, but that many Americans were willing to defy their government almost to the point of treason.

Yet Cobbett, who read the reports in the American press with the deeper understanding of one who had lived among the people there for eight years, thought differently. The bitterness with which he had been attacked when he defended the British as Peter Porcupine in the 1790s and the subsequent hatred he had inspired which had led to his prosecution and fine in 1800 had taught him that America was a proud nation which would not forever submit to the indignities which British arrogance had heaped upon her. His immediate reaction to the news of the declaration of war was to attack the widely held belief that the American government would revoke her declaration once the news of the repeal of the Orders in Council reached Washington. Repeal, he stated in his first Letter to the Prince Regent after he left prison, was not enough. The sufferings of the Americans over impressment and their fear that Britain might interfere in the Floridas on behalf of Spain would keep them to their resolve. He ended this letter:

> ... it will grieve me exceedingly to reflect that England is taxed, and that English blood is shed, for the purpose of enforcing the power to impress American seamen; but this mortification I shall, I trust, be spared by the humanity and wisdom of your Royal Highness.[14]

But while Cobbett and the ministerial papers were contradicting each other over whether repeal of the Orders in Council would end the war, the question had already become academic. Before the ship bearing the news entered American waters, blood had been spilt on the Canadian border.

If, in the United States, opinions were divided over the wisdom of declaring war on Great Britain, none could doubt that the only possible theatre of war lay on the border with Canada. For the United States to attack Britain on her own territory, on the continent of Europe or in the West Indies was obviously impossible when the Royal Navy outnumbered the American Navy by 120 ships of the line to none, and 116 frigates to 7. (Ships of the line

---

[14] *Political Register*, Vol 22, 8 August 1812.

had two or three decks with over 70 guns, frigates one deck and some 30-45 guns. The United States had also some half dozen sloops and brigs of under 20 guns.) Only in Canada was there any possibility of success in attacking the enemy, and on paper, at least, there were good grounds for optimism. After the bloody battles with the Indians, both the volunteers and the militia could be counted on to wish to prosecute the war with vigour.

Brigadier Hull's army which we have already met on its way to Detroit, arrived there early in July and was the first to invade Canada. Receiving the news that war had been declared, Hull crossed the Detroit River on July 12th, occupied the Canadian town of Sandwich on the opposite bank without encountering any opposition, and began preparations for an attack on the British Fort Malden on the Northwestern shore of Lake Erie. Four days later, an advance guard sent to reconnoitre the approaches to Fort Malden captured two prisoners and inflicted ten casualties on the British forces without the loss of any American. More encouraging still, the Proclamation Hull issued on crossing into Canadian territory, appealing to the Canadians to come over to the American side, and warning them that if any white man were to be found fighting with an Indian against American forces, he would be subject to instant death, resulted in some four to five hundred Canadian militia deserting to the United States. The supposition of the War Hawks that Canada was an easy prey ended, however, with this first success.

Discouraged by the news that the British had already captured Fort Michilimackinac, the American outpost on the far west of Lake Huron, and fearing that this success would encourage a host of Indians to join the British, Hull, instead of pressing forward, hesitated. When he heard that British forces under their energetic commander, Major-

General Brock, were on their way to reinforce Fort Malden, he decided to retire his forces back to Detroit. On August 15th, Brock with 300 regular soldiers, 400 militia, and 600 Indian allies, bombarded and attacked Detroit. Brigadier Hull, fearful that his men and the women and children in Detroit might be exposed to all the horrors of an attack by Indians (Brock had cleverly deceived the Americans into thinking that there were many more Indians than he actually had with him) surrendered his whole army of over 2000 men. Brock ordered all the regulars to be sent as prisoners-of-war to Quebec and set the American militia men free to return to their homes — a gesture perhaps humane in intention but liable to be seen in the United States as yet another example of British contempt and arrogance.

The intended American invasion of Canada was not confined to the Northwestern frontier. Larger armies were assembled at Niagara between Lakes Erie and Ontario to capture the capital of Upper Canada at York and further east still at Plattsburgh on Lake Champlain to attack Kingston and Montreal. News of the repeal of the Orders in Council which arrived before any action had taken place, led to a temporary armistice between American and British forces, but the government in Washington, as Cobbett had correctly foreseen, rejected this concession as insufficient to end hostilities. In October, the American forces assembled at Niagara succeeded in occupying the heights near Queenston, but Major-General Brock hastening east after his success at Detroit attacked and drove the invaders back across the border. A crossing of the Canadian border north of Lake Champlain by American troops and the capture of a blockhouse ended in fiasco. In the confusion among the soldiers as darkness fell, they fired upon one another and then retreated back to American territory.

With winter approaching, all the American armies sent to the Canadian border retired into winter quarters, and by the end of 1812 the only American forces in Canada were prisoners of war.

"A list of battles is not history", Cobbett was to write in a different context some years later, and he then went on to say:

> You hear enough, and you read enough, about the *glorious wars* in the reign of King Edward the Third; but you never read that, in that reign, a common labourer earned threepence-halfpenny a day, and that a fat sheep was sold, at the same time, for fourteen pence and a fat goose for twopence-half penny. These are matters of real importance, for these furnish the criterion whereby we are to judge of our condition compared with that of our forefathers.[15]

So in the chapters that follow, there will be no attempt to follow in detail the campaigns, the first of which was fought on the north western frontier of the United States under Brigadier Hull in July 1812, and the last under General Jackson in January 1815 on the battleground of New Orleans in the South. Throughout the two and a half years of war, Cobbett published official reports from both sides on many of the engagements and often devoted a large part of the *Political Register* to explaining their significance. The three thousand miles of ocean that separated England from America meant that Cobbett's comments were always two or three months late; often events had changed radically — victories turned into defeats and defeats into victories long before he put pen to paper. The interest of his comments lies not on the outcome of battles but in the fact that he saw the war as being waged on the one side by a country whose government ensured that the common

---

[15] *Advice to Young Men*, Para 74, 1829.

labourer had, if not fat sheep and fat geese in plenty, he had fat bacon and fat turkeys in abundance, and on the other side by a country whose system of government deprived the labourer of any meat at all and degraded him into the status of a pauper. This was the criterion by which he judged the merits of the two combatants. Almost as much as Jefferson, Madison and Rush, was he anxious that the "only republick" should preserve its "magnificent legacy" for future generations, and, as will be seen, he never wavered in his faith that an ill-trained army of free men under a freely elected government would be a match for the professionals, and never shrank from proclaiming that belief to his readers.

6
War 1812-1814

The first intimation to reach England that hostilities had actually begun was the news that Brigadier Hull had crossed over from Detroit into Canadian territory and captured and occupied the town of Sandwich. With the news came a report of his Proclamation to the Canadian people promising them protection if they offered no resistance, and urging them to defect to the American side. Reporting this in his *Political Register*, in the form of another letter to the Prince Regent, Cobbett said that the news of the invasion confirmed his belief that the American government was in earnest and would not disarm when it learnt of the repeal of the Orders in Council unless the concession was followed by offering reparation for wrongs inflicted and the ending of impressment. The United States, he wrote, was a nation of brave and free people, and had resources such that Britain could do little to injure her.

> Mr Madison, though a very plain-dressed, sleek-headed man; though he wears neither tails nor bags nor big wigs nor robes; though he dresses in a pepper-and-salt coat and a nice dimity waistcoat, does not want any body to tell him what is coming. He will laugh at the idea of our exhausting the resources of America, the capital of whose whole debt does not amount to a tenth part of one half year's interest upon our debt.[1]

And he ended this letter by reiterating his belief that a war

---
[1] *Political Register*, Vol 22, September 19 1812.

with the United States could only result in loss and injury to Great Britain.

> I have now done all that I am able to prevent this calamity. If the war proceeds, I shall say as little about it as circumstances will permit. I have lost no occasion of endeavouring to put aside this evil; and when the result of the contest shall be lamented; when those who now rejoice at the idea of doing mischief to free men will be weeping over their folly, I trust that your Royal Highness will have the justice to remember that this war had a decided opponent in your faithful servant, William Cobbett.[2]

Never was a promise to keep quiet more ill-kept. The very next issue led with yet another letter to the Prince Regent, this time refuting what Cobbett believed to be a false rumour that an armistice had followed the news of the repeal of the Orders in Council. Whatever other newspapers might say, Cobbett felt certain that until the practice of impressment was renounced, America would continue the war. "With impressment", he wrote, "no American in a merchant ship can sail the sea in safety; every American sails under the fear of being captured and forced to serve in a British ship, perhaps to be sent to the West Indies where he is likely to die of yellow fever, or to take part in a naval engagement with Britain's enemies and be killed or wounded. To a people so situated, war must be a relief. The American seaman will prefer war, because, if captured, the laws of war protect him and feed him as a *prisoner*".[3]

For the remaining months of 1812, Cobbett dropped his letters to the Prince Regent, but reported the news, including Hull's surrender of his whole army to the British

---

[2] *Ibid.*
[3] *Political Register,* Vol 22, September 22 1812.

at Detroit, in the Summary of Politics section of his paper, usually without comment. He did, however, draw his readers' attention to two incidents. He reacted to the news of the desertion of some Canadians to the American forces which had led to the Governor of Canada suspending Habeas Corpus, with some exultation. "What! Traitors in Canada! A few, a few, only a few. Well, then, why suspend the Habeas Corpus Act?"[4] He also drew his readers' attention to the use of Indian troops by the British, and in December published Madison's 'Message to Congress' in which he had referred to "the use made by the enemy of the merciless savages under their influence". While the United States, Madison said, had tried to dissuade Indians from taking either side, "the enemy has not scrupled to call to his aid their ruthless ferocity, armed with the horrors of those instruments of carnage and torture which are known to spare neither age nor sex".[5]

At the beginning of the following year, 1813, Cobbett spoke out in another Open Letter to the Prince Regent, begging him to consider that the war could be of no benefit to Britain.

> The love I bear my own country, and the regard I shall ever bear a great part of the people of America, will not suffer me to refrain from making one more trial to convince your Royal Highness, that the path of peace is still fairly open with that country, and that pacific measures are the only measures which ought even now to be pursued.[6]

Again he lambasted the British press which had been proved wrong in its supposition that the Americans would never dare to attack British territory; which had forecast

---

[4] *Political Register*, Vol 22, October 3 1812.
[5] *Political Register*, Vol 22, December 26 1812.
[6] *Political Register*, Vol 23, January 2 1813.

that Madison would be defeated at the next election (he had been re-elected for another term at the end of 1812); and which were now maintaining that America was destitute of resources. He asked the Prince to remember that the United States was a nation of eight million people

> none of whom are paupers; none of whom are clad in rags; none of whom are without meat upon their tables daily; not one soul of whom would condescend to pull off his hat to any human being. And this is the nation, a nation too descended from ourselves, that the hirelings of the London Press represent as destitute of resources. The Americans are active in their persons; they are enterprising; they are brave; and, which is of vast consequence, they are from education and almost from Constitution, SOBER, a virtue not at all less valuable in an army or fleet than it is in domestic life.[7]

Although by the beginning of 1813 the English press could boast of the great success of the British forces in repelling the American attempts to invade British North America, events at sea told a different story. Unlike their counterparts in the army, the commanders of the United States navy were almost without exception younger men, and many of them had had experience of war in engagements with Tripoli pirates who infested the Barbary coasts of North Africa and tried to exact tribute from ships engaged in trade with the East When war was declared, the small United States navy left port under the overall command of Commander Rodgers, and mostly sailing singly, engaged in a number of encounters with the British navy. As early as June 1812, the US frigate *Constitution* under its Commander Isaac Hull (a nephew of the General Hull who had surrendered his army at Detroit) met one British ship of the line and four British frigates, and by exceptionally

---

[7] *Political Register*, Vol 23, January 2 1813.

skilful manoeuvres escaped from these overwhelming numbers to Boston harbour where it took fresh supplies aboard and set out again to sea. There, some weeks later, Isaac Hull sighted HMS *Guerriere*. gave battle and forced the British ship to surrender. Before the year was out, Captain Decatur of the USS *United States* captured the British ship *Macedonian* and Captain Bainbridge who had taken over the command of USS *Constitution*, captured another British frigate, HMS *Java*.

When news reached England of the first of these surrenders, that of HMS *Guerriere*, it was greeted with dismay and disbelief. Although throughout the long war with France, the British army had suffered reverses on the Continent, her navy had remained the undisputed mistress of the seas and her ships had been victorious in every major engagement. The *Times* had been able to dismiss the early success of Brigadier Hull's army in crossing the Canadian border by stating:

> War is an employment so new to the people of the United States, that the humble operations of General Hull and his army are given with the most minute detail; and the driving in of a few advanced posts actually delivered in a tone of triumph not unworthy of a German campaign. (September 11th 1812)

and it could justify its belittlement less than a month later:

> The Expedition of the Americans, announced against Upper Canada in terms the most alarming, has had that issue which generally attends presumptuous boasting. It has terminated not in the possession of Canada by General Hull, but in the possession of the General and his army, and a part of his country's territories. (October 7th 1812)

But for a British ship to surrender to an American one was

something that the *Times* found difficult to stomach.

> Above all, there is one object to which our most strenuous efforts should be directed — the entire annihilation of the American navy. Nothing short of this can avenge the disgrace we have suffered by the loss of the *Guerriere*. (October 29th 1812)

Cobbett reported the affairs quite differently. He poked fun at the newspapers which had laughed at the pretensions of the US navy to fight the Royal Navy. "Let one of our frigates meet with Rodgers, and we ask no more" they had said. Yet two British frigates and one sloop had already been captured.

> Where did Isaac Hull gain his naval experience and where Mr Decatur? There are two Decaturs, the father and the son. They were my neighbours in the country in Pennsylvania. They were farmers more than seamen, though the elder went occasionally to sea as commander of a merchant ship If it be the father who has taken the Macedonian, he must be upwards of three score years of age, and, if it be the son, I am sure it is the first battle he ever was in; for twelve years ago he was but a mere lad. The father was a man of great probity and excellent sense, and I have no doubt that the son is the same; but I'll engage that both have more experience in raising Indian corn than in naval tactics.[8]

Cobbett was wrong here. It was the younger Decatur who commanded the USS *United States*. He was thirty three years old and had served with distinction in the Tripoli wars. However inaccurate in its premises, the passage is worth recording for showing Cobbett's desire to arouse in his readers' minds a picture of the "enemy" as people like themselves, a picture very different from that given by the pro-war press.

---

[8] *Political Register*, Vol 23, January 9 1813.

In 1813, a year after Hull's surrender of his army, fresh American forces were assembled on the Canadian frontier and engagements were fought along the shores of Lake Erie and around the river Raisin, when the British, aided by some six hundred Indians were successful, taking five hundred prisoners. Many of the remaining American troops were subsequently massacred by the Indians. In April the position was reversed when an American squadron of ships built on Lake Ontario crossed over to York, the capital of Upper Canada, captured a large amount of stores and burned and looted the town before returning to the southern shore. A dramatic battle in September between a squadron of British and American ships on Lake Erie ended in the surrender of the entire British squadron, and Commander Perry's famous laconic despatch: "We have met the enemy and they are ours: two ships, one schooner, and one sloop". The Americans followed up this success by recapturing Detroit, but on the eastern front north of Plattsburg an attempt to invade Canada and take Montreal was foiled, and by the end of the year the territorial situation remained almost exactly as it had existed before the war began.

The taking of prisoners during these various engagements raised the question of whether the British might apply the same criterion they used in taking seamen for impressment — the doctrine of indefeasible allegiance. If they were to do so, any American who had been born in Britain, even if by now a naturalised American, might, because he was found in arms fighting his mother country, be deemed a traitor and condemned to death. Fearing the British might apply the doctrine of indefeasible allegiance to soldiers who had been taken prisoner, the American commander, General Dearborn, took twenty-seven British prisoners-of-war into close custody as hostages, declaring that they would be treated in the same way as the American prisoners in British hands. The press in England condemned Dearborn's action and supported the British position that a man owed allegiance to the country of his birth.

In a long article in the *Political Register* Cobbett defended those British subjects who had emigrated to the United States. They had left their native country, he said, solely to improve their lot, "a motive wholly foreign to that of committing treason". He supported his stand by pointing out that the British army had in it Germans, Dutchmen, Italians and Frenchmen who had come to England expressly to join the British armed forces, but they were never considered to be traitors if captured by their countrymen in the European wars.

> I have seen hundreds of children (I might say thousands) land in America with their emigrant parents; and if either of these were to be found in arms in the American army fighting against us, would we have him hanged, his quivering bowels torn out, and his head chopped off and his body hacked into quarters for this offence?[9]

Hanging, drawing and quartering was still the punishment on the Statute Book in England at this time. Cobbett ended this article by asking that even if it were true that there were Englishmen who had left their country in order to fight against it, surely it would be wise to keep quiet about it.

> We should only blazen through the whole world the melancholy fact that *for some reason or other* there were Englishmen ready to take up arms against their country, and in that cause, not only to encounter all the dangers inseparable from war, but in addition thereto, the risk of being hanged, ripped up and chopped to pieces! Would it be to our honour to cause this fact to be known in every town, in every village, in every house, in every

---

[9] *Political Register*, Vol 24, August 7 1813.

hovel, throughout the civilised world? Where is the policy of thus astounding the world into a knowledge of a circumstance so little calculated to impress mankind with a favourable opinion of our character? I think that if I were a minister, I should do everything in my power to keep such facts from being promulgated.[10]

If during 1812 and 1813 Cobbett had been forthright in expressing his opinions of the war, he was even more so during its last year. To understand his later writings we must once again turn our attention to the dramatic events on the continent of Europe which culminated in Napoleon's surrender to the allied armies, his banishment to Elba, and the restoration of the Bourbons to the throne of France.

The withdrawal of some of Napoleon's best troops from Spain for the disastrous invasion of Russia in 1812 opened the way for the British forces under Wellington gradually to fight their way through Spain to France. In June 1813, in the fiercest engagement of the advance, sixty thousand French troops and eighty thousand British clashed at the battle of Vittoria with the loss in this one battle of some five thousand British and six thousand French troops. Inevitably, the comparative scale of the engagements fought by the British in North America paled into insignificance when contrasted with those fought in Europe, so that throughout the Anglo-American war events in Europe always overshadowed those on the other side of the Atlantic. And as the prospect of Napoleon's defeat loomed larger, so did the confidence of the British that when the Napoleonic war was over and troops could be released to cross the Atlantic, the United States would quickly capitulate. Men who had fought in those tremendous campaigns in Spain were surely a match for

---

[10] *Ibid.*

the ill-equipped and half-trained armies of the United States.

With the ending of the war in Europe in April 1814, Britain could turn her undivided attention to prosecuting the war across the Atlantic. Flushed with success, the *Times*, as did many other papers of the day, urged the transfer of troops to North America to finish the war there with the same glory as had ended the long war with Napoleonic France. It will be remembered that Cobbett, although never wishing England to become a vassal of France, had seen in Napoleon's domination of Europe the overthrow of many outstanding abuses of the regimes he had supplanted. But Napoleon's increasingly grandiose schemes for territorial conquest, and his ambition to found a dynasty of Bonapartes to rule Europe, led Cobbett to feel that he had betrayed the republic. "The French people", he wrote at the time of Napoleon's death in 1821, "sent him forth to put down despots; and he became a creator and protector of despots".[11] Nevertheless, much as Cobbett deplored Napoleon's later career as Emperor, he deplored even more the restoration of the Bourbons by the victorious allies and the reimposition of the old repressive regime which had provoked the French Revolution of 1789. He now saw with alarm and dismay that there were influential sections in England who wished completely to overthrow the American republic and to bring back some form of colonial rule from Britain. "Sentiments like these were never hazarded while Napoleon was in power; but the moment he is down, these men turn their hostile eyes towards America, the only republic left on the face of the earth".[12]

This desire to annihilate the republic, Cobbett said, was

---

[11] *Political Register*, Vol 39, July 14 1821.
[12] *Political Register*, Vol 25, April 23 1814.

aroused in some by a desire to destroy England's mercantile rival. Others

> animated solely by their hatred of whatever gives liberty to men, will see in America what indeed they have always seen, and for which they have always hated her, an asylum for the oppressed; a dwelling for real liberty; an example of a people enjoying the height of prosperity and the greatest safety of person and property without any hereditary titles; a country where there are no sinecures, no pensions, no grants of public money to individuals; where the people at large choose their representatives in the legislature, their presidents, governors and sheriffs; where bribery and corruption are unknown, and where the putting of a criminal to death is nearly as rare as an eclipse of the Sun or Moon.[13]

And once again he warned his readers that although England now had the power to waste the settlements along the eastern coast of the United States, to occupy some of the major towns, and even to capture the city of Washington and drive the government from the capital, the jubilant tone of the British press proposing that Britain should now treat Madison as it had treated Napoleon would arouse even the disaffected citizens of New England to unite behind their government.

Cobbett also pointed out to his readers that the desire to conquer the United States was actuated by other motives too.

> Then think of the delightful prospects which seventeen or eighteen provinces hold out to the hunters of places! Such cargoes of Governors, Commanders-in-Chief, Staffs, Post-Admirals and Officers, Customs House and Excise people, Attorneys and Solicitors-General,

---

[13] *Political Register*, Vol 25, April 23 1814.

> Judges, Doctors, Proctors, Paymasters, Commissaries, and, though last but not least, Bishops, Priests and Deacons! Only think of this, and wonder not that there are persons who wish for the re-colonisation of America.[14]

Throughout the months immediately following the defeat of Napoleon, Cobbett urged the people of Great Britain to press the government to make peace with the United States, and it should be remembered that he was then addressing a nation which had already endured twenty-one years of war which had brought in its train untold misery and want. All the grounds of dispute, he maintained, were now over. Peace had ended the need for blockades, for impressment, for Orders-in-Council, and for searching ships for contraband. Constantly he warned his readers of the error of assuming that if British forces were to take even great towns like New York, Charleston or Boston, the Americans would surrender. Although he admitted that the American invasion of Canada had been unpopular among some sections in the United States, he was certain that the Americans would all unite to defend their own homes and territory. "Remember", he wrote,

> they all know how to use arms; they have all been accustomed to shoot from their boyish days. They are all marks-men and so they were found to be during the last war *[he refers here to the War of Independence]*. The public should not be too sanguine as to the result of this war. The distance is so great, the conveyance of troops and of all sorts of means of war is so expensive, and attended with so many difficulties and so much delay, that it really is a war less promising of success than any other in which we could possibly have been engaged.[15]

---

[14] *Political Register*, Vol 25, May 7 1814.
[15] *Political Register*, Vol 25, June 25 1814.

Cobbett's was a lone voice. In June 1814, Sir George Prevost, Governor of Canada, received instructions from London to prepare for the invasion of the United States, and thirteen thousand officers and men, many of them veterans of the Peninsular War, were sent to reinforce the army in Canada. In September, Prevost, with his reinforced army, crossed the border with the aim of capturing Plattsburg, the American garrison town on the shores of Lake Champlain. For a successful invasion of the United States from the north it was essential for the British to obtain command of the great waterways of Lake Champlain, running down like a dagger towards Albany and New York. The Lake straddled the border between Upper Canada and the United States, and both sides had built squadrons of ships on the Lake, almost equally matched in numbers and fire power. Prevost's plan to capture Plattsburgh by storming the town from the land and bombarding it from ships on the Lake failed when the American squadron on the Lake put out of action the whole of the British squadron. With the Lake now entirely in American hands, Prevost issued orders for his army of ten thousand men to retire back across the border, for without control of the waterway he would be unable to provision and reinforce his troops if he were to use Plattsburg, as he had intended, as a springboard for further advances. This stunning victory by the Americans — the loss of the whole British squadron and the retreat of ten thousand British soldiers confronted by less than half of that number of American troops, and with two hundred British casualties against one hundred American, ended hostilities on the Canadian-American borders. Once again, now after two and a half years of war, the positions held by the belligerents were almost exactly as they were before hostilities began.

On the Atlantic seaboard, forays had been made into American territory even before the end of the European war. When the British imposed a blockade of the coast at the beginning of 1813 in order to bottle up the US navy which had so humiliated the Royal Navy in the early months of the war, the ships on station needed water and provisions, and marauding parties were sent out to obtain them. Lynnhaven in Virginia, Havre de Grace, Fredericstown and Georgetown in Maryland were all raided, provisions obtained, and property, stores and ships at their moorings burnt and destroyed. There was serious looting and pillaging by British troops later in 1813 at Hampton in the south of Virginia, and settlements in North and South Carolina and Georgia were also harassed. But with the ending of the war with France, Britain embarked on sterner measures. As well as the attack from Canada, Britain planned to invade Washington and other towns on the Atlantic coast, and assembled another large army and fleet in the West Indies in preparation for an attack on New Orleans. The attack on Washington took place at the end of August 1814. Five thousand troops under the British General Ross were landed at the mouth of the Potomac river, fought their way up to Washington, suffering some five hundred casualties from the body of militia hastily assembled to defend the capital, and entered a deserted city. So unexpected had been the attack, that they found a dinner actually prepared and spread out in the White House. Ross had been willing to spare the city from burning (its burning was justified as a retaliation for the earlier burning of York, the capital of Upper Canada, by the Americans a year earlier), but finding no one in authority with whom to bargain, he ordered the firing of the White House, the Capitol, the Arsenal and various government buildings, personally supervising himself the piling up of the furniture in the White House. But the difficulties of obtaining adequate support and supplies to hold the city decided Ross to retire his troops back to the ships. An attempt a week later to capture Baltimore was foiled by stiff resistance from American forces. Ross himself was killed, and no further attempts at invasion were made on the Atlantic seaboard.

When news eventually reached England of the destruction of Washington and the precipitate flight of President Madison and his entourage from the city, newspapers and cartoonists were merciless in pouring scorn and ridicule on the Americans, rejoicing that the burning of York had been avenged, and prophesying the imminent collapse of all American resistance. A few voices were raised in protest, the English paper *The Statesman* comparing the Russian's capture of Paris with the British action in Washington. "The Cossacks spared Paris, but we spared not the Capital of America. Is it certain, that the destruction of the public edifices for destruction-sake alone, is a legitimate method of warfare?"[16]

Cobbett's reaction in the *Political Register* was far more robust. Lambasting the "Bloody Old Times" for its glee in reporting how the Americans "ran away at the sight of our troops", how "Mr Madison and his Government have decamped", and provoked to anger by its prognostications that "the world is speedily to be delivered of the mischievous example of a Government founded on democratic rebellion", he devoted a long article to undeceiving his readers. More republican than the republicans he was defending, he even criticised the buildings in the capital city as being too grandiose for a true government of the people.

Now the truth is that the City of Washington is no

---

[16] Quoted in K Caffrey, *The Lion and the Union*, p 266, Andre Deutsch, 1978.

city at all except in name, and not at all what Johnny Bull has been led to believe. What have we done? We have entered a straggling town of wooden buildings, which our own newspapers had told us the Americans themselves had acknowledged to be defenceless; we have set fire to several buildings and some ships; we have (thank God) burnt the President's Palace and a building on a ridiculously large scale called the Capitol where the Legislature of the Union holds its sittings; we have then retreated and regained our ships with such haste that we have been compelled to leave our dead, and many of our wounded officers as well as men, to the mercy of an enemy whom our newspapers call unprincipled, cowardly and cruel.[17]

To ensure that his readers were fully aware of the insignificant nature of the supposed victory, Cobbett asked them to compare British actions with those of Napoleon. He, when he captured Berlin, Hanover, Madrid and Amsterdam, stayed there. Even in Moscow he was strong enough to remain in the city for several weeks. "But we, we capture the Metropolis of America and we decamp immediately. Oh reader! How has Napoleon been abused for leaving behind him his sick and wounded when he retreated from Russia!"[18] Cobbett did, however, give some comfort to his readers by assuring them that the British wounded were left in the hands of a "very humane people".

For most people in Britain, though, the news that Mr Madison and his government had fled from Washington made them even bolder in calling for the complete destruction of the republican system in the United States — "that system of fraud and indignity which constitutes the whole policy of the Jeffersonian school", as the

---

[17] *Political Register*, Vol 26, October 8 1814.
[18] *Ibid.*

Times described it. With all forms of democracy now extinguished in Europe, Cobbett decided to fling down a dramatic challenge. He published in full in the pages of his *Political Register* of November 11th 1814 the Declaration of Independence of 1776 and with it the Articles of the Constitution of the United States of 1789.

Still under bonds for good behaviour after his prison sentence, he was careful to preface their publication by stating that they were public documents which all the world saw at the time they were written. But, he went on to say, as many of his readers might find it difficult to procure copies, and as they had now "become somewhat interesting in consequence of the bold avowal in the press that it is our intention to overthrow the Democratic Government of the United States", he thought it opportune to acquaint his readers with their contents so that they could see just what it was that was to be overthrown. Whether the statements the documents contained were true or not, he added as a further precaution against prosecution, was not his concern. Yet even with this proviso, one is staggered at Cobbett's boldness. He was asking his readers in the middle of a war to compare their own government with that of the enemy. He went further: in introducing the texts he asked them to remember that when the Declaration of Independence was written, the Americans were merely anticipating the "blessings of freedom". Now they were actually enjoying them. Was it likely, then, that such a people, under such a government as was set out in their Constitution, would not resist to the end any attempt to destroy such a system? And was it not madness to persevere in such a project?

The ending of the Napoleonic War in April 1814 far from easing the distress of the working people, brought with it widespread unemployment. Serious outbreaks of rioting were occurring throughout the kingdom and the government was fearful of full-scale revolution. And here was Cobbett publishing a document which declared that governments derive "their just powers from the consent of the governed; that whenever any form of government becomes destructive of those ends, it is the right of the people to alter or abolish it, and to institute new government". Nor was this all, for the Declaration of Independence went on to give a "history of the repeated injuries and usurpations" perpetrated by the King of Great Britain over the colonies of America. To comprehend the enormity of Cobbett's act it must be remembered that the King of Great Britain whom the Americans had accused *inter alia* of having "obstructed the Administration of Justice", "deprived us in many cases of the benefits of Trial by Jury", "created a Multitude of New Offices and sent hither swarms of Officers to harrass our people and eat our substance" and "plundered our seas, ravaged our Coasts, burnt our towns and destroyed the lives of our people" — that King, finally and terribly condemned as a "Prince unfit to be the ruler of a free people" — was still on the throne of Great Britain. Now old, blind and mad, and represented by his son the Prince Regent, George III was still the titular head of the kingdom and the war was being waged in his name. To have published the Declaration of Independence at this particular time was perhaps the most courageous and almost certainly the most outrageous act of defiance in Cobbett's long history of defiant acts.

When he published these texts, news was already reaching England that the anticipated successes of the armies sent across the Atlantic had not been realised. Hard on the heels of the 'capture' of Washington, came news of the repulse of the attack on Baltimore and the death of General Ross, and then the even more devastating news of the retreat of Prevost's large army from Plattsburg. Against these reverses, the British could boast of a raid on and the looting of the town of Alexandria, south of Washington, and the successful invasion of the northern part of the State of Maine. This last occurred at the beginning of September 1814 when two thousand soldiers were landed at the mouth of the Penobscot River in Maine, captured and set on fire the US frigate *Adams* in harbour there, and obtained the surrender of the town of Bangor. A smaller contingent captured and occupied islands in Passamaquoddy Bay. After twenty-seven months of war, the British could at last claim to have conquered and occupied a part, though a very remote part, of the territory of the United States.

Cobbett, once again, was quick to point out the insignificance of these events. The "grand affair" of Passamaquoddy Bay and the Penobscot in the far north of the United States he compared to the taking of some remote port in the United Kingdom. "If an American privateer were to set fire to a few fishing huts on the coast of Wales, should we look upon it as a very brilliant affair?",[19] he asked. As for the attack on the town of Alexandria in Virginia, his comment was,

> The plundering of Alexandria appears to have been the most successful of our enterprises. The American papers give our people credit for their talent at the emptying of shops and the embarkation of their contents, at which, to do our army and navy (especially the latter) but bare justice, we seem to have been uncommonly adroit.[20]

As usual, Cobbett reserved his greatest scorn for the reports in the press. In an attempt to soften the hard blow to Britain of General Ross' death in the abortive attack on

---

[19] *Political Register*, Vol 26, October 29 1814.
[20] *Ibid.*

Baltimore, the papers had accused the Americans of using cowardly tactics in shooting him during the retreat from the city from behind some brushwood.

> Well, and what then? Do not troops shoot from behind parapets and walls and works of all sort? And do we suppose that the Americans will not make use of a bush when it comes in their way? If this crying tone is to be indulged in, we shall, I fear, cry our eyes out before the war be over.[21]

By November, when the full details reached England of the defeat of the British squadron on Lake Champlain and the subsequent retreat of Prevost's army of ten thousand regular soldiers before an American force of only fifteen hundred regulars and some few thousand militiamen, Cobbett once more appealed for peace. Britain, he said, was fast becoming a laughing stock and in France, in particular, the news of our defeat caused great rejoicing. Small wonder, he went on to say, when they see our great power has been shrunk and mortified by "a country without a King, without lords, without knights and squires, and without any established church, without tythes and without priests paid from compulsory levies of money, and where the press is unrestrained and the government chosen by the people".[22]

Fearing further indignities to come, Cobbett addressed a long letter to the Prince Regent asking him to recall how in earlier letters he had prophesied the consequences of going to war with America. "If we look now at the state of the war in the gross, without any particular feature being taken into view, does it not appear that we should have been fortunate if my advice had been followed?" He described to the Regent the battle of Lake Champlain and

---

[21] *Political Register*, Vol 26, October 29 1814.
[22] *Political Register*, Vol 26, November 5 1814.

how, in spite of the equality in size and numbers of the two opposing squadrons, every British ship was crippled or captured. To rub salt into the wound, he reminded the Prince that to celebrate the victory over Napoleon he had ordered a grand spectacle in London and had had built miniature fleets of British and American ships which were floated on the waters of the Serpentine in Hyde Park and a mock battle staged.

> Britannia, I am told, (for I saw it not) was seen crowning her sons with bay, while poor Jonathon, with his lank hair hanging over his drooping head, stood a captive under his own flag, which was hanging reversed over that of your Royal House.[23]

Not content with that, he went on to chide the Prince Regent for a recent speech in which he had expressed his confidence that Britain would soon regain her ascendancy after her recent reverses, and had praised "the brilliant and successful operations in the Chesapeake and at the City of Washington". These operations, Cobbett alleged, had had an effect quite different. He referred the Regent to President Madison's Message to Congress from which one gained the impression that the "successful operations" had aroused in America "the most resolute hostility to England," and he ended this Open Letter with these words.

> I have often been rebuked for endeavouring to draw the public attention to America. I have never been able to persuade any body that America was of any consequence. She has now become of consequence; and, if the war go on, as I fear it will, she will soon be of most fearful importance in the view of every nation in Europe. The world is now going to see whether a Republic, without a standing army, with half a dozen

---

[23] *Political Register*, Vol 26, November 12 1814.

frigates, and with a Chief Magistrate with a salary of about five thousands pounds a year, be able to contend, singlehanded, against a kingdom with a thousand ships of war, an army of two hundred thousand men, and with a Royal Family whose civil list amounts to more than a million pounds a year. Nothing was ever so interesting as this spectacle. May the end be favourable to the honour and happiness of this country and mankind in general.[24]

Ever more confident that a free people under a freely elected government would be a match for whatever forces were arrayed against her, and realising that the raids along the Atlantic coast and the invasion of Maine had united the nation and made it even more determined to resist, Cobbett expanded on the theme of the differences between the two forms of government. In the middle of November 1814 he published in the *Political Register* comparisons in the form of a letter to a (probably fictitious) American correspondent who, he stated, had asked him to compare the annual expenses and taxes of the two governments. His reply stated that although the populations of England and Wales and those of the United States were nearly equal at around eight million, taxes in Britain were almost twenty times higher than those in America. Indeed the expenses of merely *collecting* them in England and Wales almost equalled the whole of the taxes raised in the United States. In addition, the British had to pay another seven million pounds in poor rates and a further seven million to the established church. In England the average tax per head per annum amounted to thirty-one dollars, twenty cents, whereas in America Federal and States taxes together amounted to two dollars fifty cents.

Cobbett then went on to inform his correspondent of the

---

[24] *Political Register*, Vol 26, November 12 1814.

great differences between the two nations in their crime rates and their treatment of offenders. He compared the severity of the British penal code with its death sentences, its transportations, its whippings and fines with that of the United States.

> I lived in Philadelphia about eight years with every disposition to find fault with everything I saw, or heard of, that was amiss. During that time I never heard of any person, except in one instance, being tried for his or her life; I never heard of a murder, a highway robbery, or of a house being broken open.[25]

In that one instance three foreigners were condemned to death in the State of Delaware, and so extraordinary was the event, and so great the horror inspired, that the executioner had to be disguised and taken to and from the gallows under escort. In England, on the other hand, death sentences were passed for trivial offences, and mantraps, spring guns and gunpowder under fences were used as common deterrents against poachers and were allowable by law. How different was the situation in America where within ten or twelve miles of the city of Philadelphia "it is the common practice of the farmers to turn flocks of turkeys into the woods in the latter end of August, there to remain until towards winter, when they return half-fat".[26] An English farmer, Cobbett declared, would no more think of doing this than of depositing his purse in a public footpath.

In drawing these comparisons, Cobbett was endeavouring to persuade his readers that to make peace with such a country would not be an ignominious surrender. Since the defeat of Napoleon, Cobbett believed that the only reason for the continuation of the war was the government's

---

[25] *Political Register*, Vol 26 November 12 1814.
[26] *Ibid.*

desire to crush a mercantile rival and to discredit a system of government which they saw as a threat to their own. Negotiations between British and American Commissioners for an end to the war had begun at Ghent in Belgium but were being deliberately drawn out on the British side in the hope that harsh terms could be imposed when the armies sent across the Atlantic had inflicted defeat on the Americans. But although the planned attack on New Orleans had not yet taken place, the reverses the British had suffered in their attempt to invade the United States through Plattsburg, and their inability to capture and hold any towns on the Atlantic seaboard, did not augur well for any future engagements. The progress of the negotiations at Ghent which led to the Treaty of 1814 is the subject of the next chapter.

7
Peace 1814-1815

The strident tone of much of the British press calling on Britain "to give Jonathon a good drubbing", though encouraged and welcomed by the government, could not be acted upon while the war with France was still raging in Europe. Until Napoleon's surrender in April 1814, the American war always took second place to the European. The worst effects of America's declaration of war, the stoppage of provisions to Spain and Portugal and of raw materials to Britain, were partially overcome by the granting of licences to New England shippers which allowed them to continue to trade across the Atlantic and to the British West Indies without molestation from the Royal Navy. Throughout the war raw materials from America supplied the industrial towns in Britain, and food and equipment provisioned the armies in Spain and Portugal and even those in Canada actually engaged in operations against the Americans. In a despatch to England in July 1814, Sir George Prevost, outlining his plan to invade the United States via Plattsburgh, had written:

> The State of Vermont having shown a decided opposition to the War, and very large supplies of specie coming in daily from thence, as well as the whole of the cattle required for the use of the Troops, I mean, for the present, to confine myself in any offensive Operations which may take place to the Western side of Lake Champlain.[1] [ie to New York State rather

---
[1] Mackay Hitsou, *The Incredible War of 1812*, p 216, Univ of Toronto Press, 1965.

than to friendly Vermont on the eastern side of Lake Champlain.]

From the British government's point of view perhaps the most serious threat from the Americans was not the invasion of Canada which, early in the war, had proved to be capable of resisting the enemy, but the depredations of American privateers commissioned by the American government to harass shipping destined for Britain and her armies in the Spanish Peninsula.

> Early in the war, while one portion of the American shipping interest through the licensing system was raking in gold by supplying food for Wellington's forces, another sector was attacking his lines of supply. Repeatedly the duke [of Wellington] told the Admiralty that they were doing a poor job of keeping his communications open. On one occasion he informed their lordships of the "capture and ransom of the Canada horse transport by an American privateer, with a detachment of the 19th Light Dragoons and other troops aboard". On another, he complained that "unfortunately some vessels were taken on the coast of Portugal, which had on board equipment for our troops."[2]

However, although the losses due to American privateers were substantial, some thirteen hundred prizes being taken during the thirty months of the war, they were only a fraction of the total supplies from America reaching Europe, Canada and the West Indies. The Royal Navy, no longer needed to defend England from invasion once Napoleon had turned his eyes eastward towards the end of 1812, could, with its vast superiority in numbers over all its enemies, effectively convoy ships destined for Britain and Spain, and the ships that fell prey to the privateers were mostly stragglers and strays from these convoys, impatient

---

[2] Coles, Harry L, *The War of 1812*, p 96, Univ of Chicago Press, 1965.

to reach their destinations. Even so, the immense cost of waging a war so many thousands of miles from home, and the precarious state of Europe where differences between the victorious allied powers in agreeing the terms of a definitive Peace Treaty after the long Napoleonic wars, were causing concern to the British Ministry, made the government anxious to terminate the American war and bring her troops back to the kingdom.

America, too, was anxious for peace. The unpreparedness of her army and the defection of some of the militia men, sometimes due to lack of pay, at other times because they insisted on returning home to bring in the harvest; the difficulties of enforcing discipline amongst a people accustomed to stand on their individual rights; quarrels amongst the officers unused to obeying orders and between regulars and volunteers as to which was the senior (in some instances early in the war commanding officers felt obliged to consult their inferiors before undertaking operations, and the conflicting opinions given resulted in a plethora of orders and counter orders causing confusion and unrest among the men); these were only some of the difficulties the American government faced in the prosecution of the war. Just as serious was the lack of finance. War could only be undertaken by increasing taxation, raising duties on imports, or by Government borrowing. The first of these was anathema to a people whose newly won fight for independence had resulted in the great blessing of a vast lessening of taxes. Duties on imports, the major source of revenue since Independence, plummeted after the non-intercourse acts, and fell even further when the war put a stop to imports from Britain. The last resort, government borrowing, was dependent on the moneyed section of the population, but this was the very section most opposed to the war and the least likely to take up government stocks. Bankruptcy stalked the administration throughout the war.

When, therefore, in 1813, after Napoleon's armies had retreated from Russia with appalling losses of men and materials, the Emperor of Russia offered to act as a mediator in the Anglo-American dispute, the American government responded with alacrity. At this period of the war the small American Navy was bottled up in the harbours along the Atlantic coast by ships of the Royal Navy, there was little progress in the attempted invasion of Canada, and the New England States were threatening secession and a separate peace with Britain. Two Commissioners, Albert Gallatin, the Secretary to the Treasury, and James Bayard, a Federalist, were appointed by Madison to join John Quincy Adams, the American ambassador to Russia, and to enter into negotiations with the Emperor to initiate discussions for peace. Though anxious for an end to the war the American government was firm in its instructions to its Commissioners. There was to be no peace without a definite undertaking from Britain that she would cease her practice of impressment from American ships, and abandon her "paper blockades". Only when adequate forces were actually present to prevent ships entering and leaving harbours could she claim the right to seize and condemn neutral vessels attempting to penetrate such blockaded ports.

From the start the American Commissioners met with endless delays and prevarications. Arriving in St Petersburg in July 1813, Gallatin and Bayard found the Emperor had left Russia to be with his armies which were pursuing the defeated French across the border into Europe. It was not until five months later, in December, that Britain indicated that she would be willing to enter into negotiations with the Americans, but without the intervention of a third party.

Further delays ensued while the necessary despatches to and from Washington crossed and recrossed the Atlantic, lengthened still more by the dilatory actions of the British government in appointing their Commissioners and deciding on a suitable venue. At the beginning of August 1814, more than a year after Gallatin and Bayard had left the United States for Russia, the two sides formally met at Ghent in Belgium to begin discussions, by which time the American team had been expanded to include Henry Clay and Jonathon Russell. By then the European war was over and British troops had been sent across the Atlantic to prepare for what was hoped would be a swift and successful ending of the war.

It was then while the British and American Commissioners were beginning their struggle to try to resolve the many sources of disagreement at Ghent, that the British forces in North America, now reinforced with regiments from the Peninsular War, began to take the offensive at Plattsburg and on the Atlantic coaSt For five months the negotiations at Ghent dragged on with proposals and counter proposals, and the reports (always two months or more late) of how the war was progressing naturally affected the stances taken by the two parties — successes hardening their attitudes and reverses tending to produce concessions. The British Commissioners had instructions to insist on *uti possiditis*, ie that at the ending of hostilities each side should retain whatever territory it held at the time. Because negotiations began when British forces were assembling across the Atlantic and Britain was sanguine in her expectations that the Americans could be driven from many of their garrisons along the Canadian border and in northern Maine, and possibly from some Atlantic coast towns and New Orleans, it was in Britain's interest to prolong discussions until these hoped for successes had been achieved. As a further step for ensuring the future security of Canada, and to reward the Indians for their help in the campaigns of 1812 and 1813, they were also instructed to propose the creation of a large neutral Indian territory straddling the border between Canada and the United States.

Considering that one of the main reasons for the American decision to invade Canada had been to protect their settlers from Indians, whom they believed were armed and instigated by the British to raid the settlements, the proposition to create a neutral Indian state on their borders was completely unacceptable to the Americans. Nor was *uti posseditis* an attractive proposition to a country which had, after two years of war, gained no territory and was now facing a strongly reinforced army assembling on its borders. Equally unacceptable to the British were the American demands for Britain to end impressment and to renounce her rights to seize neutral ships. It was, in Britain's eyes, precisely because throughout the Napoleonic wars she had remained mistress of the seas that she, alone among the European nations, had remained free from invasion. After the defeat of Napoleon, she would not lightly relinquish those practices which had served her so well in the past, and of all the issues,

> The subject of impressment, which had been the most emotional of the causes which led to the declaration of war, and from which alone the war was continued after the orders-in-council had been repealed, was the main difficulty in any negotiations between the two states. Great Britain was determined not to yield in the slightest degree in her claim to the alleged right of impressment, while the United States held that it would be an added disgrace for her to submit after having resisted the claim to the extent of war.[3]

---

[3] Updyke, Frank A, *The Diplomacy of the War of 1812*, p 159, John Hopkins Press, 1915.

When negotiations began, America was in a weak position. With the ending of the war in Europe, she was demanding what had now become hypothetical rather than actual concessions from the British (both blockades and impressment had ceased after Napoleon's surrender), just at the time when the British, flushed with success in Europe and anticipating success in America, were least likely to compromise. Moreover, whereas it was in Britain's interest to prolong the discussions, for the Americans a speedy ending of the war was imperative both in view of their parlous financial position and, at the beginning of the talks, because the armies assembling on her borders seemed to pose a serious threat to the nation. In its gloomiest light, the position of America at the opening of the talks in Ghent in August 1814 can be summed up in the words of the English historian, T C Smith.

> The administration of Madison had utterly failed to secure any of the ends of the war, to inflict punishment on Great Britain, or to conquer Canada. It had also utterly failed to maintain financial solvency, to enlist an army, to create a navy capable of keeping the sea, or to prevent a movement in New England which seemed to be on the verge of breaking the country into pieces.[4]

whereas Britain's position was very different:

> When the Ministry finally sent commissioners to Ghent on August 8th 1814, it was not with any expectation of coming to a prompt agreement, but merely to engage the Americans while the various expeditions under way took Washington and Baltimore, occupied northern New York, and captured New Orleans. It was generally expected that a few months would find large portions of the United States in British possession, as was in

---

[4] Smith, T C, *The Wars between England and America*, p 235, Williams & Norgate, 1914.

fact the sea coast of Maine east of Penobscot Bay, after September 1st.[5]

In a wry twist to events, the first demand which the American Commissioners were prepared to relinquish was that for the ending of impressment. This issue of which the Secretary of State, James Monroe, had said, "this degrading practice must cease; our flag must protect our crew, or the United States cannot consider themselves as an independent nation"; this issue which was originally laid down as a *sine qua non* for any treaty, was quietly laid to rest Gallatin, the former Secretary to the Treasury, was acutely aware that the coffers of the government were empty and realised that to insist on Britain's giving an undertaking not to renew the practice in any future war would doom the discussions from the start. Neither impressment nor the imposition of blockades was so much as mentioned in the final treaty.

Ironic, too, was the fact that Britain's strong position at the beginning of the talks was eventually to lead her greatly to modify her demands. She took her stand at first by accusing the American government of waging the war not for the declared object of upholding her maritime rights, but in order to annex Canada. The United States, Britain declared, "had aimed at acquisition and aggrandizement", and, in consequence, Britain needed to ensure the security of her frontiers. To this end the Commissioners demanded that the United States should agree to have no armed vessels on the Great Lakes; no military establishments on the shores of the Lakes; there should be a revision of the boundary of northern Maine and in the area west of Lake Superior; Britain should have free access to and the right to navigate the Mississippi; and the United States should

---

[5] Smith, T C, *op cit,* p 238.

undertake not to purchase any more land from the Indians whose territories along the Canadian border were to be guaranteed to them. The American Commissioners firmly rejected all these demands and informed their government of their action.

Such harsh terms rebounded on Britain to her disadvantage. When they reached Washington in October 1814, Madison, believing that their publication would arouse the nation to a determination to unite in prosecuting the war more vigorously, put them before the people. By then the invasion of Maine, the raids along the Atlantic coast and the burning of Washington, and above all, the great success of American arms at Plattsburgh, had already given the nation new resolve and new confidence. Although a movement was afoot in the New England states for secession from the Union, the great majority of the people were now behind the war. Madison's decision to publish the rejected British terms was an astute move. The great Republican paper in Philadelphia, the *Aurora*, condemned them in these terms.

> It is impossible our Commissioners can listen to such terms without indignation... that to restrain the United States from treating with the Indians; that to despoil them in Massachusetts, Michigan, Ohio and the Lakes of their natural frontier and soil, and admit Great Britain into an exclusive right to arm the lakes and to a military occupation of both shores; to create an independent Savage power on our confines and within our domains... demands, attempts or pretensions which the United States will never submit to, but with loss of their freedom. (October 24, 1814.)

And even the Federal papers were aghast. The *United States Gazette* wrote:

> England now turns upon us in the fulness of her wrath

and power. No alternative is left us but to resist with
energy or submit with disgrace. (October 1814.)

Against such strong American determination to resist such terms, and now thwarted in her hope that the invasion from Canada or attacks on the eastern seaboard would establish a British presence in American territory, Britain began to make concessions. Towards the end of 1814, Britain gave up her demand for *uti posseditis* and agreed to the American proposal for *status quo ante bellum* (ie the positions held at the outbreak of war); yielded her demand for an exclusive military control of the Great Lakes; and abandoned her project to create a neutral guaranteed Indian territory along the borders. Her previous boast that she would overthrow the Madison government and "sweep the American navy from the ocean, not leaving a single bit of bunting or a rag or stitch behind" had come to nothing. In return, the Americans dropped their demands for an end to impressment and fictitious blockades, demands which had now become academic with the ending of the European war, and accepted the British proposals that the remaining outstanding issues of boundaries, fishing rights, reparations, etc, should be the subject of discussions between the two countries after the ending of hostilities. On Christmas Eve, 1814, the terms were agreed between the two sides at Ghent, and news that the hostilities were over despatched across the Atlantic.

Reports of the negotiations leaked out to the press before the final Treaty was signed and by November the Americans' complete rejection of the British terms and rumours that Britain was considering lowering her original demands were becoming known in England. Cobbett declared,

> These negociations show that Jonathon, poor despised Jonathon, is not much less smart in the cabinet than he is

in the field. Certainly nothing was ever better managed than these negociations on the part of Jonathon.⁶

At this time, the British government, aware that the original demands would have to be dropped if the war was to be brought to a close, began to represent the majority of the American people as basically friendly to England and the Prime Minister, Lord Liverpool, said in a speech that "in many places a disposition had been shown by the American people to put themselves under our protection". Hoping, perhaps, that if the Americans were shown in this more favourable light, some surrender of the original terms would appear less of a humiliation to British pride, Lord Liverpool referred to reports received from British prisoners of war of their kind treatment at the hands of their captors, which showed that the Americans "do not entertain any animosity against our country". But Cobbett replied:

> No, my Lord, no; this kind treatment of our officers is no sign at all that they are disaffected towards their own Government, or that they think it is wrong. The officers taken in the *Java* by Captain Bainbridge, were treated by him in the most kind and generous manner. Captain Barclay, who was defeated and captured in the Lakes by Captain Perry, spoke in the highest terms of the generosity of his conqueror and, I believe, there never was an instance of the Americans treating a prisoner-of-war unkindly.⁷

Cobbett went on to tell his readers that a perusal of American newspapers showed that, far from their wanting "to put themselves under our protection", committees of defence were springing up throughout the nation, the whole people, "merchants, labourers, lawyers and

---

⁶ *Political Register*, Vol 26, November 26 1814.
⁷ *Political Register*, Vol 26, November 19 1814.

schoolboys" were erecting fortifications, offers of money and personal service were pouring in to the government, and the Senate had recently passed a bill ordering the building of a fleet of warships.

Cobbett followed this up by publishing a series of Open Letters to the Prime Minister, the Earl of Liverpool, in which he endeavoured to show that the anti-war Federalists in the United States were very much in a minority and were becoming increasingly discredited. Since the defeat of Napoleon one of the main planks in their attacks on the Republicans, that Madison and his administration were men devoted to France and tools of Napoleon, had collapsed under them.

> They can no longer reproach the President for his attachment to France, for France now has a king, a legitimate sovereign. They are now, therefore, put in this dilemma; they must declare openly for England against their country; or, by petty cavilling, must make their opposition contemptible. So that their doom, I imagine, is sealed, and their fall will not be much less complete than that of Napoleon himself.[8]

Recalling to Lord Liverpool's mind the history of the Federal Party — how they had always hankered after titles and had seen in the French Revolution the destruction of all they held dear — he maintained that their defeat in 1801 with the election of Jefferson showed that the American *people* had always been Republicans at heart, and Cobbett warned the Prime Minister against the undue prominence being given in the British press to speeches made by prominent New England Federalists such as Goodloe Harper, H G Otis and Timothy Pickering. Cobbett had, as was mentioned earlier, referred to the use made by the press in England of Pickering's speeches to persuade

---

[8] *Political Register*, Vol 26, November 26 1814.

their readers that the Americans were hostile to their government. He now returned to the theme again.

> Timothy Pickering used to be thought a very honest man; but after he was put out of office, he seems to have abandoned himself to the revenge his disappointment created. He had not the virtue to follow the example of his venerable employer, Mr Adams (Pickering was Secretary of State during Adams' presidency), who, upon being outvoted as President by Mr Jefferson said; "I only wished to obtain a majority of voices that I might serve my country, and now I shall endeavour to serve it by supporting him who has that majority". Timothy Pickering, who had been to the astonishment of all the world his Secretary of State, who was no more fit for the office than your coachman would be fit for yours, became furious at the election of Mr Jefferson, and has ever since been in a sort of mad fit, doing a hundred things, for any of which in England, he would be sent to jail for a year or two at least[9].

Since the ending of the Napoleonic wars, Britain had not only extended her blockade to include the coast of New England, but, no longer needing supplies from America for her armies on the continent, had rescinded the licences to American shippers granting them safe passage across the Atlantic. The effect of these measures, so crippling to the New England merchants, was greatly to increase the opposition to the war among the Federalists, and when later in the year Congress passed a conscription act calling for the enlistment of one in every twenty-five men from each State into the army, the New Englanders, led by Caleb Strong, the Governor of Massachusetts, combined into an alliance to demand an end to the war. They threatened secession from the Union if it continued, and delegates were being appointed to a convention called to that end

---

[9] *Political Register*, Vol 24, December 24 1814.

in Hartford in Connecticut. In spite of his belittlement of this movement in his letter to the Earl of Liverpool, Cobbett thought it a serious enough threat to the Republic of the United States for him to denounce the movement by a direct appeal to the people of Massachusetts. Many of Cobbett's articles in the *Political Register* were at this time reprinted in American papers.

In Massachusetts, the defeat of Napoleon and the restoration of the old monarchies in Europe had been the cause of great public rejoicings. A solemn religious thanksgiving had been organised by the clergy of the State to celebrate the entry into Paris of the victorious Russian armies. Cobbett made his appeal in the form of an Open Letter addressed to "The Cossack Priesthood of the State of Massachusetts", using the soubriquet "Cossack" because of their praise of the Russians who had in their eyes "liberated" Europe from Napoleon, and deliberately choosing the loaded word "priests" with its Roman Catholic connotation, rather than the usual appellation of "pastors" or "ministers" used by the Protestant sects. How did it come about, Cobbett asked the "Cossack Priesthood", that they who as Protestants had over the years consistently attacked the Pope as "the anti-Christ, the Scarlet Whore of Babylon and the Beast of the Revelations" and condemned the Roman Catholic religion as "idolatrous, blasphemous, diabolical and as evidently tending to the eternal damnation of millions and millions of souls", had yet rejoiced at Napoleon's fall? Was it not well known that at the beginning of the French Revolution this Roman Catholic Church had been overthrown and the "Pope, Bishops, Cardinals and Monks stripped of power — images burned into firewood, relics laughed at, and religious persecution put an end to? Was this not an event calculated to call forth your gratitude to

Heaven?" How was it then, he asked, that they had reserved their thanksgiving for the time when this revolution was overthrown?

> You knew to a moral certainty that the Pope would be restored. You knew that the toleration of the Protestant sects would be instantly destroyed in the greater part of Europe. The things you praised were the return of the Holy See and the Inquisition. And yet you held a solemn thanksgiving.

Then, switching from addressing the "Cossack Priesthood" to addressing the people themselves, Cobbett continued.

> People of Massachusetts (for to your hardened Priests I will no longer address myself) what can have been the cause of this conduct on the part of your priests? The truth is that they were actuated by self-interest They began to fear that if religion became out of fashion in Europe, it might become out of fashion in Massachusetts, and leave them in a situation like that of a buckle-maker when shoe-strings came into vogue. They began to realise that the fall of the Pope and of the Romish superstition and persecutions would be to them a vast injury. They saw that France and Napoleon were snatching the very bread and meat off their plates. No more need to be said. You, the People of Massachusetts, who possess so much good sense, cannot long remain the dupes of these hypocrites, who while they have the desire of your welfare in the next world constantly on their lips, are manifestly intent upon securing to themselves in this world, ease and plenty at the public expense.[10]

Peter Porcupine's quills had not lost their sting. But within three weeks of publishing this article, Cobbett wrote as a post-script to another Open Letter to Lord Liverpool on

---

[10] *Political Register*, Vol 26, December 10 1814.

the war, the startling news:

> This moment has arrived the *Courier* newspaper with news of the PEACE. I do not know how to express the pleasure I feel at the news, or the gratitude which for this act I, in common with my countrymen, owe to your Lordship and your colleagues.[11]

The news of the Treaty of Ghent was unexpected. For some time past the Ministry had been speaking in the most sanguine terms of the great build-up of forces in the Caribbean and the prospect of a swift take-over of New Orleans. It therefore came as something of a shock that a negotiated peace surrendering nearly all the conditions originally demanded — *uti posseditis*, the control of the Great Lakes, the creation of an Indian buffer state — had been signed before these forces had yet been deployed. (The main body of these troops had, in fact, landed at the mouth of the Mississippi on December 23rd, a day before the Treaty was signed, but this of course was not known to the British government or to either of the negotiating parties at Ghent until many weeks later.)

Although Cobbett could express his relief and gratitude at the end of that war which he had striven so hard at first to avert and then to conclude, many many hundreds of his countrymen had yet to suffer and die in the swamps of the Mississippi delta. The news of the Peace agreed at Ghent on December 24th took only a week to reach England: it was not until February 1815 that the ship bearing the news to the United States touched port.

The build-up of forces to attack the United States at New Orleans had begun shortly after Napoleon's defeat in April 1814, and in August of that year a comparatively small expeditionary force had been landed in Florida

---

[11] *Political Register*, Vol 26, December 31 1814.

at the Spanish town of Pensacola east of the Perdido River, but had been forced to retire by American troops under Andrew Jackson who captured the town. It will be remembered that America had annexed part of West Florida in 1810 and 1812 when the Spanish colonists had risen against their Governor and asked the United States for protection. Much of West Florida was inhabited by Creek Indians and after the annexation, these Indians, fearful of American encroachment on their lands, raided the forts established by the United States. A bitter war between the Creek Indians and the Americans was fought during the winter and spring of 1813-1814 and, in that war, Andrew Jackson, the Commander of the Tennessee militia, once again proved himself to be a formidable and successful soldier. Promoted to the rank of Major-General in the regular army, Jackson was put in command of the forces to defend New Orleans.

After the reverses on the Atlantic coast, part of the British fleet on station on the Atlantic was moved to Jamaica to join the West Indian fleet in preparation for the attack on New Orleans. Six ships of the line, fourteen frigates and transport for over seven thousand men were finally assembled and crossed over the Gulf of Mexico, and from the fleet an advance guard was landed seven miles south of New Orleans on December 10th. The main body landed on the 23rd, a day before the Commissioners at Ghent signed the Peace Treaty. With only two sloops and a small number of gunboats, Jackson was in no position either to prevent the landing or to attack so long as the forces were in range of the powerful guns of the Royal Navy. He did, however, twice attack and stem the troops sent in advance of the main body, and it was not until January 8th that all the troops, equipment and supplies were sufficiently organised for an attack to commence. General

Pakenham, brother-in-law to the Duke of Wellington and his Adjutant General during the Peninsular war, a seasoned and successful soldier, had been sent out from England to take overall command of the operation.

The delay between the landing of the advance troops and the main body, and the further delay while the troops were assembled, allowed Jackson to prepare the defences of New Orleans, and a breastwork of sugar barrels and earth was hastily erected. Pakenham, with six thousand regular soldiers many of them, like himself, veterans of the Peninsular war and one thousand black soldiers from West Indian regiments, ordered the storming of the city. Let Cobbett himself describe the outcome.

> The American General Jackson, with the inhabitants of New Orleans aided by the militia of Tennessee and Kentucky, had assigned to him the task of defending the city against the army of regulars, and, as they were called, of invincibles. With his untutored bands, even whose officers were not in uniform, he, with inferior numbers, attacked the British army twice in the night-time, before they were ready for the main attack on him. On the 8th of January, 1815, they advanced to that attack, with rockets, bombs, an immense train of artillery, and with all the apparatus for storming, the soldiers and sailors having been previously stimulated and steeled against relaxation by assurances the most gratifying to their tastes and wishes. They finally arrived at the point of onset; the faggots, which they carried to make them a road over the works were just tossing into a ditch; in idea the city with all its spoils were in their possession. At that moment, the brave and prudent enemy, with as much coolness as if he had been aiming at harmless birds, opened his fire upon them, and swept them down like grass before the scythe of the mower. He sallied in pursuit, marching over blood and brains and mangled carcasses, and finally, to use the words of

his countrymen, "drove the survivors to their ships, and bade them carry to England the proof of the fact that the soil of freedom was not to be invaded with impunity".[12]

So ended the War of 1812. Begun while the news of the repeal of the Orders in Council was crossing the Atlantic, and continued because, having begun, the Americans could not in honour have accepted Britain's conciliatory move unless it had included the ending of impressment, it ended at New Orleans three weeks after the Peace had been signed in Europe. Britain suffered well over two thousand casualties in this last engagement, including three major-generals (Pakenham himself among them), eight colonels, six majors, eighteen captains and fifty-four subalterns. The American losses were thirteen killed and fifty-eight wounded. All Cobbett's prognostications had been fulfilled by this battle, even to the demise of the New England movement for secession, for the Hertford Convention, meeting when news of the victory was blazoned throughout the United States, broke up in confusion and shame.

As will be seen later, when the news of the stunning defeat of the British at New Orleans eventually reached England in March 1815, it was almost completely overshadowed by the extraordinary event of Napoleon's escape from Elba in that same month. But in the January and February of 1815, before the defeat was known, all the talk in England was of the Peace of Ghent. Cobbett followed up his first mention of the news by publishing in the next issues of his *Political Register* two Open Letters to Major Cartwright, a sympathetic listener because of his long fight for radical constitutional changes in the British system of government.

---

[12] *Paper Against Gold*, Letter XXXI, 1815.

> The peace with America is certainly the most auspicious event that I ever have had to record. It opens to mankind a prospect of happier days. It has, by the stroke of a pen, blasted the malignant hopes of the enemies of freedom, hurled them and their paragraphs and pamphlets and reviews down into the dirt to be trampled under foot; changed their exultation into mourning, their audacity into fear.[13]

Cobbett used these letters to remind his readers that the avowed aims of the war had not been realised. When the European war was ended, the government justified the continuation of the war with America as necessary for "the lasting tranquillity of the civilised world". One of the Lords of Admiralty had enlarged upon this theme in a speech in Parliament by stating that although Bonaparte had been deposed, "there was another gentleman whose deposition was also necessary to our interest, he meant Mr President Madison, and with a view to that deposition a considerable naval force must be kept up". In short, Cobbett maintained that the government's intention had been to destroy the last republic left because "the example of a people living under a Government such as that of America, without tumults, without commotions, would always be a handle for the friends of reform to lay hold of. It was useless, in their view of the matter, to have restored the Bourbons, the Pope, the Dominicans and the Inquisition, while America remained an example and an asylum for the oppressed of all nations".[14]

Why England had suddenly abandoned so many of her objectives and made peace with Jonathon, Cobbett found very difficult to understand at the time. Subsequent events were to provide him with an explanation. Nor was he alone

---

[13] *Political Register*, Vol 27, January 7 1815.
[14] *Ibid.*

in looking for an explanation. The more belligerent of the papers condemned the Peace as a disgrace, but most tried to pass off the doubts it aroused by emphasising that because the Americans had dropped their original demands for the ending of impressment and had exacted no concessions from Britain on blockades, Orders in Council, or any other maritime infringements of their rights as a neutral — questions which they had declared to be the cause of their declaring war — they had in fact gained nothing. But Cobbett, even though at this time still ignorant of the Battle of New Orleans, believed that Britain would never again flout America's rights now that she knew that the United States would not shrink from a resort to arms if they were ever again to be violated. How, then, he asked, could it be said that America had gained nothing?

> Has she gained no English ships? Has she gained no renown? Is it nothing to have been able, with her infant navy, to have resisted with success the maritime power of England single-handed? Is it nothing to have proved to the world that, let who will attack her, she stands in need of no foreign aid, no hired fighters of other countries; but that her own citizens are equal, not only to her defence, but to the carrying of her "bits of striped bunting" in triumph into every sea against even a superior force? Is it nothing to have proved that her Government, free as air, is perfectly adequate to the most perilous of wars? Is *this* nothing, you venal English writers? It is a gain to mankind, for who will now dare assert that political freedom, that religious freedom, that a press wholly uncontrolled, are incompatible with national safety in times of war?[15]

For Cobbett, the downfall of the Federalists, what he

---

[15] *Political Register*, Vol 27, November 14 1815.

called "the aristocratical factions" of the United States, the certainty of an immense emigration to America now that the war was over, bringing with it a rapid increase of power, and above all the fact that the republican government there remained in power with a press "to promulgate the truths of its freedom" was certain proof that America had been the victor.

Before turning to the great events on the continent and the second defeat of Napoleon at Waterloo, two last extracts from Cobbett's comments on the War of 1812 deserve to be included here. The first is from a Letter to Lord Liverpool written after the news of the Battle of New Orleans reached England. Here he chides the Prime Minister for never having thanked him for all the letters he had addressed to him throughout the war.

> You have appeared to be sulky with me, though I taught you so exactly what to do in order to avoid the great evils which were coming on you from all quarters. I told you that the Americans would beat you in fighting if you continued the war for two years. You continued the war and they did beat you. In short, you expended fifty millions of money, and lost, I dare say, thirty thousand men, and accomplished nothing excepting creating a navy in America, causing her manufacturers to flourish, and implanting in the hearts of Americans for ages a hatred of the English government.[16]

In the second extract from another Letter to Liverpool, Cobbett made it clear that in spite of all the government's protestations to contrary, the Peace of Ghent was a signal defeat for Britain. Unlike the earlier treaties ending the wars with France in the Peace of Amiens of 1801 and the Peace of Paris in 1814, which had been proclaimed by

---

[16] *Political Register*, Vol 27, May 13 1815.

heralds and celebrated in great processions from St James Palace in Westminster to the City of London, the Peace of Ghent had had no fanfares. But when it was known in America:

> There the full force of public feeling was made manifest The country resounded from New Orleans to the utmost borders of the Lakes; from the orange groves to the wheat lands buried four feet deep in snow, was heard the voice of joy, the boast of success, the shout of victory. These are mortifying recollections, my Lord, and I do not know that they will be rendered less so to you by the addition of the reflection that if you had followed my advice, there never would have been any ground for them.[17]

---

[17] *Political Register*, Vol 27, June 3 1815.

George Washington

John Adams

Thomas Jefferson

James Madison

James Monroe

John Quincy Adams

Andrew Jackson

The frontispiece to Robert Huish's *Memoirs of William Cobbett esq*, showing Cobbett in the 1790s laying low one of his detractors outside his bookshop on Second Street in Philadelphia.

" Great offices will have Great talents."

This is THE MAN—all shaven and shorn,
All cover'd with Orders—and all forlorn ;

Cruikshank's caricature of the Prince Regent, to whom Cobbett addressed many of his Open Letters in his *Political Register*

Cobbett, riding on the devil, returning to England from the United States with Paine's bones, to be welcomed by a band of reformers (bottom left). Quakers in America (bottom right) rejoice at his departure while Napoleon (centre) watches from his island of St Helena.

The USS Chesapeake being attacked by HMS Leopard three years before the outbeak of the War of 1812 as it was thought she was harbouring deserters from the Royal Navy.

In the early 1800s the threat of an invasion from France was very real. This French cartoon shows three possible methods: by sea (barges carrying troops backed by warships), by land (the army emerging from a tunnel under the Channel), by air (balloons carrying baskets conveying troops).

An anonymous artist's composite picture of the British attack on and burning of Washington city incorporating other events leading up to the destruction of the capital.

A depiction of the battle of New Orleans

The frontispiece Cobbett designed for his book *The Life of Andrew Jackson*. It depicts the ramparts at New Orleans with Pakenham's armies strewn about the plain. In the background Lord Cochrane, the British Admiral, makes off with his fleet for England, while in the foreground are two gibbets, one with a "paper money maker" the other a Creek Indian.

8

The American Political Register

The news of Napoleon's escape from Elba at the end of February 1815, little more then two months after the signing of the Peace of Ghent with the Americans, raised a host of questions in Cobbett's mind. It will be remembered that Cobbett, as did many of his countrymen, greeted the news of the Treaty with astonishment, for why should such a peace have been agreed when the great army and navy assembled in the Caribbean were known to be poised to inflict what was confidently expected to be a crushing defeat on the Americans by an invasion of New Orleans? Cobbett saw in the extraordinary circumstances surrounding Napoleon's escape from Elba a possible explanation.

> The Allies treatment of Napoleon after his first surrender in April 1814 was magnanimous. He was given the sovereignty of the island of Elba, off the coast of Italy, allowed a small army among whom were some seven hundred of his elite regiment of the Imperial Guards, given a warship, the brig *Inconstant*, and awarded a substantial income to keep up his establishment. On Elba he reigned over the native inhabitants and those who had come over with him into exile. The old etiquette of his imperial dynasty was maintained, and he received a stream of visitors who kept him in touch with events in Europe. An English Commissioner was appointed to the island whose duty it was unobtrusively

to supervise his conduct and to report any suspicious conduct of the exiled Emperor, but in many ways his status on Elba was more that of a diplomat accredited to a court.

In France itself, although the Bourbon monarchy was restored under the executed Louis XVI's younger brother Louis XVIII (Louis XVI's son, now dead, was assumed to have been King of France after the execution of his father, and given the title of Louis XVII, although he never succeeded to the throne because of the creation of a Republic), many of the reforms instituted during the Revolution remained. Lands confiscated from the Church and nobles were mostly left in the hands of those among whom they had been distributed, and the abolition of tithes, and the sweeping reductions of excise duties, taxes, levies, game laws, etc., were not repealed. Under the new Constitution, the French economy flourished and foreign visitors commented on how prosperous the country seemed to be after the long wars.

Napoleon remained on Elba for nearly a year. By the beginning of 1815 he was made fully aware by his many visitors from Europe of the quarrels among the victorious powers assembled at the Congress of Vienna over the distribution of the conquered territories in Germany and Poland, and of the unrest among the peasants in France where rumours that lands confiscated from the Church and nobles might begin to be restored to their former owners. When he believed that the time was ripe for his return to France, he ordered, during the absence on leave of the British Commissioner, the brig the *Inconstant* and his small flotilla to be stocked and made ready, and on February 26th 1815.

With bands playing and flags flying (the Imperial guard) had marched down through the twilight, past the

> windows illuminated in Napoleon's honour, under the coloured lanterns in the square, and through a crowd which called out and cried in its excitement...They were singing the Marseillaise as Napoleon went down the steps into the Caroline, which was to take him out to the *Inconstant*. There was so little wind that the men had to row all the way, and as the little craft passed each vessel in the flotilla there was a burst of cheering. It was the last of Elba. As the Emperor boarded the *Inconstant* a single cannon signalled that the escape had begun.¹

(This 'escape', glossed over by nearly all English historians even to this day, is still commonly assumed to have been undertaken in secrecy, at dead of night. The facts are very different.)

The voyage to France, delayed by the slow speed of the accompanying ships, took three nights and three days, but Napoleon succeeded in landing at Juan near Antibes, and disembarking his 1100 armed men, forty horse and four cannon without challenge or molestation on sea or land. In his progress through France to Paris, thousands of his old soldiers flocked to his standard, and thousands more deserted from the newly created Royalist army to his side; when he arrived in Paris twenty days later, the restored Louis XVIII had fled the capital and Napoleon was able to make a triumphal entry to the Palace of the Tuileries watched by a wildly cheering crowd.

> Every peasant knew that the Little Corporal would not require him to disgorge the lands which before the troubles had belonged to the seigneur and the abbot, and that whatever drawbacks might be attendant on his rule, there was at least no fear of priest or émigré under Napoleon. He was the son of the people, who could talk their language and read their hearts.²

---

[1] Mckenzie, Norman, *The Escape From Elba* pp 214-5, OUP, 1982.
[2] Fisher, H A L, *Napoleon* p 129, OUP, 1967.

By June of that year, Napoleon had established a new government in France and recruited an army of 250 thousand men. With a striking force of 120 thousand, he left France to confront the allied armies which had assembled in Belgium to crush Napoleon for a second time. These comprised some 65 thousand Belgian, Dutch and Hanoverian troops and 23 thousand British all under the command of the Duke of Wellington, and some 120 thousand Prussian troops under General Blücher some 200 thousand in all. In the ensuing battle of Waterloo of June 18th 1815, the Allied forces with a combined loss of 20 thousand men were victorious. The French lost 37 thousand killed, wounded and prisoners of war and the so-called Hundred Days of Napoleon's return to power were over. Louis XVIII was restored to the throne of France and Napoleon banished for life to the distant island of Saint Helena.

When the full facts became known, Cobbett suspected that Napoleon's escape from Elba had been deliberately engineered. He believed that the British government had come to realise that the Treaty of Paris imposed on France in April 1814 had not gone far enough. "The English government saw that enough had not been done; and that somehow or another, France must be made worse off".[3] The sight of France living under a more liberal constitution than that of Britain, with much of its land redistributed among its people and free of so many of the burdens that were causing discontent in England, was an encouragement to Jacobins at home and was a threat to established order. Another war must be fought and a new more repressive treaty imposed.

The proposition which I mean to make good, and which

---

[3] *History of The Regency and Reign of George IV*, Ch V, paras 223 and 224 (1832).

it is of the greatest possible importance to the cause of truth to make clear to the minds of my readers, is this, *that the English government most anxiously wished for the return of Napoleon to France.* Whether it actually contrived it the reader must be left to judge for himself, I wishing to lead him into no inference not fully borne out by the facts of the case.

NAPOLEON landed in the bay of Juan on the 1st of March, 1815. Common mortals were struck with surprise at this event. The government had him a safe prisoner in a small island in the Mediterranean Sea; this government had an officer living at ELBA to watch NAPOLEON; the sea was covered with English cruizers of all sizes; how was he to escape in a little sloop, and, with divers persons along with him, safely land, without interruption, in France?

The officer stationed at ELBA to watch him, came to England immediately after NAPOLEON'S return to France; and instead of being censured and disgraced, was highly honoured, and was presented to the Prince Regent, and received with every mark of Royal approbation. How is this to be accounted for, unless we believe that the English government desired to see NAPOLEON return?

Besides these circumstances there was another which Cobbett found suspect. When Napoleon landed in France the plenipotentiaries of the Allies were meeting at the Congress of Vienna, seeking to reshape Europe after the convulsions of Napoleonic domination. What puzzled Cobbett was that as early as March 13th these Allies issued a solemn Declaration stating that by landing in France with an armed force, Napoleon "had placed himself without the pale of civil and social relations, and that as an enemy and disturber of the tranquillity of the world, he has rendered himself liable to public vengeance". Cobbett maintained, quite correctly, that this Declaration was issued before there could have been any knowledge either in Vienna or in England that Napoleon would be successful in rallying the people to his side. After his landing he avoided any confrontation with the Royalist troops and it was not until March 13th, the day the Declaration was issued, when his small army reached Lyons, that it became apparent that many of the people were with him and that the Royalist armies might not be prepared to defend the restored monarchy. A whole week elapsed after the signing of the Declaration before Louis XVIII accepted defeat and fled from the capital. And yet they signed a declaration of war against Napoleon.

> How came they to take such a liberty as this? How came they to enter into an alliance for the purpose of fighting NAPOLEON? In short it is impossible not to believe that his return was in the contemplation of the English government; in its contemplation at least; and that Wellington had received instructions accordingly; for it is quite impossible to believe that any ambassador to a mere congress appointed for other matters, would, without specific authority, have joined in a declaration of war against a sovereign *de facto*, and against the French nation, beforehand, and without any act of aggression committed on their part.[4]

Some space has been given to Cobbett's supposition that Britain wished for Napoleon's escape because it is on this hypothesis that he based his second proposition explaining the hitherto puzzling *volte-face* of the British Commissioners at Ghent in agreeing peace terms with the Americans before the results of the highly organised and long planned invasion of New Orleans had taken place. Here, again in his own words, is Cobbett's second supposition.

---

[4] *Ibid*, Ch V, para 225.

After the conclusion of the Treaty of Paris in the month of May 1814, the English government had gone into the war against the United States of America with tenfold fury; the most violent warfare had been commenced; great forces had been sent thither; it had been openly declared in the House of Commons itself, that there was to be no peace with America until the President MADISON should be deposed, and that there could be no peace for regular government until the republican constitution of America should be put down. This was the tone in England; it was the fashionable talk; it was looked upon as a matter of course that there was to be no peace with America until these objects were effected; and this talk continued from the date of the Treaty of Paris all through the summer, and nearly up to Christmas. Forces were, during that time, daily going out to add to the armies and the fleets in America. The Americans, though victorious in their battles, wanted peace; were extremely anxious to obtain it; while the English government drawled out the negotiations with the manifest object of not making peace. At last it proposed a *sine qua non*; that is to say, terms without the Americans acceding to which it would never make peace. Public opinion being in this state in England, how were we all astonished, in the Christmas week of 1814, to hear that peace had all at once been concluded with the United States on Christmas-eve, without any of us having ever heard the whisper of a reason for such a thing! It was, however, concluded; and concluded, too, with an abandonment of every particle of the *sine qua non*!

Now where are we to find a sufficient reason for so sudden and so great a change of policy? The ministerial press had called Mr MADISON a "traitor" and "a rebel"; and yet, all at once, the government, this proud and insolent government, forms a treaty of peace and friendship with this same JAMES MADISON, giving up every principle for which it had contended.

It is not to be believed that this would have been done, if there had not been some cause, with which the public were never made acquainted. But, upon the supposition that the government expected the return of NAPOLEON, this sudden and disgraceful peace with the Americans was perfectly natural. By the Treaty of Ghent, the stage was cleared, as it were, for a battle of all Europe against NAPOLEON.

It should be noted that although decried and ignored at the time in Britain (though not in Europe), Cobbett's supposition that England actually wished for an opportunity to defeat Napoleon a second time and connived at his escape has recently been revived. (See particularly Norman Mackenzie's *The Escape from Elba*, OUP 1982.) Cobbett's second supposition regarding the Treaty of Ghent remains largely unexplored.

Whether or not there is any truth in these suppositions, it is undoubtedly true that the conditions imposed on France after Napoleon's second defeat were far more stringent then those imposed after the Peace of Paris of 1814. From Cobbett's point of view, this second victory of the old powers of Europe over France made the continuing existence of a republic in the New World even more important than before. Lord Grey of Falloden's despairing cry, "The lamps are going out all over Europe", uttered some one hundred years later at the outbreak of World War One, almost exactly epitomises Cobbett's reaction to the state of Europe after Waterloo, but he could discern a beacon across the Atlantic and was determined that its light should penetrate through to the Old World. After Waterloo, Cobbett took upon himself the roles of mentor, guardian and propagandist of the one remaining hope for the common man — the Republic of the United States, deeming it necessary that the Republic should preserve its purity, should be strong enough to resist attack, and that its existence should be widely known and understood.

As mentor, Cobbett thought it necessary to warn the American people against what he saw as an insidious creeping into their society of the trappings of 'aristocratical' usages. Already we saw in his report of the burning of the city of Washington his objection to the grandiose buildings of the capital as inappropriate for a republic. He returned to the subject again a little later, complaining that Members of Congress had begun to call one another "honourable gentleman" and "honourable friend". "This is indeed contemptible", he wrote. "When once the hankering after titles becomes general in that country; when once riches will have produced that effect, the country will become an easy prey to an old, compact, and easily welded country such as ours. It will proceed, unless speedily checked, to the utter destruction of that which it has essayed."[5]

As well as his fears that the American republic might, as France had under Napoleon, allow power to fall into the hands of a rich elite, he watched with alarm the financial difficulties the government had incurred in the prosecution of the war. Although, by British standards, the American national debt was miniscule, Cobbett believed that there was a real danger that it might result in a concentration of wealth in fewer and fewer hands and the pauperisation of the common people. His warnings to the Americans on the evil consequences of a national debt and the issue of paper money to fund it, first expressed in his *Paper Against Gold* written in Newgate Gaol, which he expressed at this time will be discussed later in Chapter 16.

Cobbett was anxious too that the Americans should not

---
[5] *Political Register* 26, 10 December 1814.

be under the impression that England was greatly to be admired or feared for its glorious victory at Waterloo. The *Political Register* of July 8th 1815 carried an article in the form of an Open Letter to the Proprietor of *Niles Weekly Register*, one of the leading journals in the United States, in which Cobbett said he wanted to give the people of the "last remaining republic" information on the late events in France. "The boasting here is beyond all conception. Though the fact is notorious, that we had a vast superiority of numbers and of means of all sorts, we talk here as if the victory were *wholly our own*."[6] Referring to the £200,000 voted to the Prince of Wales after the victory and a proposition for a further sum to be voted to his brother, the Duke of York, he pertinently asked: "What did you vote to Mr Jackson who won a more decided and more glorious victory at New Orleans? and continued:

> You will ask, what takes place in this respect, when we get *beaten* as in the case of Plattsburgh, Lake Champlain, Lake Erie, New Orleans, etc. Why, we hold our tongues. We do not talk about the matter except to praise the valour of our troops for a day or two. When the news of your grand achievement at New Orleans arrived, it was at once asserted that WE had *gained a great victory*. Details were even published. At the end of a fortnight, out slipped the account of the *defeat* in the middle of a Gazette, stuffed up with advertisements and promotions. We could not accuse the government of not publishing it; but, in fact, the mass of the people never either saw it or heard of it; and, to this hour, there is not a man in the village in which I am now writing who does not believe that we gave you a *hearty beating* at New Orleans.[7]

In the same Open Letter, Cobbett made plain to the

---

[6] *Political Register* 28, 8 July 1815.
[7] *Ibid.*

Americans his own views on Napoleon, praising him for those acts which consolidated the benefits bestowed on the common people in the early days of the Republic by the redistribution of land, the expulsion of nobles and priests, and a Constitution guaranteeing equality of all before the law, but also holding him up as an example of one who eventually betrayed the French people by succumbing to the temptations of power: having himself crowned Emperor, creating hereditary titles, and, most heinous of all, allying himself to the European aristocracy by marrying the daughter of the Emperor of Austria and then installing their infant son as King of Rome.

> After all his glorious deeds; after all his famous battles; after all his wise acts of legislation; all his magnanimous proceedings; all that he had done in the cause of mankind: after all this, how painful it is to see him vainly hankering after the preserving of a *crown* to his family! and, which adds to the mortification, to a son which he had by the daughter of a *king*; and of an *Austrian* too. It is melancholy to think of. If it had been the son of some tradesman's daughter! To risk the freedom and happiness of these people for the sake of a grandson of a king is horrible to think of.[8]

Sentiments echoed by the poet Shelley in his poem *Feelings of a Republican on the Fall of Bonaparte.*

> I hated thee, fallen tyrant.
> ..... Thou, mightst have built thy throne
> Where it had stood even now: thou didst prefer
> A frail and bloody pomp which Time has swept
> In fragments towards Oblivion.

And yet Cobbett was not without all hope. He said of Napoleon: "He formed a code of wise and just laws. Much of what he did will now be undone; but it will be impossible

---

[8] *Political Register* 28, 8 July 1815.

for all the kings and priests in the world to make men as ignorant and submissive as they were before he marched over the Alps", and he pointed out that the restoration of Louis XVIII to the throne did not mean that France would for ever remain a monarchy. "No, no, Louis", he wrote, "you are restored as you were before, by foreign bayonets; and the question is yet to be decided whether the bayonets will be able to keep you on the throne. The battle between light and liberty on one side, and darkness and despotism on the other; that battle, which began in 1789, is still going on.".[9]

As guardian, Cobbett warned the Americans of the animosity their very existence aroused among the powers of Europe. In an Open Letter to the People of the United States of America, Cobbett told them that some English newspapers were loudly calling for the execution of Napoleon and the punishment of all those who supported him when he returned to France from Elba. These writers, he warned, were men of great weight in the world, and they hated America because she exhibited the "great example of order, tranquillity, prosperity unparalleled under a government of such mildness and cheapness".[10] These were the men who had cheered the Convention at Hartford, hoping that it would result in the overthrow of the American government and the impeachment of Madison. Their rage and disappointment at its dissolution after the battle of New Orleans was expressed by their now saying that all Americans, regardless of party, show "a mischievous example of Democratic Rebellion". They accused the United States of wishing to renew the war with England when they heard of Bonaparte's return to France. The *Morning Post* declared: "No sooner do they learn that

---

[9] *Ibid.*
[10] *Political Register* 28, 19 August 1815.

Bonaparte has landed on the coast of France than they, his trans-Atlantic subjects, also assume the tri-coloured cockade and hoist the tri-coloured flag".

> I repeat that these men (without success I hope) will use all the means in their power to rekindle the flames of war with America. It is the duty of every man to endeavour to defeat this horrible purpose.[11]

And some months later in another letter to *Niles Register*, Cobbett wrote, "I hope you will not forget to build ships and cast cannons; for I am well convinced, that to build ships and cast cannons are the best, if not the only, security you can have for lasting peace. Therefore, again I say, build ships and cast cannons".[12]

As guardian, Cobbett also took pains to discredit the Federalist faction addressing two Open Letters to "Mr Strong, the Governor of Massachusetts", the first of which began:

> It was you, it appears, who called the government of Great Britain "the bulwark of Religion and Liberty", and assigned this as a reason against resisting by force of arms the impressment from on board of American ships on the high seas.[13]

And yet, Cobbett asked him, what had Great Britain done to defend religion and liberty. Had she not made war against France which had established liberty of conscience and freedom of worship? Had she not restored the Pope and allowed Protestants in Spain and Italy to be persecuted after Napoleon was defeated in 1814? Yet when Napoleon returned to France in 1815 to re-establish liberty, one of the Massachusetts Federalists, Mr Lemuel Shaw exclaimed

---

[11] *Ibid.*
[12] *Political Register* 30, 20 January 1816.
[13] *Political Register* 29, 25 November 1815.

"God speed the cause of the Allies, of justice, of liberty and peace".

> Vile hypocrisy! Base party spirit! Has the success produced liberty? If this be the stuff that your Federal faction is composed of, it must be the wish of every friend of justice and freedom to see that faction destroyed root and branch.[14]

As propagandist, Cobbett endeavoured to give his readers a true picture of life in the United States. His support of America during the thirty months of war with Britain had led to his acquiring a wide following in America where many of his articles in the *Political Register* were reprinted. He proudly told his readers that the city of Albany, the capital of New York State, had presented him with a suit of clothes manufactured from wool grown in the State as "a tribute for the able, independent, and masterly manner in which you have edited your Register".[15] Profiting from this goodwill, Cobbett established a network of correspondents in America and arranged for a regular supply of newspapers and journals to be sent to him in England.

In 1816 he began a series of letters in his *Political Register* entitled "The American Packet" in which he used the reports he was receiving from the United States to counteract the wrong impression of the state of the republic being given in the English newspapers, whose reports were culled almost exclusively from anti-government Federal journals and speeches.

> It is John Bull's happy turn of mind, always when he is embarrassed, to look about the world to see if there be no other nation in a state of embarrassment; and if

---

[14] *Political Register* 29, 25 November 1815.
[15] *Political Register* 28, 22 July 1815.

he find any in that state, to chuckle and hug himself in the thought that he is not suffering alone.[16]

Beginning each letter in this "American Packet" series "Dear John Bull", Cobbett maintained that the real state of affairs across the Atlantic was very different from that reported in the English press.

> Therefore, John, this is the season to call on you to reflect, and to endeavour to turn your eyes towards a country inhabited by men who are really free, who proceed, generally speaking, from the same stock as yourself, who speak the same language, who have the same common law, who talk like you, write like you, and fight like you. Come with me, John, and take a look at America."[17]

The "American Packet" letters explained the workings of democracy in the United States; why the Americans declared war on Britain in 1812; and how the country was now united and prosperous. Much of the material in this series of letters he had expounded in previous years, but the ephemeral nature of journalism and the expanding readership of his paper made it necessary for him often to repeat what he had said before. Cobbett praised the lack of a standing army, the toleration of all forms of religion, the high standard of literacy throughout the country, the comparatively small amount of crime, and above all the fact that this republican government granted no hereditary titles, no sinecures or pensions, and no gross rewards to men who held high offices in the state. Referring to the two past Presidents, now retired from office, he wrote:

> What a fine thing it is to see two men, Mr Adams and Mr Jefferson, now, living in common life, after having been Chief Magistrates of a country which has a population

---

[16] *Political Register* 30, 6 January 1816.
[17] *Political Register* 30, 27 April 1816.

and a trade nearly equal to that of England! They have gone back to their unaugmented estates. Was there ever any thing so honourable to the human mind as this sight? How it relieves one to turn one's eyes towards this scene, after having had them, for a while, fixed on those scenes of human degradation which surround us in Europe! And how anxious ought we to be that America may go on under such a government to grow in prosperity and power![18]

Alongside these "American Packet" letters addressed to John Bull, Cobbett wrote a second series addressed to "The People of the United States of America". These showed the reverse picture: the intolerable burden of taxation, the alarming numbers of bankruptcies; the appalling distress which was giving rise to outbreaks of rioting, and the draconian measures taken to suppress them, contrasting these scenes in Britain with those he had painted of life in America. Some indication was given in earlier chapters of the state of distress among the labouring classes in Britain during the war. Far from easing the situation, peace saw both increasing distress and a hardening of the government's attitude to discontent. The transition from a war-time to a peace-time economy threw thousands out of work and their numbers were swelled by discharged soldiers. When the inflated war-time prices came to an end with the opening of markets in Europe and the New World, there followed a period of acute depression. Less money caused less demand, farmers were unable to pay a living wage, manufacturers unable to keep workers in employment, and the increasing use of machinery threw even greater numbers of small-scale domestic workers out of work. The rick-burning and destruction of machinery which had broken out in 1811 and 1812 were now

---

[18] *Political Register* 30, 25 May 1816.

extensively renewed and mass meetings were held calling for redress. Whereas before 1815 the miseries could be attributed to the war, after 1815 the cruel disappointment of finding that conditions were worsening after the long and costly struggle, brought determination on the part of the people not seen before. The earlier agitations had mostly been centred around specific grievances — the high price of bread, the Orders in Council, the introduction of machinery. Now no longer able to blame the French or the Americans or the wars, men's eyes began to turn towards the system of government itself.

Cobbett, of course, had been calling for radical reform ever since the beginning of the century. His prognosis uttered over the years that the end of the war would bring no relief so long as the present system of government was retained was proving only too true. Government extravagance continued unabated in the very worst years of distress. In 1816 the government voted £60,000 for a trousseau for the Regent's daughter, the Princess Charlotte, on her marriage, and an extra £60,000 a year for life thereafter. The Duke of Wellington, already among the richest of the peers, was given a magnificent estate in the country, Stratfield Speye, as a reward for his services to the country, and these were only the grossest examples of the proliferation of gifts and pensions which continued to be given to government favourites out of taxes on the people. At the end of the war, the *Courier*, a government newspaper, had declared, "The play is over, we may now go to supper". "No", Cobbett replied, "you cannot yet go to supper. You have not yet paid for the play. And before you have paid for the play, you will find that there is no money left for the supper".[19]

---

[19] *Political Register* 31, 26 October 1816.

In issue after issue of the *Political Register* Cobbett reiterated his arguments for reform, often using his "American Packet" series of letters to John Bull to show, that there was an answer to the problems staring him in the face across the Atlantic, and using the other series of letters to the "People of the United States" as one of the vehicles to expose the true state of post-war England. "You must wish to know", he wrote in the first letter of the series, "how she is, as a nation, at the end of twenty-two years of war, and under a Debt of about a thousand million sterling".[20] It was not only the labouring classes who were now in distress — the whole country was suffering. The government's attempt to stem the growth of paper money, after its profligate spending during the war, had resulted in such a dramatic fall in prices, that those who had borrowed during the war now found themselves with insufficient income to pay even the interest on the debts they had incurred and were facing ruin. The farmer who, a few years ago, had

> a fox-hunting horse, polished boots, a spanking trot to market; wine at his dinner, a carpet on the floor, a bell in his parlour, a painted lady for a wife, novel-reading daughters, sons aping the squires and lords, a house crammed up with sofa's, piano's and all sorts of fooleries

was now sunk almost to the position of his labourers; while "Squire Crackhouse, the Army Tailor, Squire Turpentine, the spirit contractor, Squire Garbage, the meat contractor, Squire Beanmeal, the biscuit and bread contractor", were all "sallying out around him with gay equipages or numerous troops of hunters and followers".[21]

Far worse, of course, was the position of the labourers.

---

[20] *Political Register* 29, 16 December 1816.
[21] *Ibid.*

About two million were dependent on the poor-rates, and Cobbett quoted in his "Letters to the People of the United States", speeches in Parliament describing the state of the nation. "Americans, read, pause here for a minute. Look at this picture and remember it is not a Jacobin speaking, but an English County Member of Parliament".[22]

Trenchant as these criticisms were, even they, in Cobbett's opinion, did not go to the heart of the matter. Though he was confident that many of his articles would be reprinted in American journals and newspapers, he wanted the freedom to expose the British system even more clearly to the American people than the laws allowed him to do in England. Ever since his incarceration in Newgate, Cobbett had been circumspect in couching his criticisms in terms that just prevented him from opening himself to the charge of libel or sedition. Early in 1816, he arranged for an American edition of the *Political Register* to be printed and published in New York. Because the American issues of his paper bore the same format and the same number as the English ones, beginning with Volume 30, Number 1, of January 6th 1816, and ending with Volume 30, Number 26, of June 29th 1816, it has been widely assumed that they were replicas of the English issues. In fact, although every issue carried all the major articles of its English counterpart, including the series of "Letters to the People of the United States" and the "American Packet" series addressed to John Bull, they also contained articles written specially for his America readers. G D H Cole, alone among Cobbett's biographers, refers to them specifically, but apart from listing their titles, he gives no indication of the startling tenor of their contents. Because they have been so neglected, they will be quoted from at some length.

---

[22] *Political Register* 30, 16 March 1816.

The first edition of the *American Political Register*, bearing under the masthead "written in England, January 6, published in New York, May 21", began with an Introductory Address entitled "To the People of the United States in General, and to my old English Friends in that country in Particular". It opened in these words.

> Gratified, as I naturally must be, at perceiving, that what I have dared to publish here, appears to have assisted in causing many amongst you to see the character, conduct and views of our government in their true light, I am by no means content with efforts confined within the limits of a press, whence to publish, even in the most moderate language, truths disagreeable to men in power, exposes the publisher to punishment little short of death: and I am the less disposed to submit to this mental bondage, to this mere sighing under the terrors of the lash, when I see that there are many, even amongst you, who still have a hankering likeness to this government, and some who have the folly (to call it nothing worse) to hold it up as the "Bulwark of Religion and Liberty".
>
> By the *Government* I mean the whole mass of authority and power, Executive, Legislative, Ministerial, Judicial, Hierarchal, Naval and Military; and of all the deceivers of mankind, this government I regard as the greatest. Amidst the commission of innumerable acts of tyranny and cruelty, abroad and at home; in the almost constant practice of meanness and baseness, resorting to the foulest corruption and most vile hypocrisy; it has been able to make a great part of the world believe that it is the most free, most humane, most generous, most magnanimous, most pure and most frank government upon the face of the earth.[23]

Aware that such a tremendous indictment of his own

---

[23] American edition of *Political Register* 30 of 6 Jan 1816, published in New York 21 May 1816.

government might be attributed to his harbouring spite and resentment for the huge fine and two year prison sentence imposed on him so recently, Cobbett countered this objection by saying that "a fact is not less a fact, an argument is not less conclusive, because the statement of the one, or the urging of the other, has been occasioned by feelings of resentment". He promised his readers that in further issues he would justify his indictment by placing the character and conduct of "this terrible mass of power" in its true light. But before laying bare to the Americans the enormities of the British system, he needed first to counter two other objections which might cause his transatlantic readers to dismiss the expositions to come.

The first was that some of them might well remember his earlier writings as Peter Porcupine when he had been so fierce a critic of the republican system of government in America.

> Upon this occasion, bare justice to myself demands that I should hastily trace from its sources that hostility which I contracted against your political institutions, and that virulence with which that hostility was prosecuted.[24]

Later in life Cobbett was to refer in passing to his writings as Peter Porcupine as to a time when he was "a mere prater of politics", but only in this article does he set out so clearly and at such length the reasons which led him to conceive such a deep hatred of the Democratic party. In the preceding chapters some indications were given of the reasons why he so radically revised his opinions of the French Revolution and the Democrats who supported it, which was the prime cause of his hostility, and of the nature of the British system of government which as Peter Porcupine he had extolled. Cobbett had been

---

[24] *Ibid.*

attacked in England for his inconsistencies, particularly for his complete change of attitude with regard to Pitt and to the war with France, but in many ways his change of attitude with regard to American politics was even more dramatic. As Peter Porcupine, Cobbett had condemned the Jeffersonian Democratic Party with every species of invective known to him, yet here he was, in 1816, less than twenty years later, not just defending it, but holding it up as the one great hope for mankind throughout the world. His explanation needs to be told in his own words.

> When the war of 1793 broke out between England and France, I was living at Wilmington in the state of Delaware, next door to a Mr COMMONS, a carpenter, and upon a rising ground commanding a view of the Delaware. A French frigate, which had brought out the new ambassador from the republic, appeared in that river with the tri-coloured flag at her masthead. Mr Commons pointed to it, telling me, that that flag would soon drive the flag of England from the ocean. *England* was the object of attack, and I was an *Englishman*. From that time my neighbour and I became what are called *"natural enemies"*. Hence, by degrees, I imbibed the strongest desire to see England triumph in the quarrel, without knowing, and without caring, any thing about its grounds. It is probable that I never should have written for the press a single line in my life, had it not been for the discussions with my neighbour the carpenter. This set me to reading what people call politics, and reading led me to Philadelphia.
>
> (When I went to reside in Philadelphia) nothing was heard in the streets, but praises of the French and abuse of the English. Never very patient, or given to yield to a torrent, I soon became a pretty busy partizan, and sought occasions to engage in disputes. Thus become an author, I soon became known to the public, and then, I call to witness all those who lived in Philadelphia at that

time, what torrents of abuse were poured forth upon me. All manner of falsehoods were published respecting me, every sort of crime was falsely laid to my charge; and, what I believe, was never done in any other case, the foulest assertions were made respecting even my wife. Young, strong, with good health, always buoyant spirits, careless of consequences, I was a match for all my antagonists. I have laughed a thousand times, and I laugh at this moment, at the recollection of the wars that we used to carry on. My opponents contended that *nothing* was good that belonged to England. I contended that nothing was good that *did not* belong to her. I was quite sincere; and I solemnly declare that I believed that even the poultry and the apples were not half so good as those in England.

You may call this folly, enthusiasm, fanaticism; but you cannot call it baseness. The principle by which I was actuated was good. It was love for my country, which, *prima facia*, is always virtuous; and if I had had the capacity, I was in too high a state of irritation to enter into a fair discussion of the merits of her cause. Besides my antagonists were equally violent, and had, in most cases, been the aggressors. Violence begets violence, or produces submission, and the latter, with me, was wholly out of the question.[25]

The second charge that Cobbett feared could be levelled against him was that by denigrating his own country he was acting as a traitor to it. He robustly countered this charge in the following passage. (The reference to "the family of Guelph" is to the Royal Family of England, directly descended through George I from the old German family of Guelph.)

> If there be any one who is disposed to call this writing *against my country*, let me ask him, whether he looks

---

[25] American edition of *Political Register* 30 of 6 Jan, 1816, published in New York 21 May 1816.

upon the Dey and Divan of Algiers as being the country? Why then am I to look upon the family of Guelph, a band of boroughmongers, a half Hanoverian army, and a navy which impressed your seamen; why, I ask, am I to look upon these as constituting England? If, then, I show that the present government has violated all the fundamental laws of the land; that it his reduced us to the most abject slavery, insulting us all the while with the mockery of freedom: if I make these assertions out, if I establish their truth, am I, in exposing this government, to be charged with attacking *my country*? If so, Nero was Rome, Louis XVIII is France, Queen Mary was England, Ferdinand is Spain, Pizarro was Mexico, and George the Third was the United States.[26]

In this first article for his American readers, it will be remembered that Cobbett was addressing particularly those of English origins. In the second he addressed the Frenchmen in America. This time he tried to dispel the suspicions that might arise among them against any writings that came from the pen of an Englishman. "Though the treatment", he began, "which your country and your countrymen have received at the hands of this government is well calculated to make you hold in abhorrence the very names of England and Englishmen, yet, there are some of us who have not approved of them; and at any rate I am resolved to clear myself of the foul imputation."[27] This opening, directed to show that Cobbett, as indeed was true, had condemned in many numbers of his *Political Register* the actions of the British government in its relations with France, opened the way for him to go much farther. He used the article to expose the full extent of the British government's hypocrisy,

---

[26] American edition of *Political Register* 30 of 6 Jan 1816, published in New York 21 May 1816.
[27] American edition of *Political Register* 30 of 20 Jan 1816, published in New York 28 May 1816.

perfidy and double-dealing throughout the whole course of the Franco-British war and its aftermath. Until the outbreak of the French Revolution, he explained, the British government and press had represented the French system of government — the monarchy, the nobles and the Church — as a despotism ruling over "the most wretched, degraded, persecuted people". Yet when these wretched people rose up against their despots, that same British government had sheltered the very nobles and priests it had formerly condemned, subsidised and abetted the Royalists in their attempts to restore the monarchy, and when the revolution was stabilised under Napoleon, had openly supported an attempt to assassinate him, had maltreated French prisoners-of-war, contrived Napoleon's escape from Elba in order to impose harsher terms on France after his second defeat, and finally restored the Bourbons and re-established the Church which, before the Revolution, had been the objects of its bitterest hatred and scorn. It then imposed a large army of occupation on France to prop up the unpopular regime it had forced on the conquered people. Cobbett maintained throughout this article that the object of the British government had been the ruin of France. It saw from the start of the Revolution that if the French people succeeded in forming a free government on the lines of that of America, its example would be a permanent threat to the preservation of their own corrupt and oppressive system.

> They feared, too, and not without good reason, that if the people of England should see France happy and flourishing without an hereditary nobility, without tithes, and without borough elections, these things could not long last in England. They saw, in fact, that the Bourbons must be forced back upon the French, and that France must become re-enslaved, or that England must become free, and that this latter event would, and

must, be accelerated by the communications between the two nations, to which peace would inevitably give rise.[28]

Having thus prepared the ground, Cobbett's real task was yet to come. For how could such a government continue to retain its image as a Bulwark of Liberty even amongst a substantial number of Americans if what he had said so far was true? One answer lay in the Press and this was the subject of his next special article for the American edition of his Register.

Under the title "The English Press: The Corruption of it by the Government", Cobbett set out to show that it would have been impossible for the British government to have done what it had done unless it had been able to disguise the truth by the twin means of Corruption and Persecution. "The first has been the shield, the other the sword; and thus, at once covered and armed, has this government carried out a war against Truth, such as, I am fully convinced, the world has never before witnessed".[29] Noting that a number of American journals devoted much space to the reprinting of articles from English reviews, Cobbett proceeded to list the major publications from which they were taken and to expose the extent to which they were under the thumb of the government. One thing, he pointed out, that was common to most of these reviews, was the use of the word 'we', giving the impression that the gentlemen who wrote were giving utterance to their own views. But, he went on, "if the public could see them as they really are, a set of mean-spirited, dependent creatures, eating their daily bread out of the hands of a clerk of the

---

[28] American edition of *Political Register* 30 of 20 Jan 1816, published in New York 28 May 1816.
[29] American edition of *Political Register* 30 of 27 Jan 1816, published in New York 1 June 1816.

Treasury almost as completely, and with a vast deal more servility, than a spaniel eats the bits out of the hand of his master; a nest of needy men, writing for *so much a page*, and sometimes paid in advance by the editor, who acts under the Treasury, their pompous WE would not stand them in much stead."[30] Hiding under this WE, Cobbett informed his readers, was the editor of the pro-government paper the *Quarterly Review*, a William Gifford. From humble beginnings, he was educated by a clergyman, became a tutor to a nobleman's son, and through him was given a sinecure appointment of £300 a year and appointed editor of the *Quarterly Review*.

> Thus was he enlisted a literary *hack* for life; and, having been called upon to edit, or overlook the workmen of the Quarterly Review, any article that should be found to contain one single sentence favourable to political, civil or religious liberty, or any appearance of a want of zeal in the cause of this government, would in one month take from him his 300 pounds a year, and drive him from the first floor, where he now lives, to the shabby second floor which he formerly inhabited. Now must it not be mortifying to the last degree to see the American Reviews and Magazines conveying to the people of that country the contents of a work thus established and sustained, as if they proceeded from the pens of independent and honourable men, actuated by a love of truth.[31]

In similar vein Cobbett exposed the motives which lay behind the writers for many other of the journals and magazines of the day.

> So much for the corruption of Reviewers. And will any man, with pretensions to common sense, profess

---

[30] *Ibid.*
[31] *Ibid.*

to believe that a press thus sustained, thus influenced, thus rewarded, is not one of the greatest scourges that ever was inflicted on a nation? If our press were free; if any man dared to state the truths that I have here stated, these outrageous acts of oppression and insult would never be endured. There is yet enough spirit left in the people to protest against such things, if they could be duly informed of them; if they could be placed clearly before their eyes. But to do this no one dares. Though I have here put upon paper not a single fact, which is not true to the very letter, the publishing of these facts would cause me to end my days, in all probability, in a prison.[32]

From the Press, Cobbett turned his searchlight on to Parliament and the Parliamentary system in an article entitled "English Parliament: The mockery of its pretended elections. Its sham debates and divisions." The corruption in the electoral system of Britain at this time — its pocket boroughs and its rotten boroughs, the open buying and selling of seats, the bribery and intimidation during elections — that whole system which Cobbett lumped together under the name of Boroughmongering, is too well known for it to be repeated here. The interest of this article lies in the manner in which Cobbett tried to dispel the misconceptions of the many "good and able men in America" who regarded the English Parliament as being in some degree "a protection to the rights of the people". Although it had never been representative in that it had always been elected under a very restricted franchise, Cobbett was at pains to point out that its whole character had altered out of recognition during the last thirty or forty years. Up to then, Cobbett maintained that the House of Commons consisted for the most part of

---

[32] American edition of *Political Register* 30 of 27 Jan 1816, published in New York, 1 June 1816.

country gentlemen who resided on their estates and were in close touch with those of the people at large. "In this sort of natural magistracy of the country, the people had, in spite of the partial distribution of the elective rights, a tolerable security for their liberties and properties."

> But when Bute, and North, and Pitt, and George the Third, with their tools, the Jenkinsons, and Percevals and Addingtons, had, by their loads of taxes, swept all this race of gentry away as completely as a hurricane sweeps away the sugar canes in Jamaica, and had, by their contracts and commissions, and loans and grants, and bribes, created a new and grasping race of moneyed men and officers and lawyers to supply their place, the character of the Members became wholly changed; and the parliament, having no longer any common interest with the people, became, as we have seen, a mere set of scramblers for pelf and power, falling, each party in turn, upon the devoted people, as warring dens of wolves from the Pyrenees fall alternately upon the bleating flocks in the valleys below. [33]

After giving many examples of the machinations employed in buying and selling seats in Parliament, the hypocrisy displayed in debates and the treatment meted out to any who dared to expose its notorious and flagrant abuses, Cobbett appealed to those Americans who still defended the English system to think again.

> Such, Americans, is the situation of that "land of your forefathers" the government of which some good and weak men amongst you still hold up as worthy of your imitation, or, at least, of your respect. Let me ask the Quakers of Pennsylvania, amongst whom I have spent so many happy days, the recollection of whose virtuous lives is so pleasant to me, and whose kindness

---

[33] American edition of *Political Register* 30 of 3 Feb 1816, published in New York, 4 June 1816.

and hospitality are so deeply engraven on my heart; let me ask *them* whether they approve of the corruption, the bribery, the fraud, the cruelty, that I have described? And whether they do not think, that all these ought to be held up as a warning to mankind?[34]

In describing the English Parliamentary system to his American readers, Cobbett was largely repeating, though in less cautious terms, what he had been telling his English readers since the early 1800s. The next article "The Royal Family of England" is different, for here one can feel that Cobbett has at last found the freedom and the opportunity to put in print whet he had been burning to say for years. With obviously intense enjoyment, he launches into the subject and describes the nature of the monarchy.

> We usually call this branch of authority the *Crown* or the *Throne*, and with great propriety, for the poor creature who wears the one and sits on the other, is neither more nor less than a passive tool in the hands of those who own the Seats in Parliament and who, in fact, appoint all the Ministers, Ambassadors, Judges and Commanders, and who, if they were to meet with a refractory king, or one who, from excessive folly, was troublesome to them, would very soon dispose of him by shutting him up for life, or by some other contrivance so as never to be pestered by him again.
>
> Of all the objects which the Boroughmongers would most dread, next after free elections, would certainly be a king of sound understanding, good talents, aptness for business, and really desirous to promote the honour and happiness of the country. And, it must be confessed, that in this view of the matter, they could hardly have been more fortunate than they are in the Guelphs, not one of whom, since their being pitched upon to fill the throne of England, has ever discovered symptoms of a

---

[34] *Ibid.*

mind much more than sufficient to qualify the possessor for the post of exciseman.[35]

It was, Cobbett went on to say, not without significance that the Royal Family had, after the death of Queen Anne without issue, been selected from the German family of Guelph. The Boroughmongers were well aware of the fact that the English had an almost rooted contempt for foreigners, and by keeping the throne in foreign hands and seeing to it that the monarchs always selected foreigners for their wives (so that ever since the accession of George I the Royal Family had not had "a single drop of English blood in their veins"), they kept the Crown distant from the people. The notion that the Royal Family had an influence on public affairs, assiduously put about by the government, was, Cobbett considered, "one of the numerous cheats that have been practised upon the world." How deep was the contempt in which they were really held by all sections of the public, Cobbett described in the following passage.

> The language that is made use of in conversation, with regard to this family, would astonish any stranger. All sorts of names, expressions of contempt, are constantly used by all ranks of people towards them.
>
> The "d——d Germans", they are called in a lump by the common people; and when the nobility and gentry reject vulgar epithets and terms, it is only to choose others more severe. This abuse is made use of by all parties; by all men in, as well as out of, office. When the war was declared against France, at the rupture of the peace of Amiens, the princes went to the House of Lords to support the address to the Throne. The Duke of Clarence (the Prince Regent's brother later to become William IV) made a speech on this occasion and I was standing with a crowd of others below the Bar (as it is

---

[35] American edition of *Political Register* 30 of 10 Feb 1816, published in New York, 8 June 1816.

called) at the time. The House, which was exceedingly full, were very merry at his expense; and two Peers, who sat close to the bar at the side of the House on which I stood, indulged themselves in this sort: "What a Jackass!" said one: "What a great fool!" said the other: "did you ever hear such a beast?" And, towards the close of the speech, the Royal Duke having declared that he spoke the sentiments *of his whole family*, a third Peer exclaimed: "*his* family! who the d——l cares about his family!" All this was said loud enough for twenty or thirty persons to hear, who stood or sat nearest to them. Other Peers were smothering a laugh; some affected to be blowing their noses; and the Lord Chancellor, ELDON, sat and looked at the Duke with one of those smiles which contain the double expression of pity and contempt. To be sure the speech was a foolish rant; but, if it came from a Duke of Newcastle or an Earl of Lonsdale, or any other great Boroughmonger, it would have been listened to with the greatest attention and apparent respect.[36]

That the King himself was merely the tool of his ministers, Cobbett illustrated by an account of how Bishops, allegedly appointed by the monarch as Head of the Church, are in reality appointed by the Boroughmongers, combining his criticisms of the monarchy with a devastating attack on the Established Church.

> When a Bishop dies, another must be put in his place. The Bishop is elected by the Dean and Prebends of the Cathedral Church of the Diocese. The king, who is called the *head* of the Church, sends these gentleman, who are called the Dean and Chapter, a conge d'élire, or a leave to elect; but he sends them, at the same time, the *name of the man* whom, and whom only, they are to elect. With this name in their possession, away they go into the Cathedral, chant psalms and anthems, and

---

[36] *Ibid.*

then in a set form of words *invoke the Holy Ghost to assist them in their choice*. After these invocations, they, by a series of good luck wholly without a parallel, always find that the dictates of the Holy Ghost agree with the *recommendation* of the king. But even this shockingly impious farce loses part of its qualities, unless we bear in mind, that it is not the *king*, but some Boroughmonger, in virtue of some bargain for votes, who has really nominated the Bishop, and that the King, the Minister, the Dean and Chapter, and the Holy Ghost proceeding, all neither more nor less than so many tools in the hands of the said Boroughmonger. Good and pious people wondered amazingly that the Holy Ghost, or even the king should have pitched upon the present gentleman to fill the Archbishop's Chair of Canterbury; but these good and pious Church people did not know that the Duke of Rutland had, as he still has, seven or eight votes of his own in the two Houses, besides perhaps twenty more that he could, upon a hard pinch, make shift to borrow.

It is interesting to note that Cobbett's attitude to the Royal Family, in contrast to his attitude to the government, is one of contemptuous pity, and he even defends the poor mad King's wife and daughters from some of the calumnies directed against them. Referring in this article to the "dirty stories about the Queen and her Daughters" which the public greedily devour, he wrote that he himself had never heard of anything even bordering on the nature of proof for these calumnies. He pitied, too, the "Royal Dukes", the sons of George III, who endeavoured to gain some popularity by patronising various charitable societies. "Their names are in all the great subscription Lists; and they make speeches on many of these occasions, and always give away some of their money. All this only exposes them to ridicule". Cobbett was referring here, of course, to their known extravagant styles of living, and to the fact that nearly all the sons of George III kept mistresses.

Free at last from the restrictions imposed on the press in England, and from the need so to couch his opinions as not to shock and alienate his increasingly wide following at home in his battle for Reform, Cobbett ended this article by expressing his real feelings about that "mass of authority and power" which made up the government of Britain.

> What name to give such a government it is difficult to say. It is like nothing that ever was heard of before. It is neither a monarchy, an aristocracy, nor a democracy; it is a band of great nobles who, by sham elections, and by means of all sorts of bribery and corruption, have obtained an absolute sway in the country, having under them, for the purposes of show and of execution, a thing they call a *king*, sharp and unprincipled fellows whom they call *Ministers*, a mummery which they call a *Church*, experienced and well-tried and steel-hearted men whom they call *Judges*, a company of false money-makers whom they call a *Bank*, numerous bands of brave and needy persons whom they call *soldiers and sailors*, and a talking, corrupt and impudent set, whom they call a *House of Commons*. Such is the government of England; such is the thing, which has been able to bribe one half of Europe to oppress the other half; such is the famous "Bulwark of religion and social order" which is now about, as will be soon seen, to surround itself with a permanent standing army of at least, a hundred thousand men, and very wisely, for without such an army, the Bulwark would not exist a month.[37]
>
> WILLIAM COBBETT

---

[37] *Ibid.*

9

Exile on Long Island

Had Cobbett included in his English edition of the *Political Register* the articles he wrote for his American edition, he would undoubtedly have been prosecuted for seditious writing. But although much of the English press was, as he maintained, subsidised by the government, the laws of England still allowed freedom of speech within certain limits, and Cobbett knew well just how far he could go in his English publications without falling foul of the law. In June 1816 he heard that copies of the American edition of his paper were being sent back to England to Lord Castlereagh, the Foreign Secretary, and, realising that if he were ever to overstep the mark in England and find himself subject to prosecution, his American articles could be used as supplementary evidence against him, he ceased publication of his American edition and directed all his energies to uniting the English people in a mass movement for the complete overthrow of the whole network of institutions represented by the present system of government — activities which, in less than a year, were to lead him to seek asylum in the United States.

He became at this time increasingly alarmed at the spread of rioting throughout the kingdom, fearing that it could only lead to a closing of ranks among the ruling classes, further repressive measures, and a weakening of the case for reform. Already his writings were being read among the labouring classes, but the price of the *Political Register* with its stamp duties necessarily limited its circulation.

In November 1816 he decided to issue parallel with the Register, a single sheet containing only the 'leading' article without the advertisements and the news, despatches and reports contained in the weekly paper, and so not subject to tax. This cheap Register he sold at 2d a copy and the circulation rose astonishingly, some forty-four thousand copies being sold of each issue. In the first broadsheet Cobbett wrote his famous *Address to the Journeymen and Labourers*, reminding the working people that it was *they* who produced the wealth of the nation, *their* labour which made the nation abound in resources, and it was to *them* that the country looked to secure its safety.

> With this correct idea of your own worth, with what indignation must you hear yourselves called the Populace, the Rabble, the Mob, the Swinish Multitude; and with what greater indignation, if possible, must you hear the projects of those cool and cruel and insolent men, who, now that you have been, without any fault of your own, brought into a state of misery, propose to narrow the limits of parish relief, to prevent you marrying in the days of your youth, or to thrust you out to seek your bread in foreign lands, never more to behold your parents or friends?
>
> The remedy is what we have now to look to, and that remedy consists wholly and solely of a reform of the Common's, or People's, House of Parliament. We must have that *first*, or we shall have nothing good.[1]

Already by this time, the government feared revolution. Spies were sent about the country to infiltrate and pinpoint seed-beds of possible revolutionary activities, and troops were quartered in industrial centres to quell rioting. A Magistrate in Manchester wrote to the Home Secretary, Lord Sidmouth:

---

[1] *Political Register* 31, 3 November 1816.

> I am very sorry to inform your Lordship that from all I can learn Messrs Drummond, Bagueley, Ogden and Knight, have been most active for several months past in disseminating among the lower orders at meetings convened for the purpose in the different lesser towns in the neighbourhood, the most poisonous and alarming sentiments with respect to the government of the country. They are certainly much bolder grown than they were last year, and if they can avail themselves of the present temper of the working people to throw this populous district into disorder, and I might, I think, truly add rebellion, they will certainly attempt it.[2]

Of all the seditious propaganda being distributed at the time, Cobbett's, with its vast circulation, was considered to be among the most dangerous; but try as it might, the government found that no case against him could be brought to prosecution. He was, in fact, appealing to the people to desist from unlawful activities and to turn their attention to constitutional measures — an appeal even more threatening to the existing government than the actual disturbances. A government cannot prosecute a man for advocating an end to rioting, or for setting out side by side the differences between the amount of taxes imposed on the people by a republican government and a monarchical one, or for publishing the salary of the President of the United States and comparing it with that granted to the Royal Family of Great Britain; or even for reprinting the Declaration of Independence which, in spite of its seditious doctrines, was a public document widely distributed at the time. But a government faced with alarming disturbances of the public peace, can pass laws to curb such disturbances. A Report from a Secret Committee set up to enquire into the disturbed state of the country,

---

[2] Christopher Hampton, ed, *A Radical Reader* pp 417-8, Penguin Books 1984.

wrote of "the existence of widespread conspiracies" to "infect the minds of all classes of the community with a spirit of discontent and disaffection, of insubordination, and contempt of all law, religion and morality", which aimed at "a total overthrow of all existing establishments and a division of the landed, and extinction of the funded, property of the country". In March 1817, acting on this Report, a series of Acts were passed restricting public meetings, placing all public meeting-halls, reading rooms, etc. under the supervision of magistrates, and suspending the Habeas Corpus Act, giving the authorities the power to imprison "agitators" without trial.

Cobbett saw these laws as passed expressly for silencing him. Because the government could find nothing in his writings which they could prosecute with success,

> Therefore, the Power of Imprisonment Bill was passed! a law to enable some of *themselves* to shut me up in prison *at their pleasure*; to keep me in a dungeon as long as they pleased; and this too without even telling me what I was accused of; and all this they did, as expressly stated by Sidmouth, because I had committed no offence against the laws; because the law-officers could find nothing to prosecute in my publications.[3]

There can be little question that had Cobbett continued writing after the suspension of the Habeas Corpus Act he would have been imprisoned, and this time without any opportunity to continue his publications. He was offered a substantial bribe for his future silence (Cobbett said the sum was ten thousand pounds), but instead of accepting it he quietly slipped out of the country with his two eldest sons and took ship for America.

Cobbett has been criticised both by some of his

---

[3] *Political Register* 53, 1 Jan 1825.

contemporary reformers and by later writers for deserting his country at a time of acute distress. Such criticisms arise from a misunderstanding of his nature: his was not the stuff that martyrs are made of. From his earliest writings condemning the atrocities committed during the Years of Terror in France, he saw his mission as one to alleviate sufferings, not to court them. How could his incarceration have bettered in any way the lot of the people he was striving to serve? He suffered from no false modesty; his opinion of himself suffered, if it suffered at all, from an overestimation of his powers. He saw himself not only as the ablest and most persuasive champion of the working people — which he probably was — but as a man who saw into the very heart of the problems and knew, as no-one else did, how the problems could be overcome. It was this certainty that he was right in his diagnosis (a diagnosis intimately bound up with his views on banking, borrowing and the existence of a huge National Debt), and right in his proposals for a radical restructuring of society, that made him see his continuing freedom to publish as imperative. That he was aware that his action in leaving his country might be misinterpreted is apparent in a long article headed *Mr Cobbett's Taking Leave of his Countrymen* which appeared in the issue of the *Political Register* published just after he had embarked from Liverpool.

> I have reasoned thus with myself: What is now left to be done? We have urged our claims with so much truth; we have established them so clearly on the ground of both law and reason, that there is no answer to us to be found, other than that of a suspension of our personal safety. If I still write in support of those claims, I must be blind not to see, that a dungeon is my doom. If I remain here, I must, therefore, cease to write; therefore it is impossible to do any good to the cause of my country by remaining in it; but if I remove to a country where I

can write with perfect freedom, it is not only possible, but very probable, that I shall, sooner or later, be able to render that cause important and lasting services.

What! shall I submit in silence? Shall I be as dumb as one of my horses? Shall that indignation which burns within me, be quenched? Shall truth never again be uttered?

My countrymen, be you well assured, that though I shall, if I live, be at a distance from you; though the ocean will roll between us, not all the barriers that nature as well as art can raise, shall be sufficient to prevent you from reading some parts, at least, of what I write.

Though I quit my country, far be it from me to look upon her cause as desperate, and still farther be it from me to wish to infuse despondency into your minds. *I can serve that cause no longer by remaining here*; but the cause itself is so good, so just, so manifestly right and virtuous, and it has been combated by means so unusual, so unnatural, and so violent, that it must triumph in the end.

A mutual affection, a powerful impulse, will, I hope, always exist between me and my hard-used countrymen; an affection, which my heart assures me, no time, no distance, no new connections, no new association of ideas, however enchanting, can ever destroy, or, in any degree, enfeeble or impair. A splendid mansion in America will be an object less dear to me than a cottage on the skirts of Waltham Chace or of Botley Common. Never will I own as my friend him who is not a friend of the people of England. I will never become a *Subject* or a *Citizen* in any other state, and will always be a *foreigner* in every country but England. All the celebrity which my writings have obtained, and which they will preserve, long and long after Lords Liverpool and Sidmouth and Castlereagh are rotten and forgotten, I owe less to my own talents than to the discernment and that noble spirit in you, which have at once instructed my mind and warmed my heart: and, my beloved countrymen, be you assured, that the last beatings of that heart will be, love for the people, for the happiness, and the renown of England; and hatred of their corrupt, hypocritical, dastardly, and merciless foes.

The beautiful country, through which I have lately travelled, bearing upon every inch of it, such striking marks of the industry and skill of the people, never can be destined to be inhabited by slaves. To suppose such a thing possible would be at once to libel the nation and to blaspheme against providence.

Dated: Liverpool, 28 March 1817[4]

True to his word that he would continue to concern himself with the plight of his countrymen, Cobbett began his first article for the *Political Register* which he would send back to England for publication, three days after his landing at New York on May 5th 1817. "I have hardly recovered from the rocking of the waves, than I sit down for the purpose of convincing you that I am not unmindful of that promise";[5] he wrote to his readers, though they had to wait until July before this first Register arrived in England for printing and distribution. Thereafter, his copy arrived regularly and the *Political Register* was able to be issued weekly as before, a striking tribute to the navigational skills of those seamen plying across the Atlantic in the days of sail.

In marked contrast to his first visit to the United States in the 1790s, this time Cobbett took no part in American internal polities. One of his first major articles was a devastating attack on the British government entitled *A History of the last Hundred Days of English Freedom* in which he detailed the draconian measures the government had adopted to quell discontent and stifle demands for reforms

---

[4] *Political Register* 32, 29 March, 1817.
[5] *Political Register* 32, 12 July, 1817.

leading up to the repressive Acts and the suspension of the Habeas Corpus Act. Throughout his stay, Cobbett took a keen interest in the fate of reformers imprisoned under the new Acts, in the insurrections of the labourers and in the proceedings of Parliament, and he commented on them at length.

> He was thus very present in spirit among his countrymen all through those troublous years. Nor was he compelled to rely wholly on letters and newspapers for his knowledge of English events. One result of the bad times in England was that a stream of emigrants including many substantial farmers crossed the Atlantic, while the repression sent with them a steady trickle of political refugees. He was constantly visited by Englishmen who, for political or economic reasons, had come to the United States; from them he got the latest news of English affairs.[6]

The fact that the main thrust of his articles was directed to the parlous state of England, does not mean that Cobbett neglected to inform his readers about the situation in the United States. Of American politics he said little; of the conditions of the people he said much. And besides this, he also wrote a book *A Year's Residence in the United States of America*, which he published in 1818, in which he spoke of his experiences as a farmer in Long Island and of his journey through Pennsylvania to Harrisburgh which he visited in January 1818, unsuccessfully as it turned out, to try to obtain some redress for the losses he had sustained in the lawsuits brought against him in the 1790s.

Almost from the moment he landed in New York, Cobbett found abundant proof that he had not misled his readers in his praises of the American system of government. Everything delighted him: the cheapness and abundance

---
[6] Cole, G D H, *The Life of William Cobbett*, p 225, W Collins & Sons, 1924.

of food, the friendliness of innkeepers and strangers, the absence of signs of want among the labourers, and the countryside itself.

> The people are engaged busily in planting their Indian corn. The Cherry Trees, of which there are multitudes, planted in long avenues, or rows, or round the fields, have dropped their blossom and begin to show their loads of fruit. The apple and pear orchards, in extent from one to twenty acres on each farm, are in full and beautiful bloom. The farms are small in extent: no appearance of *great* riches amongst the farmers and not the smallest appearance of want among the labourers, who receive, in the country, about 2/3d a day, with board and lodging and which board consists of plenty of excellent meat and fish of all sorts, the best of bread, butter, cheese and eggs.[7]

Cobbett made up his mind from the start that his first concern would be to establish himself in independence as a small farmer. "It is my intention to be a downright farmer and to *depend* solely on what I can get in that way. I begin by counting on nothing but what I can raise from the ground."[8] He leased a farm on Long Island in Queen's County near North Hempstead "with an avenue of trees before it the most beautiful I ever saw. The orchard, the fine shade and fine grass all about the house, the abundant garden, the beautiful turnip field; the whole a subject of admiration; and not a single drawback."[9]

Cobbett, it should be noted here, was a man of superlatives and never more so than in his descriptions of the countryside. When in the 1820s, he travelled widely in England to see for himself the state of the country preparatory to standing as a candidate for Parliament, he

---

[7] *Political Register* 32, 12 July, 1817.
[8] *Political Register* 32, 26 July 1817.
[9] *Political Register* 34, 6 March 1819.

was constantly coming across "the most fertile valley", "the finest corn" or "the prettiest village", though this did not prevent him from seeing the misery of the people living in the midst of plenty. His enthusiasm ought, therefore, always to be taken with a pinch of salt; nevertheless. Long Island did seem admirably suited for the life he had chosen, albeit he sadly missed his own people. Much as he eulogised the fertility of the soil and the weather: "the rains come about once in fifteen days; they come in abundance for about twenty-four hours and then all is dry again immediately";[10] or, from his Journal of June 16th: "Fine beautiful day. Never saw such fine weather. Not a morsel of dirt. The ground sucks up all. I walk about and work on the land in shoes made of deerskin. They are dressed *white* like breeches-leather",[11] but he was not entirely uncritical. Comparing the dwellings, gardens and outhouses of the labourers in southern England with those he saw on Long Island, he wrote,

> Instead of the neat and warm little cottage, the yard, the cow-stable, pig-sty, hen-house, all in miniature, and the garden nicely laid out and the paths bordered with flowers, while the cottage door is crowned with a garland of roses or honeysuckle; instead of these, we here see the labourer content with a shell of boards, while all around him is as barren as the sea-beach. This want of attention in such cases is hereditary from the first settlers. They found, land so plenty, that they treated small spots with contempt.[12]

Nor was Cobbett above introducing improvements into American methods of farming. In his book *A Year's Residence* he wrote on his own methods of cultivating cabbages and Swedish turnips, on transplanting Indian

---

[10] *Journal of a Year's Residence in the United States of America*, para 14.
[11] *Ibid*, para 20.
[12] *Ibid*, para 18.

corn, and on other agricultural topics. He prided himself on innovations he made on his farm at North Hempstead. One of these concerned hens. The practice on Long Island was to allow hens to roost out on trees in winter, but Cobbett decided "to give the poor things a chance". He converted an outbuilding into a hen-house, lined it with cornstalks and leaves and "made ladders for the fowls to go in at holes six feet from the ground". Sure enough, after peeping at the ladders for some two or three days, the hens took to sleeping in the roost and by March Cobbett was able to report his first young chickens. "I hear of no others in the neighbourhood. This is the effect of my warm fowl-house; The house has been supplied with eggs *all the winter* without any interruption. I am told this has been the case at no other house hereabouts."[13] Another improvement he was proud of was his method of keeping at bay the flies and mosquitoes which so plagued households throughout the summer months. He detailed his tactics.

> June 19. Fine day. But now comes my alarm! The *musquitoes* and still worse the common *house fly* which used to plague us so in Pennsylvania, and which were the only things I ever disliked belonging to the climate of America. Flies are bred in *filth* of which none shall be near me as long as I can use a shovel and broom. They follow *fresh meat and fish*. Have neither, or be very careful. I have this day put all these precautions in practice: and, now let us see the result
>
> July 21 Fine hot day; but heavy rain at night. *Flies a few*. Not more than in England. But, then, I cause all *wash* and *slops* to be carried forty yards from the house. I suffer no peelings, or greens, or any rubbish to lie near the house. I proscribe all fish. Do not suffer a dog to enter the house. Keep all pigs at a distance of sixty

---

[13] *Ibid*, para 20.

yards. And sweep all round about once every week at least.

August 17   Fine hot day. Very hot. I live on salads and other garden vegetables, apple-puddings and pies, butter, cheese (*very good* from Rhode Island), eggs and bacon. Resolved to have no more fresh meat, 'till cooler weather comes. Those who have a mind to swallow, or be swallowed by, *flies*, may eat fresh meat for me.[14]

Both in his book *A Year's Residence* and in his descriptions of America in the *Political Register*, Cobbett attempted to give a true picture of the life he found there. "The account which I shall give, shall be that of actual *experience*. I will say what I *know* and what I have *seen* and what I have *done*."[15] Ever since the War of Independence, reports from travellers from Britain and Europe, anxious to see this new nation under its new form of government, had aroused great interest. Conflicting stories abounded: some travellers coming, as Cobbett said "with a resolution to find everything better than at home", described a kind of demi-paradise; others travelling "in the stages from place to place, have lounged away their time with the idle part of their own countrymen and, taking every thing different from what they left at home for the effect of ignorance, and every thing not servile to be the effect of insolence, have described the country as unfit for a civilized being to reside in".[16]

Cobbett approached the subject in a different way. He did not want to leave England: he wanted England to be itself a good place to live in. With his thoughts and energies always directed to improving the lot of his fellow countrymen, his comments on the customs and life-style

---

[14] *Journal of a Year's Residence in the United States of America*, para 20.
[15] *Ibid*, para 3.
[16] *Journal of a Year's Residence in the United States of America*, para 2.

of the American people are unique. Although, like other visitors, he dwells on the many differences between the Old World and the New, he attributed the differences to the superior form of government in the United States and held it up as an example of what Britain might be like if all the corruption and malpractices were swept away. Nowhere is this more apparent than in his reactions to the relations between employers and employed, masters and servants. In his *Address to the Journeymen and Labourers* published shortly before he left England, Cobbett had striven to make English work people aware and proud of their worth. In Long Island he found the American labourer did truly have "a correct idea of his own worth", and he praised him accordingly.

> The American labourers, like the tavern-keepers, are never *servile*, but always *civil*. Employed about your house as day-labourers, they never come to interlope for victuals or drink. They have no idea of such a thing. Their pride would restrain them if their plenty did not; and thus it would be with all labourers, in all countries, were they left to enjoy the fair produce of their labour. Full pocket or empty pocket, these American labourers are always the *same men*; no saucy cunning in the one case, and no base crawling in the other. This, too, arises from the free institutions of government. A man has a voice because *he is a man*, and not because he is the *possessor of money*. And, shall I *never* see our English labourers in this happy state?[17]

This spirit of independence was commented on by other visitors. Fearon, who was in America at the same time as Cobbett, described the labourers he saw in New York as "not better clothed than men in a similar condition in England, but they were more erect in their posture,

---

[17] *Ibid*, para 320.

less careworn in their countenances, and there were no beggars".[18] Hamilton, writing of his experience some ten years later, was surprised to see on his travels servants dining with their masters: "all the passengers on the stage coach eat at the same table" he wrote, and explained this phenomenon as due to the short time allowed for meals at the stages, so that "unless John dines with his master, the chances are that he goes without his dinner altogether".[19] And Harriet Martineau commented on "the absence of poverty, of gross ignorance, of all servility, of all insolence". [20] For some, though, this spirit of independence could be carried too far. Sir Augustus Foster, British Minister to the United States from 1810 to 1812, tells how his secretary returned from a stormy voyage in Chesapeake Bay to Norfolk in Virginia "with a sad account of the state of discipline on board, every individual sailor wanting to command, and the steersman hollering in accents of despair, 'Sons of Liberty, boys, for the love of Jesus hawl down the mainsail'".[21]

The spirit of independence among the people was matched in Cobbett's eyes by their skill.

> These Americans are the best that *I ever saw*. They mow four acres of *oats, wheat, rye* or *barley* in a day, and, with a cradle, lay it so smooth in the swarths, that it is tied up in sheathes with the greatest neatness and ease. So that our men, who come from England, must not expect that, in the common labours of the country, they are to surpass, or even equal, these "Yankees", who, of all the men that I ever saw, are the most *active* and the most

---

[18] Fearson, Henry, *Sketches of America*, p 5, Longman, Hunt, Rees, Orme, Brown, 1819.
[19] Hamilton, Thomas, *Men and Manners in America*, p 226, Wm Blackwood & Sons, 1843.
[20] Martineau, Harriet, *Society in America*, Vol 1, p 39, Saunders & Otley, 1839.
[21] Sir Augustus Foster, *Jeffersonian America*, p 128, Huntingdon Library Press, 1954.

hardy. They skip over a fence like a greyhound. They will catch you a pig by racing him down; and they are afraid of nothing.[22]

The abundance and cheapness of food surprised all travellers. Cobbett experienced this immediately he landed when he put up in an inn with his two sons. "It really was eating", he wrote. "Not an egg, but a dish full of eggs, not a snip of meat or of fish, but a plateful. For dinner we had the finest of fish, bass, mackerel, lobsters; of meat, lamb, veal, ham, etc."[23] Thomas Hamilton was even more eloquent.

> The table, instead of displaying as with us, a mere beggarly account of fish and soup, exhibits an array of dishes wedged in close columns, which would require at least an acre of mahogany to deploy into line — plates various appear and disappear as if by magic — the flight of ham and turkey is incessant; venison bounds from one end of the table to the other with a velocity scarcely exceeded in its native forest.[24]

Here as elsewhere Cobbett pointed the moral. It was, he stated, the absence of taxes that made all this possible.

> It is not with a little bit of toast, so neatly put in a rack; a bit of butter so round and so small; a little milk pot so pretty and so empty; an egg *for you*, the host and hostess *not liking eggs*. It is not with looks that seem to say 'don't eat too much for the taxgatherer is coming'. It is not thus that you are received in America. You are not much asked, not much pressed, to eat and drink; but such an abundance is spread before you, and so hearty and so cordial is your reception, that you instantly lose all restraint, and are tempted to feast whether you be hungry or not. And though the manner and style are

---

[22] *Journal of a Year's Residence in the United States of America*, paras 314 and 318.
[23] *Political Register* 32, 12 July 1817.
[24] Hamilton, Thomas, *op cit* p 68.

widely different in different homes, the *abundance* every where prevails. This is the strength of the government: a happy people; and no government ought to have any other strength.[25]

Over and over again in his descriptions of America, Cobbett referred to the low taxation under the American system of government. In Britain at this time, there were not only taxes on land, houses, windows, carriages and so on, affecting the middle classes, but a host of other taxes on necessities falling most heavily on the poor. Sydney Smith, an English clergyman and one of the great wits of the age, described some of them in this memorable passage.

> TAXES upon every article which enters into the mouth, or covers the back, or is placed under the foot — taxes upon every thing which is pleasant to see, hear, feel, smell or taste — taxes upon warmth, light, and locomotion — taxes upon every thing on earth — on every thing that comes from abroad or is grown at home — on the ermine that decorates the judge, and the rope that hangs the criminals — on the poor man's salt and the rich man's spice — on the brass nails of the coffin, and the ribands of the bride — at bed or board, couchant or levant, we must pay. The school boy whips his taxed top — the beardless youth manages his taxed horse with a taxed bridle, on a taxed road; and the dying Englishman, pouring his medicine, which has paid 7 per cent, into a spoon which has paid 15 per cent — flings himself back upon his chintz bed which has paid 22 per cent -- and expires in the arms of an apothecary who has paid a licence of a hundred pounds for the privilege of putting him to death.[26]

How different was the situation in America. In *A Year's Residence*, Cobbett tried to convey to his English readers

---

[25] *Journal of a Year's Residence in the United States of America*, para 353.
[26] Smith, S, *Works Vol 1 Review of Seybert's Statistical Annals of the United States.*

what it was like not to be worried by taxgatherers and excisemen.

> It is a state of such blessedness, when compared with the state of things in England, that I despair of being able to make you fully comprehend what it is. Here a man may make a new window, or shut up old windows, as often as he pleases, without being compelled under a penalty to give notice to some insolent tax-gathering spy. Here he may keep as many horses as he likes, he may ride them or drive them at his pleasure, he may sell them or keep them, he may lend them or breed from them; he may employ his servants in his house, in his stables, in his garden, or in his fields just as he pleases; he may, if he be foolish enough, have armorial bearings on his carriage, his watch-seals, on his plate, and, if he likes, on his very buckets and porridge pots. You dare not make candles or soap, though you have the fat and ashes in abundance. If you attempt to do this, you are taken up and imprisoned; and, if you resist, soldiers are brought to shoot you. Now, we *here*, make our own candles and soap. A labouring man, or a mechanic, buys a sheep now and then. Three or four days' work will buy a labourer a sheep to weigh sixty pounds, with seven or eight pounds of fat. The wool makes stockings. And the loose fat is made into candles and soap. The year before I left Hampshire, a poor woman at Holly Hill had *dipped* some *rushes* in grease to use instead of candles. An Exciseman found it out; went and ransacked her house; and told her that if the rushes had had *another dip*, they would have been *candles* and she must have gone to jail! Why, my friends, if such a thing were told here, nobody would believe it. The Americans could not bring their minds to believe that Englishmen would submit to such atrocious, such degrading tyranny.[27]

For Cobbett, the great benefits the Americans derived from

---

[27] *Journal of a Year's Residence in the United States of America*, para 423.

low taxation and the absence of government interference, was paralleled by the absence of a tithing system. The Established Church in Britain, itself a huge landowner receiving rents, was also supported by tithes. One tenth of all the produce of the land was forfeited to the Church, regardless of whether the farmer or cottager was himself a member of that Church. For years Cobbett had been carrying on a feud with his own parson, the Reverend Baker of Botley, accusing him of poking and prying into the nooks and crannies of every man's garden in the village to see if he was receiving his legal tenth of the eggs, the vegetables or the corn it produced.

> And then, think of the *tithes*! I have talked to several farmers here about the tithes in England; and they *laugh*. They sometimes almost make me angry; for they seem, at last, not to believe what I say, when I tell them that the English farmer gives, and is compelled to give, the Parson a tenth part of his whole crop and of his fruit and milk and eggs and calves and lambs and pigs and wool and honey. They cannot believe this. They treat it as a sort of *romance*.
>
> But, my Botley neighbours, you will exclaim, "No tithes! Why then there can be no Churches and no Parsons!" By no means, my friends. Here are plenty of Churches. No less than three Episcopal (or English) Churches; three Presbyterian Churches; three Lutheran Churches; one or two Quaker Meeting-houses; and two Methodist places; all within six miles of the spot where I am sitting. Oh no! Tithes are not necessary to promote religion. Religion means a reverence for God. And what has this to do with tithes? Why cannot you reverence God, without Baker and his wife and children eating up a tenth part of the corn and milk and eggs and lambs and calves that are produced in Botley parish? The Parsons, in this country, are supported by those who choose to employ them. A man belongs to what congregation he

pleases. He pays what is required by the rules of the congregation. And if he thinks that it is not necessary to belong to any congregation, he pays nothing at all. And the consequence is, that all is harmony and good neighbourhood.[28]

And Cobbett clinched his argument by declaring that the absence of an Established Church, far from creating a society of "wicked, disorderly and criminal people" had produced "the most orderly, sensible, and least criminal people in the whole world".[29]

Here, then, in America, Cobbett found a people free of just those abuses which he had for nearly a quarter of a century been striving to expose and eradicate in his own country. Of almost equal importance to him was the absence of an aristocracy. Cobbett was the very antithesis of the Englishman "who loves a lord". He prided himself on being the grandson of a day-labourer. "With respect to my ancestors, I shall go no further than my grandfather, and for this plain reason, that I never heard talk of any prior to him".[30] The conferring of titles, in his opinion, encouraged haughtiness on the part of the ennobled and sycophantic cringing or envy among the rest. In America he found neither.

> this people contains very few persons very much raised in men's estimation, above the general mass; for though there are some men of immense *fortunes*, their wealth does very little indeed in the way of purchasing even the outward signs of respect; and as to *adulation*, it is not to be purchased with love or money. Men, be they what they may, are generally called by their *two names*, without any thing prefixed or added.[31]

---

[28] *Journal of a Year's Residence in the United States of America*, paras 431 and 432.
[29] *Journal of a Year's Residence in the United States of America*, para 434.
[30] Life and Adventures of Peter Porcupine (1796).
[31] *Journal of a Year's Residence in the United States of America*, para 343.

And again:

> One of the most aimiable features of American society is this: that men never boast of their riches, and never disguise their poverty; but they talk of both as of any other matter fit for public conversation. No man shuns another because he is poor; no man is preferred to another because he is rich. In hundreds and hundreds of instances, men not worth a shilling have been chosen by the people and entrusted with their rights and interests in preference to men who ride in their carriages.[32]

In the absence of titles, however, there was one mode of address which travellers from the Old World commented on with some derision, and that was the use of military titles. Charles Dickens, for instance, describes how in a boarding house in New York, Martin Chuzzlewit "found that there were no fewer than four majors present, two colonels, one general and a captain, so that he could not help thinking how strongly officered the American militia must be; and wondering very much whether the officers commanded each other; or, if they did not, where on earth the privates came from". Cobbett had no such condescending attitude. As was seen earlier, the absence of a standing army, the immediate discharge of soldiers once the war was over, and the bravery displayed by the militia fighting the professionals of the British army, were all, for him, the subject of admiration. Compared with the overpaid, overdressed and idle British peace-time officers, "My neighbour, Colonel Mitchell, who in hot weather, ploughs and hoes his Indian corn without stockings on his legs or shoes on his feet, is the sort of Colonel that I like", Cobbett declared, and he went on to tell his readers that his servant, Mrs Churcher, who with her husband had come over from Botley to keep house for him and his

---

[32] *Advice to Young Men*, para 57, 1829.

sons on Long Island, had laughed when she had heard this neighbour called 'Colonel'.

> "Stop", said I, "Mrs Churcher. Think a little. Mr Mitchell may be as brave or braver than the gay-dressed, long sworded, strutting, impudent fellow that you used to see at Portsmouth or Gosport. They helped to swallow what you earned. It was to support them and set them up to walk over you, that you were compelled to pay so dearly for your beer, your tea, sugar, candles and soap. Colonel Mitchell takes nothing from you here. He lets us make our fat into candles and soap. He lets us make our malt and brew our beer. And he lets you keep your dollars till they fill a stocking or two. He will let you buy a farm and have a dairy of your own by-and-by; and he will never knock Churcher down for not pulling his hat off to him, and never will kick you for not making him a curtsey. In short, Mrs. Churcher, always bear in mind that a country of pretty Colonels is, and must be, a country of poor and degraded people![33]

And was this society, lightly taxed, free of government interference, unburdened by tithes and egalitarian in its relationships, so preferable to that of the Old World? Cobbett had no hesitation in answering in the affirmative. He believed that all these advantages permeated the whole fabric of social intercourse: between men and women, parents and children, masters and servants, neighbours, friends and strangers.

> It is supposed, in England, that this equality of estimation must beget a general coarseness and rudeness of behaviour. Never was there a greater mistake. No man likes to be treated with disrespect; and when he finds that he can obtain respect only by treating others with respect, he will use that only means. When he finds

---

[33] *Political Register* 34, 5 September 1819.

that neither haughtiness nor wealth will bring him a civil word, he becomes civil himself; and I repeat it again and again, this is a country of *universal civility*.[34]

An impression echoed by a French writer as early as 1792 who spoke of the Americans he met as "hospitable to strangers and obliging to friends; they are tender husbands and almost idolatrous parents, and kind masters";[35] and by Harriet Martineau travelling in the 1830s. "I believe it is not so much the outward plenty, or the mutual freedom, or the simplicity of manners, or the incessant play of humour, which characterize the whole people, as the sweet temper which is diffused like sunshine over the land. They have been called the most good-tempered people in the world: and I think they must be so".[36]

Cobbett was impressed, too, by the lack of ignorance among the farmers he met, and how they and their wives and daughters "all read a good deal". He confirmed Harriet Martineau's later impressions of the American people's good temper, telling how the ladies "can converse with you upon almost any subject" and speaking of "the ease and gracefulness of their behaviour". All this, he believed, was due to the gentle treatment they received from their parents and husbands due to the absence among them of so many causes of racking anxiety. As for the men themselves, "they always hear with patience. I do not know that I ever heard a native American interrupt another man while he was speaking".[37]

Were there then no drawbacks? Looming over the whole society there was the huge question of the blacks, both

---

[34] *Journal of a Year's Residence in the United States of America*, para 345.
[35] J P Brissot de Warville. *The New Travels in the United States of America*, p 14, J S Jordan, 1792.
[36] Martineau, H, *op cit* Vol 3, p 54.
[37] *Journal of a Year's Residence in the United States of America*, para 356.

slave and free. But before considering Cobbett's attitude to this, some brief mention must be made of a custom that attracted the attention of nearly every visitor from the Old World: the habit of chewing tobacco and squirting out the juice, a habit indulged in from the top to the bottom of society. (Thomas Jefferson had special mahogany spittoons installed in every room in his house in Monticello, and President Jackson's addiction is described below.) The three extracts that follow typify the reactions at the time: the first from Fanny Trollope describing the cabins of a steam-ship on the Mississippi.

> both this (the ladies) and the gentlemen's cabin were handsomely fitted, and the latter well carpeted; but oh! that carpet! I will not, I may not, describe its condition: indeed it requires the pen of a Swift to do it justice. I hardly know of any annoyance so deeply repugnant to English feelings, as the incessant, remorseless spitting of Americans.[38]

The second, Dicken's description of the Congress buildings in Washington.

> Both Houses are handsomely carpeted; but the state to which these carpets are reduced by the universal disregard of the spittoon with which every honourable gentleman is accommodated, and the extraordinary improvements in the pattern which are squirted and dabbled upon it in every direction, do not admit of being described. I will merely observe, that I strongly recommend strangers not to look at the floor; and if they happen to drop anything, though it be their purse, not to pick it up with an ungloved hand on any account.[39]

---

[38] Trollope, Frances. *Domestic Manners of the Americans*, Vol 1, pp 19-20, Treacher & Co, 1832.
[39] Dickens, *American Notes*.

Lastly, Hamilton's description of his visit to President Jackson in 1830.

> He is a very decent-looking old gentleman, something like a country minister in Scotland, and kind, though somewhat vulgar in manner. He chews tobacco, and kept rolling an enormous quid about in his mouth and squirting his saliva on the carpet, which, and his chair, was really covered with a fluid of the most disgusting description.[40]

In spite of the almost universal condemnation expressed about this habit, Cobbett refers to it only once during his second visit. Leaving Trenton, in New Jersey, on his way back to Long Island after his journey to Pennsylvania, he wrote, "and now I bid adieu to Trenton, which I would have liked better, if I had not seen so many young fellows lounging about the streets, and leaning against the doorposts, with quids of tobacco in their mouths, or segars stuck between their lips, and with dirty hands and faces".[41] He was, however, very censorious about the drinking habits of Americans, though he was reluctant to write about it.

> There is one thing in the Americans, which I have reserved, or rather kept back to the last moment. It has presented itself several times; but I have turned from the thought, as men do from thinking of any mortal disease that is at work in their frame. It is not covetousness; it is not niggardliness; it is not insincerity; it is not enviousness; it is not cowardice above all things: it is DRINKING. You cannot go into hardly any man's house, without being asked to drink wine, or spirits, *even in the morning*. The scenes that I witnessed at Harrisburgh I shall never forget. To see this beastly vice in *young men* is shocking. At one of the taverns in Harrisburgh

---

[40] Hamilton, Thomas, *op cit,* p 248.
[41] *Journal of a Year's Residence in the United States of America*, para 20.

there were several as fine young men as I ever saw. Well dressed, well educated, polite, and everything but *sober*. What a squalid, drooping, sickly set they looked in the morning! Even little boys at, or under, *twelve* years of age, go into stores and tip off their drams! However, I must not be understood as meaning that this tippling is universal amongst gentlemen; and, God be thanked, the *women* of any figure in life do by no means give in to the practice, but abhor it as much as well-bred women in England, who, in general, no more think of drinking strong liquors, than they do of drinking poison.[42]

The glaring anomaly of a slave-owning society boasting of liberty and equality was commented on by almost every traveller who visited the United States after Independence. Those who visited Washington and the southern States, where they saw slaves being bought and sold were unanimous in their condemnation, although some spoke of the kindly treatment of house-slaves in the homes where they stayed. It will be remembered that as Peter Porcupine Cobbett had used the practice of slavery as one of his weapons to castigate those Democrats who, after having sung-hymns to the Goddess of Liberty, went back to their homes in the South to sleep with their 'property' in their arms, enhancing their value by making them bear to their owners "the proofs of their democratic delicacy". In both his sojourns in America, Cobbett lived and travelled exclusively in the northern States where slavery either had been or was in the process of being extinguished. When he was living in Philadelphia in the 1790s, the resident black population comprised about 5% of the total, some three thousand in all, of whom half were already freed, although the number of slaves was swelled by those which the Senators and Representatives from the South brought

---

[42] *Journal of a Year's Residence in the United States of America*, para 359, 361-3.

with them as servants during the sessions of Congress.

The manumission of slaves in the northern States did not necessarily bring benefits to the freed. Dependent since birth on their owners for housing, clothing and food, deprived of education and so often unable to read or write, unaccustomed to the use of money or to any concept of making provision for the future, the freed slave faced formidable difficulties. Thomas Jefferson, himself a slave-owner, although sympathetic to the cause of freedom for all blacks, told Augustus Foster that he believed that emancipation often brought misery with it. "He told me", Foster wrote in his memoirs, "that Negroes have, in general, so little foresight that though they receive blankets very thankfully from their masters on the commencement of winter, and use them to keep off the cold, yet when the warm weather returns, they frequently cast them off without a thought as to what may become of them, wherever they may happen to be at the time, and then not seldom lose them in the woods or fields from mere carelessness".[43] And later in a letter to a friend Jefferson wrote,

> For men probably of any color, but of this color we know, brought from their infancy without necessity for thought or forecast are by their habits rendered as incapable as children of taking care of themselves. My opinion has ever been that, until more can be done for them, we should endeavour, with those whom fortune has thrown on our hands, to feed and clothe them well, protect them from all ill-usage, require such reasonable labor only as is performed voluntarily by freemen, and be led by no repugnancies to abdicate them, and our duties to them.[44]

---

[43] Sir Augustus Foster, *op cit* p 149.
[44] Jefferson, *Letter to Edward Coles*, 25 August 1814.

The freeing of slaves was, in fact, deliberately slowed down in some of the northern States, for the problem of caring for the sick, the destitute and the old now fell on the community as a whole instead of on the owners as heretofore. In Pennsylvania, under the influence of the Quakers, some creditable attempts were made to provide schooling for blacks and to make provision for the sick. As early as 1788 a French traveller, Brissot de Warville, was astonished to see in a hospital in Philadelphia blacks mingled with whites "and lodged in the same apartments. I saw a negro woman spinning with activity by the side of her bed and another taking tea. Her tea! My friend you are astonished at this luxury in a hospital. It is because there is humanity in its administration"[45]. Nevertheless, the majority of the freed slaves even in the Quaker influenced State of Pennsylvania lived in miserable conditions. During his first sojourn in America, Cobbett referred in passing to the "dark lanes and alleys" of Philadelphia where could be found "Paddy's filthy cabin and Pompey's hovel" implying that Irish immigrants and free blacks lived in unsavoury slums in the city.

When Cobbett arrived in New York some twenty years later, the blacks in New York State numbered about forty thousand out of a total population of one million people. The majority, about three-quarters, were free though the State did not completely abolish slavery until 1827. A large number of the free blacks in the State migrated to the flourishing city of New York where they found employment as drivers, waiters, labourers in the docks and on the farms, and in domestic service. Fearon, arriving in the city shortly after Cobbett, wrote, "One striking feature consists of the number of blacks, many of whom are

---

[45] J P Brissot de Warville, *op cit*.

finely dressed, the females very ludicrously so, showing a partiality to white muslin dresses, artificial flowers and pink shoes"[46]. One can sympathise with these former slaves vaunting their freedom by showy clothes, for in what other way could they present themselves as free members of society when they were branded for life by their colour as belonging to the lowest strata? The prejudice of whites against blacks tended to increase rather than diminish when whites met blacks as competitors in the labour market. De Toqueville, visiting the United States in 1832, gives a sad picture of the position of the freed slaves. "As he becomes free, independence is often felt by him to be a heavier burden than slavery.... In short, he sinks to such a depth of wretchedness, that while servitude brutalises, liberty destroys him."[47] And again "The negro is free, but he can share neither the rights nor the pleasures, nor the labour, nor the afflictions, nor the tomb of him whose equal he has been declared to be; and he cannot meet him on fair terms in life or in death."[48] Thomas Hamilton, describing his impressions at about the same time as De Toqueville, confirms his views on the sorry position of the free black. "Be his acquirements what they may, a Negro is still a Negro, or, in other words, a creature marked out for degradation and exclusion from those objects which stimulate the hopes and powers of other men!", and commented on the "tyranny of that prejudice which, regarding the poor black as being of an inferior order, works its own fulfilment in making him so."[49]

While Cobbett was living in Long Island, there was little pressure in the northern States, all of which had either

---

[46] Fearson, Henry, *op cit.*
[47] Alexis de Tocqueville *Democracy in America* p 336, Longman Green & Co, 1875.
[48] *Ibid*, p 365.
[49] Hamilton, Thomas, *op cit,* p 52-3.

freed or were in the-process of freeing their slaves, to persuade their southern neighbours to do the same. (It is worth noting here, that with the exception of John Adams of Massachusetts' four-year-term of office from 1796 to 1800, all the Presidents, Washington, Jefferson, Madison and Monroe had come from the slave-owning State of Virginia, and were themselves slave owners.) Aware of the difficulties of freeing slaves even when their numbers were only a very small percentage of the total population, the northerners could accept the arguments of the southerners that with blacks actually outnumbering whites in some States, emancipation would unleash a host of almost insuperable problems. Although a number of enlightened southerners, Washington and Jefferson prominent among them, abhorred the institution, the logistics of manumission persuaded them that at the present time emancipation would benefit neither blacks nor whites. It was not until the 1830s that a nation-wide movement for the abolition of slavery, led by W L Garrison and fanned by the publication of Harriet Beecher Stowe's *Uncle Tom's Cabin* in 1852 gained momentum, and not until the whole nation had suffered the frightful tragedy of the Civil War of the 1860s that slavery was finally abolished throughout the Union.

Cobbett writing only of 'what he knew and what he had seen' made no reference to the plight of the slaves in the South during his second stay in America. His references to the black people were confined to remarks on those whom he himself had seen in New York City and on Long Island and during his visit to Pennsylvania. They were few. In praising the skill of American labourers in cutting down and cutting up -trees, and comparing them with the efforts of a recent Irish immigrant who was sent to cut a load of wood to burn, he wrote. "An American, black or white, would have had half a dozen trees cut down, cut up into lengths, put upon the carriage, and brought home"⁵⁰ in the time it had taken this Irishman to hack down just part of one hickory tree. And the pride and independence of spirit he found among blacks as well as whites. After dining in a tavern at Trenton and finding the bill exceptionally low, he wrote "I had not the face to pay the waiter a quarter of a dollar; but gave him half a dollar, and told him to keep the change. He is a black man. He thanked me. But they never *ask* for any thing."⁵¹

The only direct reference Cobbett made to freeing slaves was to criticise the plans of the recently formed Colonisation Society in America for repatriating blacks to Africa. He had warned Englishmen of the difficulties they would be likely to encounter if they considered emigrating to the United States, a land using the same language as themselves and inheriting many of the same traditions and customs. Furthermore, while serving in the British army in Canada in the 1780s, Cobbett had himself been closely involved in a resettlement project in New Brunswick for American loyalists who had supported the British side during the War of Independence and fled the country for fear of reprisals being taken against them. He was in consequence aware of the enormous amount of support and equipment needed for a resettlement enterprise. Those settlers, he explained, had been given provisions (pork, flour, butter and rice) for four years, blankets and clothing for two to three years, tools, nails, ploughs, harrows, spades, etc. as well as cattle and food for the cattle, and these were for men accustomed to independence and many of them practising farmers.⁵² To imagine that freed slaves sent

---

[50] *Journal of a Year's Residence in the United States of America*, para 317.
[51] *Journal of a Year's Residence in the United States of America*, para 20.
[52] See *Political Register* 51, 3 July 1824.

to a country as different from America as Africa could start a new life there was, in Cobbett's opinion, a cruel delusion.

From other references he made to the subject, it is apparent that Cobbett tended to accept the prevalent view that the blacks were an inferior race to the whites (his eldest son William in an early letter home to Botley, said that the thing he disliked most was that "all the servants here are black"). Cobbett himself certainly abhorred any notion of miscegenation, and referred to the blacks' "absence of reasoning faculties". He asserted that it was the blacks that were responsible for nearly all the cases of thieving in the country round about where he lived, that "biting dogs and ready loaded guns are kept in exact proportion to the number of free negroes in a township", and that blacks "form nine tenths of the paupers and criminals of the country". On the other hand, he roundly condemned the fact that free blacks were captured in the north and sent south to be sold as slaves, and after his return to England, he publicised a book sent to him by a Mr James Torry entitled *A Picture of Domestic Slavery in the United States* which detailed the cruelties to which slaves were exposed. In general terms it would be true to say that Cobbett shared the opinions and prejudices of the majority of white Americans in the north, and believed that abominable as was the institution of slavery, its extinction was fraught with difficulties. Writing on the subject after his return to England he said,

> I insinuate nothing here either to the government or the people of America. Generally speaking, never was a kinder or more humane people. But what is the conclusion then? Why, that this Slavery is a curse entailed upon the country; that it is a thing not to be got rid of by visionary means; that the wisest of men and

the most sincere lovers of liberty have been and still are baffled in all their attempts not only to remove the evil, but to prevent it from increasing in magnitude.[53]

Before leaving the subject of slaves, a word should be said about Cobbett's violent antipathy to the Englishman William Wilberforce who devoted virtually the whole of his career as a Member of Parliament to the abolition of the slave trade and the emancipation of the slaves in the British West Indies. Four years older than Cobbett, Wilberforce was born of well-to-do Yorkshire merchants and educated at Cambridge. In 1780 he entered Parliament at the age of twenty-one, and early in his career became interested in the slave question. Deeply religious, he founded in 1797 the Society for the Suppression of Vice to counteract what he considered the loose morality of the times. ("A corporation of informers", Sydney Smith described it, "bent on suppressing not the vices of the rich but the pleasures of the poor" and on reducing their life "to its regular standard of decorous gloom" while "the gambling houses of St James remain untouched".)[54] In the same year — a year in which he underwent a kind of religious and spiritual awakening — he took up the question of the slave trade in the House of Commons. Against powerful vested interests Wilberforce succeeded in 1807 in pushing through Parliament a bill forbidding British ships to take part in dealing and trading in slaves. Having succeeded in that objective, he continued unremittingly to work for emancipation, and slavery was finally abolished in the British West Indies, very shortly after his death in 1834. He himself lived long enough to know that the bill would be passed.

Cobbett had begun attacking Wilberforce as early as 1802.

---

[53] *Political Register* 40, 22 September 1821.
[54] Quoted in Oliver Warner, *William Wilberforce and his Times*, B T Batsford Ltd, 1962.

His forming the Society for the Suppression of Vice in itself condemned him, for in Cobbett's eyes, as in Sydney Smith's, all attempts to 'improve' or 'better' the morals of the people were shot through with hypocrisy. Charity Schools, Bible Societies, Methodist preachers and the distribution of moral tracts Cobbett saw as measures taken to keep the poor in their place and make them contented with their lot. As for Wilberforce's efforts to alleviate the lot of blacks so many thousands of miles away, was not his first duty as a Member of the House of Commons to his own people? Was it not hypocrisy to appeal for justice and humanity to be shown to the five hundred thousand blacks in the West Indies when there were at the time more than one million paupers in Britain? One by one, Cobbett challenged Wilberforce's emotive appeals for humanity to be shown to West Indian slaves as being equally applicable to Englishmen. Slaves were flogged, but was Wilberforce not aware that English soldiers and sailors were flogged quite as brutally? Slaves were sold, but it was public knowledge that "shiploads of Irish and Welsh, and some English and Scotch, were yearly sent to America and there sold by advertisements". (Cobbett was referring here to the practice of indentured service whereby the poor were given free passage to the United States and then sold by the shipowners as domestic servants and bound to their employers for periods of up to seven years.) The cruelty of removing children from their parents was practised in England as well as in the West Indies. "How many thousands, and hundreds of thousands, of English children are at this moment in such a state of separation from their parents?", Cobbett asked. Were there not currently advertisements in the press put out by the Guardians of the Poor asking citizens to contract for the labour of pauper children? "Why, then, while they are contracted for and let out; why should we seek for objects of compassion elsewhere?"⁵⁵ Taunting Wilberforce with the fact that he had never set foot in a country holding slaves, whereas, "I have seen negroes in a state of slavery and I have seen free negroes; in all sorts of employment and under all sorts of treatment, I have had a fair opportunity of observing them", Cobbett maintained that negro slaves in the West Indies were fed better, lodged better, and received more medical attention than the English poor, and said that he was convinced that there was more misery in the parish of St Margarets, Westminster than in all the British West Indies. And if Wilberforce were to reply that these Englishmen were freemen and not slaves, "Say rather, Sir, that they are not black; a circumstance which they may, seeing the preference which is given to that colour, well regard as extremely unfortunate".⁵⁶ (It should be pointed out here, that in spite of Cobbett's attack on Wilberforce as a man who had never been in a slave-owning country, Cobbett too, had never seen plantation slaves either in the southern States or in the West Indies.)

Such, then, was Cobbett's opinion of Wilberforce during the first decade of the nineteenth century. His single minded devotion to the cause of the blacks when over a million of his own countrymen were in a state of deep distress and reduced to dependence on the poor laws which degraded them to a position comparable to slavery was not the only cause of Cobbett's hatred. During the disturbances which followed the ending of the Napoleonic Wars, Wilberforce was a member of that Secret Committee of the House of Commons set up to enquire into the state of the country which, instead of addressing itself to the causes of the disturbances, attributed them to 'Jacobin principles' and 'seditious propaganda'. Wilberforce was

---

⁵⁵ *Political Register* 5, 16 June 1804.
⁵⁶ *Political Register* 5, 16 June 1804.

foremost amongst those in the Commons who pressed for the draconian measures of repression and the suspension of Habeas Corpus which had forced Cobbett to flee to America, so it is not surprising that when in America Cobbett returned to the attack. In an Open Letter to Wilberforce in the *Political Register* of November 1817, Cobbett referred to his opposition in the Commons to a proposal for extending the franchise in Britain, on the grounds that the people must be educated before they were given the vote. And what, Cobbett asked him, was the difference between a free man and a slave? Was it not that "the free man, if he be in a state of civil society, partakes in the making of the laws by which he is governed; and the slave is governed by the will of another or of others?" The great legal authority, Blackstone, had stated that a man can be punished for breaking the law only because he has given his consent to the making of that law; and yet "many poor wretches in England have suffered death under laws to which they never assented. Therefore, as you found the people of England slaves, ought you not to have begun at home?"[57]

So great was Cobbett's detestation of Wilberforce that in one of the many eulogistic passages he wrote at this time in praise of the United States, the absence of a Wilberforce was given pride of place. In an Open Letter to Henry Hunt, one of the leading reformers in England, Cobbett wrote from Long Island:

> And then, to see a free country for once, and to see every labourer with plenty to eat and drink! Think of that! And never to see the hang-dog face of a tax-gatherer! Think of that! No long-sworded and whiskered captains. No judges escorted from town to town and sitting under a guard of Dragoons. No packed juries of

---

[57] *Political Register* 32, 15 November 1817.

tenants. No Cannings, Liverpools, Castlereaghs, Eldons, Ellenboroughs, or Sidmouths. No Wilberforces. Think of that!   No Wilberforces![58]

---

[58] *Political Register* 34, 3 October 1818.

10

Spanish America: Thomas Paine

Cobbett lived and farmed on Long Island for twenty-seven months, from May 1817 to October 1819. His family came to join him in the autumn of 1817 but returned to England early the following summer, leaving his eldest son, William, who had come over with his father from the start, and his third son, James, behind with their father. Towards the end of Cobbett's stay William junior returned home, and during Cobbett's last months in America only James, then aged 16, remained with him. Little is known of why the family found life in Long Island unsatisfactory, but it seems that the house in North Hempstead was somewhat primitive. "As to our living *here*", Cobbett wrote to his eldest daughter after she had returned home, "in a way suitable to my state of life, is out of the question. Simply to preserve *life* and *health* is all that reason or common sense will permit me to go to the expense of".[1] When the Act suspending Habeas Corpus expired in 1818, Cobbett was urged by his fellow reformers in England to return home, but a number of reasons were responsible for his extending his stay. Life on Long Island gave him the freedom to embark on a number of projects which he hoped would be financially successful: his books *A Year's Residence in The United States*, *The American Gardener* and *A Grammar of the English Language*

---

[1] Letter to his daughter Anne, June 19, 1818, (Nuffield Library, Oxford).

were all written and published before he returned home. Cobbett had a number of debts hanging over him (his enthusiasm for his farm in Botley had led him constantly to overstretch his resources) and he had been forced to borrow extensively to pay his fine and the high cost of his rooms in Newgate and simultaneously to keep his family of seven children. Cobbett also hoped, while in America, to recover some of the losses he had sustained during his previous sojourn in Philadelphia.

Cobbett lived on Long Island during the period which, in the United States, has been termed the Era of Good Feelings. After the Peace of Ghent and the final ending of the Napoleonic Wars, many of the reasons for divisions in the nation had disappeared. Once the European war was over, the pro-English (and anti-French) and the pro-French (and anti-English) factions necessarily ceased to exist, and the secessionist movement in New England during the war of 1812 had come to an ignominious end with the crushing defeat of the British at New Orleans. When President Madison's term of office expired in 1816, he was succeeded by James Monroe, his Secretary of State, just as Madison himself, Secretary of State in the previous administration, had succeeded Jefferson in 1808. When Cobbett arrived in America in 1817, the Democratic Party had held the reins of government without a break since Jefferson's election, in 1800, and the feeling of relief at the ending of all the restraints and indignities which the nation had suffered at the hands of both the belligerents during the twenty-two years of the European conflict, coupled with a justifiable pride that America had resisted the might of the British navy and the seasoned veterans of the British army, was shared by and tended to unite the whole country.

So in this second period Cobbett spent in the United States, we have from his pen no vivid descriptions of what went on in Congress, no wicked vignettes of the protagonists in the debates, no feuds with newspaper editors, or judges, or doctors, or Spanish dons. Even when he failed to recover the losses he had sustained in the Law Courts of Pennsylvania in the 1790s, we find a surprising absence of recrimination.

But, though careful to steer clear of any involvement in the internal affairs of the American government, Cobbett did, while he was in America, embroil himself in American foreign policy over the question of the United States' attitude to the Spanish American colonies which were at the time engaged in a struggle for independence from Spain. The vicissitudes Spain suffered during the Napoleonic Wars, invaded by France, riven with internal dissensions, and used as a battlefield by the English during Wellington's advance into France in 1813 and 1814, necessarily weakened her authority over her possessions in the New World. With the colonists already chafing under mercantile restrictions and the preference given to officials sent over from the mother country to those of the colonists themselves, there broke out a series of revolts throughout Central and South America in 1809 and 1810 against the Spanish administrations. When the Bourbon monarchy was re-established after Napoleon's first surrender in 1814, Spain, now with a fleet and army at her disposal, succeeded in restoring some semblance of colonial rule in most of her territories in the New World. However in 1817 further risings in La Plata (Argentina), Colombia (then comprising the present Colombia and Panama, Ecuador and Venezuela) succeeded in overthrowing the restored Spanish administrations and declaring their territories to be independent republics owing no allegiance to Spain.

These self-created republics naturally looked for recognition to the United States as the nation which had, by its own revolution of 1776, blazed the way for the independence of the New World from the Old, and it is probably true to say that the great majority of the American people echoed the sentiments of Henry Clay, the speaker of the House of Representatives, who saw the revolt of the Spanish patriots as "the glorious spectacle of eighteen millions of people struggling to burst their chains and be free". The government itself was more cautious. After 1815, with the outstanding differences with Britain over her northern borders being hammered out by Commissioners appointed under the Treaty of Ghent, the United States could turn her attention to the differences with Spain over her southern borders — those between Louisiana and the Floridas in the east, and between Louisiana and Texas (then part of Mexico) in the west, neither of which had been clearly defined at the time of the Louisiana Purchase. In an earlier chapter brief mention was made of the lax and unsatisfactory nature of the Spanish administration in the Floridas which allowed Creek Indians to harass American settlers along the border, and of the actions of Andrew Jackson in 1808-10 in crushing the Indians followed by the virtual annexation by the United States of part of the Spanish territory of West Florida.

It had long been the aim of the United States to gain possession of both East and West Florida, and negotiations to this end were begun early in 1818 with Spain. In the opinion of the American government, this was a greater priority than to accede to the request of the South American republics for recognition as independent states. At this time, recognition would have jeopardised all negotiations with Spain and antagonised all the Great Powers in Europe who supported Spain in her efforts to re-establish her authority in her colonies. On the other hand, there was strong pressure in Congress and in the country as a whole to recognise the de facto Spanish republics and to give aid to those Spanish patriots who were still engaged in a struggle with their colonial rulers. Individual Americans had from the start of the revolts been active in supplying arms and fitting out ships to support the patriots and the United States government thought it necessary, in order to avoid a break with Spain during her negotiations over the Floridas, to pass a law entitled "An Act more effectively to preserve the neutral relations of the United States". This forbade American citizens to give any succour or aid to colonists in revolt against any country with which the United States was at peace. It was at this point that Cobbett entered the scene.

Cobbett's detestation of all the restored dynasties in Europe led him strongly to sympathise with the Spanish revolutionaries and to deplore the action of the American government making it a criminal offence for an American citizen to aid them. He saw the recent Act as favouring Old Spain; although professedly neutral, by forbidding the arming or fitting out of ships to commit hostilities, the Act denied arms and assistance to the Spanish revolutionaries, whose only source of supply was from neutral powers. Yet it allowed the use of American ports to Spanish ships because, in quelling disturbances in her colonies Spain was not technically at war with a country with which the United States was at peace. It is easy to perceive that Cobbett was now in a position of some delicacy. If he were to condemn the American government for aiding a Bourbon King against a people struggling for their freedom, he would be attacking a government which, in other respects, he greatly admired, be criticising a nation which had afforded him protection from persecution in his own country, and be taking sides in internal dissensions within the United States. His resolution of the problem was to use an instrument which had served him so well in the past in publicizing his views — an appeal to his own Sovereign, the Prince Regent, but this time not by an Open Letter, but by a formal Petition.

Cobbett's Petition to the Prince Regent which, after it had reached England, he published in full in the *Political Register*, began by stating that the present situation in the Spanish colonies of South America was of great interest to England because it gave her the opportunity "to crown herself with the unfading glory of having given freedom to 20 millions of people, who now groan out their lives under the double-thonged scourge of Civil and Religious tyranny". An appeal to the head of a government which had sacrificed thousands of men and spent millions of money in restoring the Spanish monarchy, to aid that monarch's colonial subjects to rebel against him was impudence personified, particularly when one is aware of Cobbett's attitude to the British monarchy. But, as will be seen, Cobbett used the form of a Petition to disguise his criticisms of the American government under the cloak of a patriotic subject anxious to further his own country's interests. Using the stilted phrases of a subject appealing to his Sovereign, Cobbett introduced his exposition. "Deep is the sorrow of your Petitioner when he reflects on his incapacity to perform this task in a manner worthy of the subject", and he proceeded to detail the present state of the Spanish colonies in the New World. He reminded the Regent of their huge extent, four thousand miles in length and sometimes three thousand miles in breadth, containing vast mineral wealth and producing timber, cotton, tobacco, indigo and grains. Much of this rich region was already in the hands of the Spanish patriots, and even in those areas where Old Spain had recovered some control, many of her Royalist troops were disaffected. One English frigate,

Cobbett maintained, carrying arms for the patriots would suffice to capture the port of La Vera Cruz in Mexico', and enable a country of seven to eight million people to free themselves from Spanish domination. In other areas, it needed only the provision of arms and "trifling naval forces" for the patriots to succeed. Having thus sketched in the background, Cobbett arrived at the crux of his Petition: that the recent Act of the United States to preserve neutral relations would, by cutting off aid and supplies to the Spanish patriots, enable Old Spain to re-establish her authority, and that this would be damaging to Britain's interests. Independent republics in Central and South America, free to trade with whomsoever they pleased, would provide a huge and ready market for British exports, and an almost inexhaustible supply of the raw materials and minerals Britain needed; whereas if they were restored to full colonial rule, all these benefits would accrue to Spain. It therefore behoved England, in her own interests, to recognise by the exchange of envoys those colonies which had succeeded in establishing de facto governments, and to render every assistance in her power to those engaged in throwing off the Spanish yoke.

In reading Cobbett's Petition it is important to keep in mind the audience he was addressing. Every British subject had a right to petition his Sovereign, and Cobbett's use of this right was cunningly contrived. He well knew that a Petition from "William Cobbett of Botley, in the County of Southampton, now residing at North Hempstead in the State of New York", a known calumniator of the government and a known purveyor of seditious doctrines, would have no hope of reaching the eyes of the Regent. He couched his views in the form of a Petition for quite other reasons. The quaint language of its title and the occasional deliberate lapses into stilted phraseology were a sure way of arresting his readers' attention, and, as in his previous Letters to the Prince Regent, it was his newspaper readers and not the Prince he was trying to convince. That it was particularly his American readers he had in mind is shown by the tact he used in explaining why the American government had passed its Act of Neutrality. That a government founded on a revolt against oppression, and granting citizenship to all who chose to live under its protection,

> that a government, thus implanted, thus growing up, thus extending its sheltering branches and dropping its nourishing fruits; that such a government should have voluntarily passed an Act punishing with severity such of its own citizens as may aid or abet the colonists of Spain, must necessarily excite throughout the world the utmost degree of sorrow and surprize."[2]

Yet, he maintained, in passing the Act, Congress had shown foresight and wisdom. Spanish America had abundant supplies of precisely the same goods as those that the United States exported and on which it depended for its prosperity. If it were freed from the mercantile restrictions imposed on it as a Spanish colony, it could usurp much of the trade and seriously diminish the customs duties that provided the United States with the bulk of its revenue. Nor should it be overlooked that Mexico, containing nearly as large a population as that of the whole of the United States, could, if it became independent and exploited its resources, become a maritime power and a powerful and possibly threatening neighbour of the United States. Therefore, Cobbett concluded, it was perfectly natural for the Congress to feel "anxiety and alarm" at the prospect of independent states on its borders.

---

[2] Petition of 17 October 1817 published in *Political Register 32*, 27 December 1817.

So in this Petition Cobbett skilfully steered a course which not only avoided any overt criticism of the American government, but gave him an opportunity to praise its wisdom and express his admiration for the principles upon which it was founded. Yet by stressing how the recent Act harmed the cause of the Spanish patriots, and attributing the motives behind it to self interest, Cobbett was indirectly appealing to and siding with those Americans who deplored the betrayal of the Spanish patriots as an act unworthy of a government based on the ideals of freedom. Furthermore, by underlining the fact that if England were to forestall the Americans in recognising those colonies that had overthrown the Spanish administration and in giving aid to those others still engaged in their struggle for independence, she would become the protector and ally of the whole of Central and South America, his intention was partly to alert the Americans to the threat this would impose to the security of the United States. If independent republics on her borders were a threat, how much more so would they be if they were closely allied to Great Britain and could look to her to support them in any differences that arose between them and the United States.

A few weeks later Cobbett returned to the subject again by publishing two Open Letters to his fellow reformer in England, Major Cartwright. This time he could express somewhat different feelings, talking, as it were, to someone who was likely to share his views. In the first he expressed his sorrow at the passing of America's Act of Neutrality denying Americans the opportunity to aid the Spanish patriots, and he followed this up by a second in which he said he was thrilled to find his sentiments echoed in Congress where it had been decided to institute an enquiry to ensure that the Spanish people in the colonies received a just observance of their rights from the United States. "But this"; he went on, "is nothing to what followed, this is only a glimpse through the gloom". In a speech in Congress, Henry Clay had compared the unfortunate position of the Spanish patriots to that of the American colonists during their War of Independence. Here, in this speech, which he published in full, he told Major Cartwright

> you will see the Sun of Liberty dissipating all the clouds of every description that obscured his rays;

> Here was this gentleman, plainly and honestly asserting all that I had asserted, and a great deal more; the assertion of the people's real sympathy with the Spanish Colonies; the assertion that the measures of the Government, had all been in favour of Old Spain.[3]

Particularly gratifying to him, also, was that during the debates in Congress, his Petition to the Prince Regent had been quoted to support the arguments of those who favoured the cause of the Spanish Patriots. He made plain his own views on the refusal of the American government to receive Envoys from those Spanish colonies which had succeeded in establishing independent governments, while Envoys from Old Spain were granted full diplomatic privileges.

> Old Spain: the beloved Ferdinand; his most Catholic Majesty; that pink of the Holy Alliance: that devout worshipper of the Virgin Mary: that darling son of his Holiness the Pope: that pattern of Princes: he has an envoy here; his Envoy is received by the Government of the United States. Why then, I should be glad to know, are not the Envoys of the New Republics received, if they have, with regard to neutral nations, "equal rights" with that blessed son of the Church and restorer of the Holy Inquisition?[4]

---

[3] *Political Register* 33, 21 February 1818.
[4] *Political Register* 33, 14 February 1818.

(Once again, it should be noted, by addressing his remarks to an Englishman, Cobbett steered clear of embroiling himself in American politics.)

After these letters of February 1818, Cobbett made no further reference to the subject of Spanish America while he was in the United States. The fate of the Spanish colonists was not to be resolved until after Cobbett returned to England, and his involvement with the controversies which surrounded their eventual recognition will be discussed later. But before following Cobbett back across the Atlantic there remains to be discussed the motives which led him to disinter the coffin of Thomas Paine from its grave near New York and bring it back with him to England.

It will be remembered that during his first sojourn in America Cobbett had, as Peter Porcupine, attacked Paine as a supporter of the French Revolution, as a calumniator of George Washington, and as an infidel. His first realisation that his condemnations of Paine might have been based on a misconception of his true nature occurred when he read Paine's *Decline and Fall of the English System of Finance* shortly after he returned to England in 1800. When he read Paine's treatise on money he greatly regretted his early writings against him. Now that Cobbett had come to consider the government of the United States to be a model for the Old World to copy, his admiration of Paine for his great contribution to the freeing of America from its colonial dependence on Great Britain needs no explanation. Referring to Paine's statement in one of his Crisis papers during the War of Independence that "We fight not to enslave, but to set a country free and to make room upon the earth for honest men", Cobbett wrote; "He himself contributed more than any other man to *make room for us*: to make for us a place of safety; to prepare for us a place of refuge from dungeons and banishment bills"[5]. And later "No one man, since the world began, ever produced so great effect on the minds of mankind".[6] As for Paine's *The Rights of Man*, which Cobbett had criticised for justifying revolt against established governments, the arguments put forward in that book were just those which Cobbett was now using for a complete reform of the system of government in Britain.

While in Newgate prison, Cobbett had taken up the cause of a Daniel Eaton who had at that time been stood in the pillory and condemned to prison for publishing *The Age of Reason* which was proscribed by law as blasphemous and subversive to Christian religion and morality. What aroused such deep rooted hostility to the book was Paine's open questioning of the divine origin of the Scriptures and his attack on the Christian churches which he accused of misinterpreting Christ's teachings, and of using religion as a means to dull the people into an acquiesence with their lot and make them obedient to their superiors. Even more dangerous was that Paine wrote in a language which ordinary people could readily understand. When Cobbett re-read *The Age of Reason* in prison, he realised that his previous denunciation of the book was based on false premises. As Peter Porcupine, he had equated Paine's book with the atheistical principles of the French Revolution. There, atheism had led to terror and persecution, and it was because Paine's thesis would, he believed, incite others to similar bloody outrages that he attacked the book so viciously. He saw it now in a very different light. Far from being the blasphemer he had supposed him to be, Paine, though questioning the divinity of Christ, honoured and revered his teachings, and his attack on Christianity was

---

[5] *Political Register* 35, 15 January 1820.
[6] *Ibid*.

an attack on the institutions of Christian churches, not on the teachings of Christ.

Cobbett's criticisms of churches and churchmen have been touched upon in previous chapters in his denunciation of the tithing system in England, and his attacks on the "Cossack Priesthood" of Massachusetts. Throughout his life, both before and after reading Paine, he was outspoken in exposing hypocrisy and cant wherever he found it, and Methodists, Quakers and Jews, as well as the Church of England, all came under the lash of his tongue. Paine's influence on his thinking on the far deeper questions of the authenticity of the Scriptures can clearly be discerned in his writings after he left Newgate, particularly in two series of articles he wrote in 1813 entitled "Ecce Homo" and "The Trinity".[7] But he was always to tread very carefully in his writings on religion, knowing that to be so much as tainted with blasphemy would immediately alienate a huge section of his readers. He subtly avoided any overt identification of his own views with those of Paine by adopting the stand that he, as one born and bred up in the Church of England, found Paine's arguments very difficult to refute, and calling on those better versed in theology than himself to supply him with an answer. Nor was he shy, whenever opportunity occurred, to mention that he was still awaiting a refutation.

Cobbett's debt to Paine was great: it was through Paine's writings on the subject of finance that he had first been alerted to the depths of corruption in the British government; it was Paine's clearly reasoned arguments in *The Rights of Man* that gave strength to and justification for his call for radical reform; and Cobbett felt that the presence of a republican government in the United States

---

[7] See *Political Register* 24, 4 December 1813.

where he was now enjoying the freedom to continue his fight for the rights of the labouring classes in England, was in part due to Paine's brilliant pamphleteering skills in rallying the American people during the War of Independence. As G K Chesterton perceptively observes of Cobbett:

> He found that Paine, of all men, and apparently alone among all men, had really tried to say some of these things that needed so excruciatingly to be said; and about which all mankind walked about gagged and in a ghastly silence. He had cruelly calumniated a man who might have been his friend and was certainly his ally. And it was too late to tell him so. For that which he had madly splashed with mud had already returned to dust, and Thomas Paine was dead.[8]

The caution which prevented Cobbett from openly endorsing the views put forward by Paine in his *The Age of Reason*, although perhaps justified by his belief that had he done so, all his subsequent writings would have been derided and ignored as coming from an atheist and a blasphemer, as Paine's had been, may have been influential in determining him to make reparation. But there is another fact to be taken into consideration. Paine's life after he returned from France to America in 1802 had been a sad one. Although Jefferson, then President of the United States, received and befriended him, Paine found himself ostracised and subjected to a series of humiliations. His letter to George Washington accusing him of falsehood and treachery was never forgotten or forgiven, and his *The Age of Reason* caused him to be shunned by all professed Christians. For his services to the nation during the War of Independence the government had given him a small

---

[8] Chesterton, G K, *Cobbett* p 118, Hodder & Stoughton 1924.

estate at New Rochelle outside New York City. (This was, of course, before he had written his letter to George Washington or published his *The Age of Reason*.) Among other indignities he underwent after his return to America, he was refused the right to vote in elections on the grounds that he was not an American citizen, and when, finding it difficult to live on the income he received from his estate, he applied for a small pension, his application was refused. He ended his life in lodgings in New York City and died in 1809. Such was the effect of his writings on religion that he was denied a Christian burial and his remains were interred in unconsecrated ground in a corner of his place in New Rochelle.

Cobbett's very genuine love of his country and his own people, caused him to view with deep concern the fate of his fellow-Englishman buried in an obscure and untended grave, thousands of miles from his native land. If Paine's remains were to be interred in his own country with a fitting memorial, Cobbett felt that he would have gone some way to make amends to the man he had so greatly wronged and now so greatly admired. His feelings about the disposal of his own remains after his own death give an insight into his action: at the end of his book *A History of the Protestant Reformation,* itself a searing indictment of the Church of England, he wrote that in spite of all he had written against that Church, he hoped that "Having the remains of most dearly beloved parents lying in a Protestant churchyard", he trusted his survivors would place his by their side.

> The man had been buried in his land of exile; and Cobbett, himself an exile, realised as few could realise, the horror of dying far away from home. He believed, as only he could believe, that the one perfect act of piety which could be done to the body of an Englishman was

to bring it back to England..... Cobbett was a son of the earth, or what used to be called a child of nature; and these rude and natural people are all ritualists.[9]

The first intimation of Cobbett's desire to make amends was expressed in an Open Letter he addressed to Major Cartwright in January 1818. Cartwright was at this time urging him to come back to England to lend his weight to the growing movement for Reform, and Cobbett's reply stated that he had first another task to fulfil.

> However, there is one thing, which if I have life and health, I am resolved to do while in this country: to write an account of the Life, Labours and Death of that famous Englishman, THOMAS PAINE; and, perhaps, to collect and republish the whole of his writings complete in a Cheap form and with some explanatory notes to *The Rights of Man* particularly. I am here upon the spot. I have within my reach all the means of correct information. There are only Long Island Sound and a very few miles of land between me and the spot where he died. Justice to his memory, justice to the cause of freedom, justice to the country that gave him birth, justice to his friends on both sides of the Atlantic, demand at my hands an earnest endeavour to perform this task in a manner worthy of the subject.[10]

Stories current about Paine's last years in New York included accusations that he ended his days as a drunkard living in filthy conditions, that he had lived with a married woman and fathered children by her, and even that he had been overheard conversing with the devil. False as these rumours were, they give some indication of how he was looked upon towards the end of his life: he was feared and hated, hissed in the streets, and ended his days almost as

---

[9] Chesterton, G K, *op cit*, p 119-20.
[10] *Political Register* 33, 24 January 1818.

an outcast. When Cobbett published in his *Political Register* his intention to write a life of Paine and to republish his works, the old fears and antipathies were still alive, even though he had now been dead for nine years, and a Quaker, Charles Collins, visited Cobbett telling him that he had proof that on his deathbed Paine had retracted all he had said and written against the Holy Bible.

> I laughed at him and sent him away. But he returned again and again to the charge. He wanted me to promise him that I would say 'that it was said' that Paine had recanted. 'No', said I 'but I will say that you say it, and that you tell a lie unless you prove the truth of what you say; and if you do prove the truth of what you say, if you do that, I shall gladly insert the fact'.[11]

After a great deal of prodding from Cobbett, Charles Collins at last produced a document which he alleged was the statement of a Quaker woman who had lived near Paine and had visited him during his last illness. Among other things, she said that she had sometimes found Paine in an attitude of prayer, and that when she had told Paine that she had begun to read his *The Age of Reason*, but finding that it "estranged her mind from all that is right" had thereupon burnt it, Paine replied that he wished that all had done so, for "if ever the Devil had an agent on earth, I have been one". Armed with this document, Cobbett searched out the woman in New York. She turned out to be the servant-maid of a neighbour of Paine's who had been sent across to Paine's house from time to time with little delicacies while he was ill. She was now living in a back room up one flight of stairs, earning her living by sewing. Cobbett read her Charles Collins' statement of what she had said "stopping at several points to ask her

---

[11] *Political Register* 36, 19 February 1820.

if it were true".

> She shuffled; she evaded, she equivocated, she warded off; she affected not to understand the paper, not to remember. The result was: that it was so long ago that she could not speak positively; and that she had never given 'friend Charley' authority to say any thing about the matter in her name. "Oh! No! Friend, I tell thee that I have no recollection of any person or anything that I saw at Thomas Paine's house".[12]

Cobbett at once sought out Charles Collins to "bring his nose to the grindstone", but Charley "though so pious a man, and doubtless in great haste to get to everlasting bliss, had moved out of the city for fear of the Fever. And thus he escaped me, who sailed from New York in four days afterwards."[13]

Before he sailed, Cobbett had obtained permission to disinter Paine's coffin, and with this addition to his baggage he arrived in Liverpool on November 21st 1819. Although the sales of his *Political Register* in England had somewhat fallen off during his stay in America, he still had a wide following: huge crowds were waiting on the quay to receive him, and a public dinner in his honour was organised by his fellow radicals. Amidst such publicity, the news that he had brought back Paine's bones was seized upon by the press and

> set loose a concourse of rhymesters and cartoonists who celebrated the exploit with extreme gusto. This was not wholly disinterested sprightliness of wit; for Paine's name was regularly made the political synonym for all forms of atheism, treason and immorality, and the chance of linking Cobbett's name with it was too

---

[12] *Ibid.*
[13] *Ibid.*

good for any political opponent to miss.¹⁴

The sequel to this story is a mixture of tragedy and farce. George Spater in his biography of Cobbett writes that Cobbett thought he was bringing back the bones "of the author of *The Decline and Fall of the English System of Finance* but discovered that to most Englishmen he had brought back the bones of the author of *The Age of Reason*, the book that defended deism and taught that the Bible was largely mythology".¹⁵ Although the second half of this sentence is undoubtedly true, the first half needs some qualification: Cobbett wanted Paine to be remembered quite as much for his exposure of hypocrisy under the cloak of religion and for his advocacy of the rights of man, as for his writings on economics. The furore which surrounded his return with Paine's bones Cobbett himself described in a letter which he published in the *Political Register* to his son James whom he had left behind in America to look after his publishing interests there. He told him that

> about three hundred newspapers had proclaimed me to be coming with a design to carry the bones at the head of a Revolutionary army. They had called me blasphemer and had prefixed to my name every appellation calculated to fill the minds of the people against me. The Times and the Courier newspapers, more especially, teemed with the most abominable calumnies, descending, at last, to sheer execrations.¹⁶

Receiving news that Cobbett was shortly arriving in England from America, *The Times* wrote a long article on November 17th. "This rascal is now returning, or said to be returning to England. He pretends that he has pulled TOM PAINE'S carcass out of the earth by night and is

---

¹⁴ Cole, G D H, *op cit*, p 236.
¹⁵ Spater, George, *op cit*, Vol 2, p 387.
¹⁶ *Political Register* 35, 27 January 1820.

bringing it over to England with him", and poured scorn on the notion that the bone's were really those of Paine. On the next two days, November 18th and 19th, (and this was still before Cobbett actually landed) *The Times* devoted two articles to publishing at length Cobbett's earlier writings condemning Paine and his *The Age of Reason*, ending by quoting his own words that all that is base and malignant can be summed up "by the single monosyllable PAINE". Cobbett was by no means exaggerating in his Open Letter to his son when he spoke of the efforts made "to fill the minds of the people against him" and of the fear of the authorities of his influence. After his enthusiastic reception at Liverpool, he was invited by reformers to visit Manchester. Manchester had been the scene of a huge mass meeting some three months previously, when, in an effort to disperse the crowds, at least eleven peaceful demonstrators had been killed and many hundreds injured. This so-called massacre of Peterloo had inflamed the people, and enormous precautions were taken to ensure that no such meeting would be repeated. A reporter on the spot wrote that "a troop of the 15th Hussars and a large body of infantry and, I believe, two field pieces were stationed close to the New Bailey by which Cobbett was expected to pass. Other bodies of soldiery were posted in other quarters of the town".[17] Cobbett wisely decided to refuse the invitation and did not pass through the town. But even two months later, *The Times* felt it necessary to return to the attack. On January 6th 1820, it wrote:

> As to the bones which he calls THOMAS PAINE'S (this, we may observe nobody believes), but as to the bones to whatsoever animal they may have belonged, we will advise what to do with them. There is nearly opposite to Shoreditch church a sign to the effect "The

---

[17] Quoted in *The Times*, December 2, 1819.

best prices given for old bones". Thither let Cobbett take them, and sell them for as much as they will fetch; and let the world hear no more about them.

For some months after his return to England Cobbett was optimistic that when the furore had died down he would be able to carry out his intention to inter Paine's coffin in England and collect enough money to build a fitting memorial over the grave. He tried to organise a huge dinner on Paine's birthday, January 29th, at the Crown and Anchor in London where, he believed, "there would have been such a company as this Crown and Anchor never yet saw and never will see". His plan was frustrated by the Landlord refusing permission to use his rooms under the pretext that the law did not allow money to be taken for admission to meetings for political discussion. "Envy, hatred, malice, revenge, fear; but above all Envy, mean black dastardly Envy, interfered to prevent the triumph of reason and of truth, and the Landlord refused us the house".[18] Cobbett also spoke of his intention to put Paine's hair into gold rings and himself to watch the women he employed to do so, in order that he could write in his own hand a certificate on parchment to attest that they were genuine. These rings he would sell at a guinea a piece above the cost of the gold and the workmanship, and the money received would be put towards the cost of the memorial.[19] But this plan, like that of the dinner at the Crown and Anchor, came to naught.

The subject of Cobbett and Paine's bones was never allowed to lapse. In a speech in the House of Lords on emigration, Earl Grosvenor referred to Cobbett's having brought back to England "Paine's miserable bones". After

---

[18] *Political Register* 36, 27 January 1820.
[19] See *Political Register* 35, 27 January 1820.

chiding him for his speech and having once again praised the prosperity of the United States, the cheapness and abundance of food and clothing, so that "even the servant girls in New York are seen sweeping down the doorways dressed in China crepe; nay even the *black girls* are frequently seen wearing them", Cobbett went on to say.

> And now, my Lord, does not common justice call on us to remember, and to do honour to the memory of the man who took the lead in the glorious work of American Independence? That man whose bones I have done myself the great honour to bring to this country?[20]

Far from despising these bones, Cobbett maintained that the people of England had made hundreds upon hundreds of applications to him to see the relics, and "and as your Lordship has yet to see, they will honour them more than they have ever honoured any thing dead or alive". Countering the objection that a man who had written against religion should have no memorial, Cobbett reminded the earl that

> The Scotch, who have been extolled for superiority in morality and religion, have erected fine monuments to David Hume, though he was a notorious atheist. But then he was a good politician; that is to say an enemy of freedom and an advocate of despots. So is Gibbon praised, though a deadly enemy of Christian religion, but he too was against giving rights to the people.[21]

The publicity given to Paine and his writings by Cobbett's exploit struck fear in the government, and in January 1820, just two months after Cobbett's return, a bill was passed by Parliament "for the more effectual prevention and punishment of blasphemy and seditious libels". In

---

[20] *Political Register* 35, 15 January 1820.
[21] *Political Register* 35, 15 January 1820.

retaliation, Cobbett published an Open Letter to the Bishop of Landaff who had strongly supported the bill in the House of Lords and who had referred to Paine's *The Age of Reason* as peculiarly dangerous because it was written "in a style suited to the lowest capacity". Cobbett denied that any part of the book was blasphemous. "Though Mr Paine is no Christian, he is no blasphemer; he offers no indignity to God himself". Indeed, Cobbett continued, Paine professed a belief in God and "calls on his readers to reverence his name, and that, too, in a strain of eloquence the equal of which I never happened to meet with in any sermon, or homily, or any other composition written by layman or clergyman". In the same debate, Earl Grosvenor had said of *The Age of Reason* that it was destitute of argument. Cobbett pounced to the attack. If there be no argument in it, how can it be dangerous? he asked. Hundreds of pounds were spent on publishing religious tracts in England supporting Christianity and "Are the people so very perverse and obdurate as to be blind and deaf to what five millions of publications say on one side, in answer to one single publication?" Not only were Paine's writings proscribed, but everything was done to persuade the people to despise and detest him. Boys and girls twenty years ago, Cobbett said, were led on to burn Paine in effigy, and for some time burning Tom Paine had supplanted burning Guy Fawkes on November 5th.

> And after all this, do we, my Lord, come to the conclusion that it is necessary to make it a crime to put forth this book of Mr Paine, which book is (as your Lordship says) wholly destitute of argument?[22]

But in spite of this spirited defence, Cobbett had to accept defeat. Parliament, Bishops, newspapers and cartoonists made it impossible for Cobbett to carry out his design,

---

[22] *Political Register* 35, 27 January 1820.

and we find him a year later acknowledging that the time is not auspicious and sadly accepting the fact that he may die before he can accomplish the great task, but with his customary optimism, he wrote that if that were to happen, "there will be alive those that will perform this sacred duty in my stead".[23] The bones remained in his possession until his death, moving with him wherever he lived and last heard of at his farm near Farnham where he died. Cobbett died in debt and the bones were lost during the sale of his effects in 1835. Nor did Cobbett fulfil his intention of writing Paine's biography and republishing his works. It was not until the twentieth century that a group of Americans erected a monument to Paine in his birthplace at Thatcham.

The extreme virulence with which the campaign was waged to ridicule Cobbett's action is a striking tribute to the powerful arguments of *The Age of Reason*, and also to the influence the government believed Cobbett himself exerted in Britain, but Cobbett's quixotic action in attempting to make amends utterly failed in its intention. For many years he was depicted in cartoons as staggering under a coffin or holding a bag in his hand labelled "Tom Paine's bones", and by associating Paine's name with that figure of fun, the press was partially successful in its efforts. Though Cobbett retained and indeed greatly extended his influence among the people of Britain, Paine and his works remain to this day unjustly neglected by the great majority of his countrymen.

---

[23] *Political Register* 40, 8 September 1821.

11

The Monroe Doctrine

After Cobbett returned home in November 1819, he soon found himself plunged into the upheavals of domestic politics. Before he left England he had resolved to contest the seat at Coventry at the next election, and the death of George III in January 1820 and the accession of the Prince Regent to the throne as George IV, made it necessary to call a General Election in March of that year. Cobbett, as had been expected, polled only a small proportion of the votes — his refusal to treat and bribe electors alienating a large proportion of the electorate — but the expenses he had to incur in the contest was one of the causes which forced him to declare himself bankrupt in the spring of 1820.

A second cause was the passing of the so-called Six Acts by Parliament in December 1819 and January 1820. The suspension of Habeas Corpus from March 1817 to January 1818 and the Acts restricting public meetings and the freedom of the press, had been insufficient to quell the demands for reform. Cheap publications, many of them clandestine, were issued in greater numbers than ever. The Six Acts which succeeded them in 1819 and 1820, though not suspending the Habeas Corpus Act, were in some ways more draconian in their powers, and among them was one which subjected pamphlets and newspapers issued more than once a month and costing less than sixpence, to a stamp duty of fourpence a copy. This meant for Cobbett a heavy fall in the sales of the cheap twopenny edition of his *Political Register*, and a consequent diminution of his income. This, added to his expenses in the Coventry election and the drain of his resources by having to maintain himself in Long Island and his family in England, plus the debts he had already incurred before leaving home in 1817, left him no option but to default on his debts. His farm at Botley passed out of his hands, and the family rented a house with a few acres of ground on the western outskirts of London.

Cobbett was now fifty-seven years old, but the last fifteen years of his life — he died in 1835 at the age of seventy-two, were to be even more active than the previous fifty seven. Freed, albeit with reluctance, from the ties and cares of farming, he devoted the remainder of his life to Parliamentary Reform, achieving his ambition to become a Member of Parliament in 1832, a few months before his sixty-ninth birthday. Throughout the 1820s he travelled extensively through the counties of England to see for himself the state of the country and to attend and address the large meetings that were being organised throughout the kingdom to petition Parliament for redress of grievances. In January 1822, his daughter Anne wrote to her brother James who was still in America but was to return home later in the year,

> Papa is going about the country, making fine speeches at great dinners and making such a stir as you never heard. He and John are just gone off to Huntingdon where he has been invited to a dinner, and there are all sorts of preparations making to do him honour.[1]

Cobbett reported on these travels in his *Political Register* and it was these articles which were later collected together and incorporated into his most famous book for

---
[1] Quoted in Spater, G S, *William Cobbett: the Poor Man's Friend*, Vol 2, p 416, CUP, 1982.

later generations, *Rural Rides*. In 1832 Cobbett visited Scotland, and during the Parliamentary recess of 1834 toured Ireland. Throughout his journeyings he preached the need for a reform of Parliament, and we find him at the age of seventy-one addressing packed meetings in the Fishamble Theatre in Dublin on three successive nights, before embarking on an extended tour of Ireland and further speechmaking.

Yet Cobbett still found time to keep himself abreast of current affairs and the *Political Register* continued week by week to carry comments on the major political issues at home and abroad. Among them, those concerning the United States were seldom neglected, and Cobbett had much to say regarding the fate of the Spanish Colonies in Central and South America. Shortly after returning home, Cobbett informed his readers that during his sojourn in Long Island:

> Though living in an obscure part of the country, gentlemen from South America, agents from the Provinces, found me out. I had opportunity of knowing every thing relating to the contest, relating to the views and wishes of the insurgents; and I was put in possession of numerous most interesting facts, accompanied with an anxious expression of the desire of the parties that I would cause them to be communicated to the government in England.[2]

The general election of 1820 in which Cobbett was unsuccessful at Coventry, resulted in little change in the government. Lord Liverpool, Prime Minister since 1812, retained his Ministry, and the only major changes occurred two years later when George Canning succeeded Lord Castlereagh as the Foreign Secretary and Robert Peel

---

[2] *Political Register* 36, 19 February 1820.

succeeded Viscount Sidmouth as Home Secretary. Both Castlereagh and Sidmouth had been the special objects of Cobbett's attacks on the government, for he considered them to be the prime architects in the repressive Acts of 1817 which had forced him to flee the country, and of the Six Acts which had succeeded them in 1819 and 1820. How he judged Canning, who was to play a major role in the relations between Britain and the United States over the South American question, will be seen in the course of this chapter.

Events in Europe in the years 1819 and 1820 were greatly to influence the outcome of the struggle in the Spanish colonies for independence. It was at this time that liberal elements in Europe began to revolt against the new order imposed by the great powers after Napoleon's defeat. Beginning in the German states, revolts broke out in Naples, Portugal, Greece and Spain. In Spain, Ferdinand VII ("the beloved Ferdinand, his most Catholic Majesty, that darling son of his Holiness the Pope" as Cobbett had earlier described him) was forced to accept a more democratic and liberal constitution. The great powers, Russia, Austria, Prussia and France herself, now under her restored monarchy, viewed the success of the Spanish in wresting concessions from their king with alarm. They considered armed intervention to restore to Ferdinand VII the powers he had been forced to relinquish, but dissensions among them, and the refusal of Great Britain to support them, led to their taking no immediate action. Two years later, in 1822, Ferdinand VII, hoping to profit by continuing divisions in the country, attempted to stage a coup d'état. He was defeated, made virtually a prisoner in his own land, and shorn of his remaining powers. The success of a revolution which had replaced a Bourbon king by a liberal constitution struck fear into all the

European monarchies. But it was France most of all who viewed the success of the Spanish liberals as a threat to her existence.

> Ferdinand's predicament greatly increased the pressure on the ultra-royalist government of France to intervene in Spain. The French were still sore from the humiliation of defeat. The desire for some assertion of national independence was strong and what better excuse than to rescue a Bourbon prince and restore him to his throne? There was also the danger that if revolutionary principles triumphed in Spain, they might spread across the Pyrenees to France.[3]

In April 1823 the French invaded Spain. By October France had succeeded in restoring Ferdinand VII to power, and for the next five years Spain was occupied by French troops and the Spanish monarchy was secure. The disorder into which Spain fell at this time still further weakened her authority in her remaining colonies in the New World, and by 1822 the whole of mainland Spanish America, with the exception of Upper Peru, had established *de facto* governments independent of the mother country. But the restoration of a firm government after France's invasion and occupation of Spain posed problems. Would France and Spain combine to attempt to restore colonial rule in Spain's provinces in the New World? Throughout the convulsions in Spain and Spanish America, the island of Cuba had remained under the control of Spanish administration. With Cuba as a base it would be possible for France and Spain to assemble troops and ships and launch offensives against the rebellious colonies. It was this possibility that exercised the minds of the governments of both Great Britain and the United States. Both deplored the invasion of Spain by France, but for different reasons.

---

[3] Hinde, W, *George Canning*, p 325, Collins, 1973.

Great Britain's stance was complex. With such deep unrest at home, the government did not look favourably on the success of Spanish liberals, and though paying lip service to liberal constitutions, saw the rebellion in Old Spain as a threat to kingly government. Castlereagh, Foreign Secretary until 1822, had refused to join the European powers in an attempt to restore to Ferdinand the powers he lost in 1820, not because he approved of the revolution in that country, but because owing to the huge debts England had incurred during the Napoleonic Wars, the government was unwilling to increase that debt by intervening in the affairs of another European nation which at the time seemed to impose no immediate threat to Britain. His successor, Canning, a younger and far more flamboyant character than his aristocratic predecessor in the Foreign Office, loudly condemned France's invasion of Spain in 1823 and strove to persuade her to withdraw her troops from that country, but his efforts were in vain. It was always in Britain's interests to keep the balance of power evenly distributed in Europe, and after her wars with France in the eighteenth and nineteenth centuries, she feared the results of a powerful alliance between France and Spain. Throughout this period, Britain stood aloof from the absolutist monarchies of Russia, Prussia, Austria, France and Spain who were determined that all stirrings of revolt should be ruthlessly crushed, and equally aloof from the strivings of the subjected peoples of Europe to replace those autocratic governments with more liberal and democratic regimes.

The United States, as might be expected, welcomed the rise of liberal sentiments in Europe, and once she had succeeded in her negotiations with Spain and obtained possession of the Floridas in 1819 for a sum of $5 million, she was free to be more open in her attitude towards the Spanish Patriots. But just as Britain kept aloof from openly supporting the liberal elements in Old Spain, so did the United States refrain from actively supporting the Spanish Patriots in the New World. By this time Henry Clay's vision of "eighteen million of peoples struggling to be free" was not shared by all Americans. John Quincy Adams, the Secretary of State's far more realistic appraisal of the situation sums up the official attitude of the American administration. He saw "no prospect that they would establish free or liberal institutions of government. Arbitrary power, military and ecclesiastical, was stamped upon their habits, and upon all their institutions. Civil dissension was infused into all their seminal principles".[4] There was, in fact, little basis for the comparison between the revolutions in Spanish America and the earlier War of Independence in the North. Except that both were aimed to throw off colonial rule, there were few parallels to be drawn. Although the Spanish Patriots may have mouthed some of the phrases of the Declaration of Independence and Paine's *The Crisis* Papers, most of the Spanish Provinces were feudal in outlook and hierarchical in structure. Spanish America had never been a refuge for the persecuted or disaffected as North America had been, for instance, for the Puritans in New England, for the Catholics in Maryland, or for the Quakers in Pennsylvania: hence the ideals of creating democratically elected self-governing communities which exercised so powerful an influence during the War of Independence on its northern neighbour, was almost absent in the Spanish south. There the revolutions resulted in power passing from the officials sent over from Old Spain mainly to the long settled landed proprietors and had led to the imposition of dictatorial regimes constantly in danger of being overthrown and

---

[4] Morison, *op cit*, pp 411-412.

replaced by rival factions.

Yet whatever reservations the government of the United States may have had about the new forms of government being established in the former Spanish provinces, it was adamant in opposing any intervention by Europe and, confident that the convulsions in Spain would preclude any attempt at recolonisation, the United States recognised the independence of La Plata, Chile, Peru, Colombia and Mexico in 1822.

The invasion of Spain by France and the restoration of the Spanish monarchy to power in 1823 was as unwelcome to the United States as it was to Britain. America foresaw the possibility of a Franco-Spanish expedition to the New World which would bring in its train all the ugly questions of the rights of neutrals which had so harmed America during the twenty-two years of the Napoleonic Wars. The War of 1812 seemed to many in the United States the culmination of the previous War of Independence in that America had finally proved that she was a nation powerful enough to defend her integrity as a sovereign power. She was now determined to maintain that integrity and to frustrate any intervention in the affairs of the New World by any European power.

The interests of the United States therefore coincided with those of Britain. And for Britain, as strong a motive as her fear of a powerful France allied with Spain was the benefit she had gained by her commercial links with the newly independent states in South America. If they were recolonised commercial restrictions would ensue. Cobbett's vision of the advantages to Britain of independent states in South America, which he had expressed so forcefully in his Petition to the Prince Regent in 1817, had been proved to be true. British merchants had early seized the opportunities of trading with the de facto governments, foreseeing a huge new market for manufactured goods which would amply compensate for the loss of markets in the United States which had resulted from the growth of manufacturing in America during the years of the Embargo and the War of 1812. Even though the British had not granted the new states formal recognition, by 1822 British exports to South America actually exceeded those to the United States; British merchants had established commercial houses and obtained mining concessions in many of the new states and British financiers had been active in providing loans to the *de facto* governments. Until the invasion of Spain by France in 1823, the weakness of the Spanish government in Europe had seemed to guarantee the continuing existence of the de facto governments, but after the restoration of Ferdinand VII by the French, the prospects were far less auspicious. Ominously, the French ambassador to Britain, the Prince de Polignac, declared: "that in the interests of humanity, it would be worthy of the European governments to concert together the means of calming, in those distant and scarcely civilised regions, passions blinded by party spirit; and to endeavour to bring back a principle of union in government, whether monarchical or aristocratic, to a people amongst whom absurd and dangerous theories were now keeping up agitation and disunion".[5]

The new British Foreign Secretary, George Canning, aware of the great commercial advantages of free markets in South America, had been pressing for some time for a recognition of the Spanish republics, but the King and the ultra-Tories felt, as did Polignac of France and the other great powers of Europe, that recognition would be seen as condoning rebellion and would give encouragement to

---

[5] Quoted in Harriet Martineau, *The History of the Thirty Years of Peace* Vol II, Ch V.

rebellion nearer to home. But after 1823, the prospect of France aiding Spain to recover her colonies and even of taking over for herself some of Spain's former territories posed a serious threat to the government's desire to curb the power of France. Even the most intransigent Tories were forced to recognise the common interests of Britain and the United States in preventing any recolonisation in the New World, and Canning was encouraged to make overtures to America. One of his early moves in this direction was to take advantage of the arrival in Liverpool of an American envoy, who was en route to take up his duties in the American Embassy in Sweden. In a widely publicised speech, Canning welcomed the "distinguished stranger" and spoke of the positions of the two nations as not unlike that in a family "where a child, having, perhaps, displeased a parent — a daughter, for instance, in contracting a connexion offensive to that parent's feelings — some estrangement would for a while necessarily ensue; but after a lapse of time, the irritation is forgotten, the force of blood again prevails, and the daughter and the mother stand together against the world". Cobbett could hardly contain his feelings.

> The comparison about the child and the parent is worthy of a female boarding school, and perhaps I even do the young ladies injustice. The daughter "contracting a connexion offensive to the parent's feelings". What beastly nonsense! For the daughter rebelled against the mother, not in forming a connexion a la boarding school; but in refusing to give the old lady the fruit of her earnings. The old dame wanted to have the daughter's earnings, and the daughter gave the old lady a good scratching in the face and a good thumping upon the back, and thereby kept her earnings to herself.[6]

---

[6] *Political Register* 47, 20 September 1823.

Perhaps even worse in Cobbett's eyes was the hypocrisy of a man who had been so full of derogatory phrases about America during the recent war. Addressing Canning, he continued:

> you who so glibly talked of the "half dozen frigates with bits of striped bunting at their head"; you, who even in your despatches in the insolent days of PITT, made a jest of the Congress of America! What! you who made part of a crew called a Ministry, who expended our money by hundreds of thousands of pounds with exhibitions to celebrate the fall of republican government. You who made an exhibition of flags on that occasion at Portsmouth, in which exhibition the American flag was hanging reversed under those of England, Holland, Prussia, aye, and France! What! do you now call upon those Americans to make a stand with you against the world![7]

The conceit and impudence of Canning's Liverpool speech were matched in Cobbett's eyes by a misunderstanding of America's position. He still believed that the independence of the former Spanish colonies, and particularly that of Mexico, encompassing as it did at this time the present States of Texas, California, Utah, Arizona, New Mexico and parts of Colorado, posed a threat to the United States.

> There are those who imagine that the United States of America would take part with us in a war preventing the recolonisation of South America. If we go to war with France or Spain, the United States will carry on their commerce; they will not suffer us to search their ships for enemy goods; and if we insist on doing this, they will take part in the war *against* us.[8]

Cobbett taunted the government with its inability to prevent

---
[7] *Ibid.*
[8] *Political Register* 48, 15 November 1823.

France from occupying Spain. The costly Peninsular War had been fought to oust the French from Spain, and at the time Spain had actually been referred to as the great outwork of England.

> And now, after spending a hundred and fifty millions of sterling in getting this "outwork of England" out of the hands of the French, we, without pulling a single trigger, suffer the French to go and take complete possession of this *outwork*, and our Minister for Foreign Affairs tells us from his dinner seat at Plymouth that, to have interfered for the Spaniards would have been "Quixotic", romantic in its object and thankless in its end![9]

In spite of the fact that England had an army more costly than that of France, and a fleet more costly than that of all Europe, "we can borrow no more, we can give subsidies and make loans to Foreign powers no more; we are at the end of our tether". Her parlous financial situation had brought England to impotence.

Cobbett had now come to revise his opinion of the Spanish Patriots, believing that by accepting British loans and granting concessions to British merchants, they had betrayed their peoples. He thought that it was likely that Spanish America would be recolonised by Spain and France "an event which one shall scarcely regret when one reflects that the "liberty" which the "Patriots" have given to the people of South America is, to have their country and their labour mortgaged to the Jews and Jobbers of London, and to have the advantages of their commerce turned over from Old Spain to the Boroughmongers".[10] He castigated the British government for not acting on his advice to recognise the new republics earlier and even went so far as to say that Britain's pusillanimity had encouraged

---

[9] *Political Register* 48, 8 November 1823.
[10] *Ibid.*

France to invade Spain, because it led her to the belief that South America remained open to recolonisation and that she could share in the spoils. Instead, the British government did "not what the interests of the country demanded, but what the interests of the enemies of Reform demanded".[11]

The failure of Britain to recognise the new states adversely affected its relations with the United States which viewed Britain's stance with suspicion. Canning was at this time entering into discussions with the American ambassador to Britain, Richard Rush, with a view to a joint declaration by the two nations that they would not view "with indifference" any attempts by Europe to recolonise the Spanish provinces in South America, coupled with a declaration that neither country aimed at the possession of any portion of the former colonies for herself. In his book *A Residence at the Court of London*, Rush gives a detailed account of the many discussions he had with Canning during the second half of 1823. Canning tried to persuade him that a joint declaration by Britain and America would be enough to ward off expeditions from Europe aimed at retrieving any of the former Spanish colonies, and Rush reported to his government that Canning had framed his suggestion "in a spirit of great cordiality and expressed an opinion that seldom perhaps at any time among nations, had an opportunity occurred when so small an effort of two friendly Governments might produce so unequivocal a good and prevent such extensive calamities".[12]

Rush's reaction was cautious. He told Canning that the value of such a declaration would depend on its being made formally known to Europe and that such step would

---

[11] *Ibid.*
[12] Rush, Richard, *A Residence at the Court of London from 1819-1825,* Vol II, p 26, Richard Bentley, 1845.

"wear the appearance of the United States implicating themselves in the political connexions of Europe. Would it not be acceding, in this instance, at least, to the policy of one of the Great European Powers, in opposition to the projects avowed by others of the first rank?"[13] The policy of the United States, he told Canning, was formed on the maxim of preserving peace with all nations without forming entangling alliances with any. Canning's proposed joint statement by Britain and the United States would be seen by the other European powers as forming an alliance with Britain against them. The matter could be better resolved, he told Canning, in another way.

> Let Great Britain immediately and unequivocally acknowledge the independence of the new States. This will put an end to all difficulty; the moment is auspicious; everything invites to the measure; ... let Britain but adopt this measure, so just in itself, so recommended by the point of time before us, and the cause of all Spanish America triumphs.[14]

Canning put forward various reasons why Britain felt that the time was not ripe to acknowledge the independence of the new states, the chief among them being the uncertainties of the stability of the new regimes, but Rush stood firmly by his statement that he was certain that his government would not put itself in the invidious position of appearing to collude with Britain against other powers in Europe by issuing a joint statement. The stance he took in rejecting Canning's proposal met with approbation and was confirmed by the American government, and particularly by the American Secretary of State, John Quincy Adams:

> The object of Canning appears to have been to obtain

---

[13] *Ibid*, p 43.
[14] Rush, Richard, *op cit*, p 49.

some public pledge from the Government of the United States, ostensibly against the forcible interference of the Holy Alliance between Spain and South America, but really or especially against the acquisition by the United States themselves of any part of the Spanish American possessions.[15]

Cobbett was perhaps not wrong in his supposition that the British government was over optimistic in imagining that America would welcome an offer of an alliance with Britain.

Frustrated in his efforts to woo the Americans, Canning turned to the French Ambassador to Britain, the Prince de Polignac. Intimating to him that Britain would use her naval power to prevent any attempts by the European powers to intervene in Spanish America, Canning obtained from him a written statement that France had neither the intention nor the desire to appropriate any part of the former Spanish Provinces. His approach to the French Minister was far more successful than that to the American but it will hardly be supposed that Cobbett allowed it to pass without comment. When he became aware that Britain was warning France against intervention, he published an Open Letter to Canning once again accusing him of hypocrisy.

> Will you say, that one nation is not to interfere in the affairs of another nation? You will hardly say this after your wars in Spain and Portugal, after, in short, expending 700 millions of pounds sterling in order to interfere, and hire others to interfere in the affairs of France. And if you say Mexico is an independent nation well *you* interfered for the lawful sovereign of France against his rebellious or misled subjects, and will not France now interfere for the lawful sovereign of Mexico against his rebellious or misled subjects? But then you

---

[15] Quoted in Dexter Perkins, *The Monroe Doctrine*, p 92, Harvard University Press, 1927.

will say but France's subjects were JACOBINS, whereas those of Mexico are patriots. What is the difference? Both are men; both walk upon two legs; both eat and drink from a table; both cover their bodies with clothes of some sort or another. Let us see, then, what difference there is in their public conduct to give the name Jacobin to the one and to the other Patriot.[16]

Throughout the last months of 1823, Cobbett continued to believe that the European powers would be successful in overthrowing the new republics in the New World and that the United States would not intervene. At the beginning of November, he boldly prophesied that in two and a half years Spanish America would be recolonised, and that the United States would acquiesce in the event because the existence of large independent nations on her borders would threaten her security and her .commercial interests. He was, however, to be proved to be wrong in his prognostication. On December 1st 1823 President Monroe delivered his famous Message to Congress in which he declared: that the American continents were henceforth not to be considered as subjects for future colonisation by any European power, and that the United States would consider any attempt on their part to extend their system to any portion of that hemisphere as dangerous to the peace and safety of the United States. Canning's proposition to Richard Rush for a bilateral declaration had been pre-empted by America, and her unilateral declaration would result in her, and her alone, appearing as the champions of the new states with all the advantages Canning had hoped Britain might have obtained if his proposal to Rush had been adopted.

Holding the view that the United States feared the creation of powerful independent states on her borders,

---

[16] *Political Register* 48, 22 November 1823.

Cobbett was unprepared for the President's declaration, and reported his speech in the *Political Register* with the comment that its matter had "most agreeably surprised me". His explanation of the reasons which had led the President to proclaim what has come to be called the Monroe Doctrine deserves attention, for even if his interpretation is sometimes open to question it illustrates his abiding interest in the politics of the United States. This was at a time when he was also deeply involved in the movement for Reform in England, completing his long work *A History of the Protestant Reformation* which he published in 1824, and writing series of articles in his paper on such varied subjects as the plight of Irish Catholics, the sufferings of the common people under the Game Laws, the turnpike system, banking and paper money, and even on the superiority of the American type of open-hearth fireplaces on the ground over the English barred grate system with space below to receive the ashes.

In describing the background to Monroe's declaration, Cobbett informed his readers that the question of recognising the independence of the Spanish republics had long been a party question in the United States: President Monroe, strongly backed by Henry Clay, being in favour of early recognition, and his opponents accusing him of wishing to involve his country "in scenes of commotion, robbery and bloodshed and espousing the cause of revolution and rebellion".

> This is indeed the Devil rebuking sin! These people meet, every fourth of July, in bodies all over the country, to listen to orations in praise of revolution, rebellion and declarations of independence. They themselves were Colonists. They boast they have cast off the authority of the King. And yet there are men among them who openly rail against revolution and rebellion![17]

---

[17] *Political Register* 49, 3 January 1824.

He reminded his readers of the decision of Congress in 1817 to make it a criminal offence for an American citizen to give aid to the Spanish Patriots. "And now we hear the President of the same Congress talking just as if he had always been the warm friend of South American independence".[18] However he exonerated President Monroe himself. "He is an honest man", he wrote, "and a real lover of freedom", a point of view confirmed by Dexter Perkins in his history of the Monroe Doctrine who relates how Monroe had been in favour of recognition as early as 1818, and goes on to say:

> His views, it is true, were to be overruled or modified by his advisers. But his interest in positive action was very real, and is quite consistent with the character of the man whose flaming sympathies with French republicanism had been so obvious in his earlier career.[19]

But why, Cobbett asked, had the government of the United States decided after all to act as the protectors of these independent states when they, and Mexico in particular, threatened their security and their commercial interests? He attributed Monroe's decision to issue a warning to the European powers to keep out of the New World as due to a fear that if France and Spain were successful in recolonising Spanish America they might turn their attention to wresting back from the United States some of their former possessions in the Floridas and Louisiana. Unwelcome as were the emergent new states on her borders, the threat to Louisiana and Florida was considered more serious. It is interesting to speculate why Cobbett clung so persistently to his notion that the American government viewed the matter in this light. It had, in fact, recognised some of the republics in 1822 after the

---

[18] *Ibid.*
[19] Dexter Perkins, *op cit,* p 43.

negotiations with Spain over the Floridas were concluded, and there appears to be little corroborating evidence to suggest that the government ever considered colluding with France and Spain in attempts to recolonise them or that it feared that those two countries might have designs on Florida or Louisiana. Some possible explanations are put forward towards the end of this chapter, but first it is necessary to see how the British government reacted to Monroe's declaration and how Cobbett assessed those reactions.

The promulgation of the Monroe Doctrine caught the British government, as it had caught Cobbett, unawares. It was welcome in that it helped to guarantee the continuing independence of the new republics, but it had done so by stealing a significant march over Britain. John Quincy Adams had rebuffed Canning's overtures to Rush on the grounds that he did not wish the United States to "come in as a cockboat in the wake of a British man-of-war", interestingly using the same arguments, but in the interests of the United States, that Cobbett had put forward six years earlier in his petition to the Prince Regent that it was in the interests of Britain to forestall the Americans in granting recognition to the rebels. Canning was fully aware that Monroe's public support of the new republics would greatly lessen Britain's standing in the eyes of the new rulers of Spanish America, and was determined that America should not gain all the credit for protecting them. He went to great lengths to publicise the statement he had obtained from Polignac, the French Ambassador to Britain, in October 1823, declaring that France had neither the intention nor the desire to appropriate any part of Spanish America. He saw to it that copies of this so-called Polignac Memorandum were widely circulated in South America and that it was made clear that Britain had obtained this promise from France two months before Monroe made his speech warning off all European powers. Canning was not unsuccessful in his efforts.

> The Chilean authorities even went so far as to describe Canning as the "redeemer of Chile". The fact that the United States had recognised the new states, whereas Britain had not, does not seem to have affected the success of the campaign. What really mattered was that Britain's naval supremacy was unchallenged, and her protection was more effective than anything the United States could offer.[20]

Canning's astute move in winning for Britain acknowledgement that she, too, had been instrumental in defending the new republics, did not mean that the threat was extinguished. Ferdinand VII of Spain, backed by France, still viewed the revolt of his former colonies as a challenge to established order. The other great powers, Russia, Austria and Prussia, — the so-called Holy Alliance — were at one in wishing to overthrow the new republics, and although it was considered unlikely that they would submit to full colonial status, moves were afoot to attempt to restore Bourbon princes to head their governments, giving some measure of independence but establishing strong connections with their former mother country.

Although the British tried to hail the Monroe Doctrine as a triumph in that its own success in obtaining from France an undertaking not to interfere had now been supported by the United States, Cobbett was far less sanguine.

> It is curious to observe that, in our eagerness to take shelter under the wings of the United States, we seem to lose ourselves; we seem, not only to regard the President's speech as a *law* of Congress, but as a law

---

[20] Hinde, *op cit,* p 355.

which is sure to be carried into execution without any hindrance.[21]

Cobbett thought the American declaration would probably be successful in keeping Europe from intervening in the New World for the present, but he warned that Monroe's successors might pursue a different line. He did not see the Monroe doctrine as a sign that the United States was drawing nearer to Britain. He quoted from an article in an American newspaper which accused England of trying to push the United States into defending the new republics so that she could continue to benefit from trading with them. The article put forward the hypothesis that England "might, if there were war between the United States and the Holy Alliance, join the latter to recover her own colonies. She is unquestionably playing a deep game, and it behoves us to be more than ever cautious in the nature of our intercourse with her".[22]

Cobbett's reaction to the promulgation of the Monroe Doctrine was, therefore, one of unease. He greatly feared that America, suspicious of Britain's and Europe's intentions, might create a large army and navy in order to secure her borders and possibly enlarge them into Mexican territory. He urged the British government to counter this threat by immediately declaring Mexico independent and send out "a good strong fleet with twenty thousand men to establish that independence."

> We ought to make Mexico independent, form a treaty with her, offensive and defensive, and thus put an everlasting bridle in the mouth of the United States.[23]

If Britain failed to do so, Cobbett continued, and the United States were to incorporate Mexico into the Union,

---

[21] *Political Register* 49, 31 January 1824.
[22] *Political Register* 49, 3 January 1824.
[23] *Ibid.*

America would control the whole of the Gulf of Mexico and threaten the sea routes and British possessions in the Caribbean.

These are unexpected sentiments to be uttered by a man who for years had been so great an admirer of America, but one must not forget that Cobbett considered it his duty first and foremost to defend the interests of his own country. One senses in his writings at this time a feeling of humiliation at the sorry role Britain was now playing in the world. She had stood impotently by when France invaded Spain, and she had been outwitted by America's declaration of the Monroe Doctrine. Much as he despised and deplored the present government, he looked forward confidently to the time when the Reform movement would triumph and a democratic, representative government be installed in its place. Such a Britain would need to retain her supremacy of the seas if she was to be secure against any intervention from hostile powers. It may be, too, that Cobbett felt he needed to be circumspect in his utterances now that he was becoming so influential a leader in the reform movement and putting himself forward as a Parliamentary candidate in elections. To rally the people behind him, he needed to counter the vociferous criticisms of his detractors who labelled him as a Jacobin and an infidel, seeking to sow the seeds of dissension and anarchy in his native country. This is confirmed by his repeatedly reminding his readers that, much as he wished well to the Americans, he had always been open in declaring that great as was his friendship for the United States, he wished them to prosper only if this could be done "without injury or danger to England".

Nor should it be overlooked that Cobbett had, by this time, realised that he had been mistaken in espousing so whole-heartedly the cause of the Spanish Patriots.

Underlying his vicious attacks on their having sold out their people to the Jews and Jobbers in London, is a feeling that he had been betrayed. He had accepted Henry Clay's portrayal of the revolutions as a struggle of fifteen million of peoples to break their chains and be free: he now found that this had never been a true picture of those events. "They have been, and are", he wrote in 1824, "bands of ruffians intent on plunder, and that man must be next to a monster who wishes to see those fine countries under their fangs".[24] Equally galling to him was the increasing clamour of British cotton merchants with interests in South America, who were petitioning the government to recognise the new states, for after France's occupation of Spain their saw their trading concerns threatened by recolonisation. These merchants were now full of phrases about giving freedom to an oppressed people.

> Seigneurs of the Twist, Sovereigns of the Spinning Jenny, great Yeoman of the Yarn, give me leave to approach you with some remarks on your Petition to the House. You are pretty fellows to talk about *giving freedom* to South America. The negroes who gather the cotton and put it into bags, are a thousand times better off, better fed, and more gently treated, more happy and *more free*, than the poor creatures who work and weep for your profit, and whose squalid looks, and lungs choked up with cotton fuz, tell every beholder that they can never live out half their natural lives.[25]

The cotton lords then turned on Cobbett and accused him of inconsistency in no longer espousing the cause of the Spanish Patriots. But, Cobbett answered them, it was in 1817 when Spain was in convulsions and the Americans not yet recovered from the War of 1812 that he had urged recognition.

---

[24] *Political Register* 50, 8 May 1824.
[25] *Political Register* 51, 26 June 1824.

To have issued a proclamation acknowledging the independence of the Spanish colonies, to have proclaimed the rights of man; to have proclaimed the rights of representative government; to have declared that Spaniards had a right to choose their own rulers; to do this, while the numerous dungeons of England, under the warrants of Sidmouth, were tenanted by men who were not informed of their crime, who were never brought to trial, and whose only offence was seeking for such a change as would have given Englishmen a right to vote at elections; to proclaim the right of Spaniards to make entirely new governments for themselves while Englishmen were treated thus; to do this would have been a glorious occurrence indeed.[26]

Now, he went on, the situation was very different: the rulers of the new republics had sold their countries to Jews and Jobbers, and their cause was no longer that of freedom. Furthermore, recognition might now lead to war between Britain and the Holy Alliance. Continuing to address the cotton merchants, he wrote:

> you abuse me, call me all sorts of names, because I do not join you; because I am not for a *war* to secure you a market for your calicoes and to prolong your power of keeping large portions of the people of England in a state most abject, shut up in a heat of eighty-four degrees, to toil away their lives for your benefit. You can look with an eye perfectly calm on the poor souls that are thus toiling for you. You can see the poor children pining away their lives in these hells upon earth; you can see them actually gaping for breath, swallowing the hot and foul air, and sucking the deadly cotton-fuz into their lungs; and at the very moment when you are thus engaged, you are pouring forth your souls in the cause of Spanish American "freedom".[27]

---

[26] *Political Register* 51, 10 July 1824.
[27] *Political Register* 51, 10 July 1824.

Cobbett's reference to war in this paragraph was not without foundation. Early in 1824 preparations were in hand in Britain for raising regiments and fitting out ships on the grounds that an alliance would soon be made between Britain and the United States to prevent any intervention in Spanish America. There were rumours of a French fleet off Brazil and of ships and troops being prepared in Europe for expeditions to cross the Atlantic. Cobbett again warned the government that it was mistaken in thinking that Britain and America had mutual interests. His belief that the Monroe Doctrine did not necessarily imply that the United States would actively intervene if forces were sent across from Europe were partially confirmed. In July 1824 the Colombians, fearing that the French were seeking to install some form of monarchical government in their country, asked what would be the reactions of the United States if an expedition was sent from Europe to impose such a government. John Quincy Adams, the Secretary of State, sent a somewhat equivocal reply. He stated that the employment of a small European force in South America would not "constitute a case upon which the United States would feel themselves justified in departing from the neutrality which they have hitherto observed".[28] The unwillingness of the American government to commit itself to armed intervention if forces were sent over to South America was confirmed by the Russian Envoy to the United States, Baron Tuyll, who. writing to his government, reported that he thought that the United States might aid Britain if she opposed expeditions sent across the Atlantic, but by words rather than deeds, and by using privateers to prey on shipping rather than taking part in open hostilities. "In this manner", he wrote "the American government would risk nothing, would spend little, and would finish in

---

[28] Quoted in Dexter Perkins, *op cit,* p 191.

case of success by attributing to itself a great part of the glory of having assured the independence of its allies".[29]

In the months following Monroe's declaration, Cobbett felt not only shame but anger and frustration. His repeated warnings of the consequences of prolonging the War of 1812 had been unheeded. It was the government's stubborn refusal to give up the right of impressment, even after that war, that had alienated the United States from Britain. "They hate England as a power, with a perfect hatred. As a power it is their duty to hate her". So long as Britain maintained her naval supremacy, the independence of the United States was always precarious; "their ships can be ransacked if they do not take our part in all our wars; we can meddle in their affairs, setting one part of the Union against another, give export licenses to some and not to others". Small wonder, therefore, that "there is hardly a man employed in hoeing corn, who has not, at some time or other, coolly calculated how long it will be before America shall make England bow the flag to her upon the seas".[30]

Cobbett believed, not without some justification, that by ignoring all his advice, before, during and after the War of 1812, the British government had created in America, a dangerous and hostile power. He maintained that had the government listened to him in 1817 and 1818 and recognised the Spanish republics, the suspicion and hatred they had engendered might have been lessened, and the great powers of Europe would have been far more hesitant in planning to impose some form of monarchical government in the Spanish provinces. By refusing to acknowledge the republics, the government had once again mishandled the situation and thrown away the opportunity

---

[29] Quoted in Dexter Perkins, *op cit,* p 172.
[30] *Political Register* 51, 25 September 1824.

of creating a better climate in the relations between Britain and America. The government's persistent neglect of his advice, when all along he had had the interests of Britain at heart, was, for Cobbett, a source of bitterness for it had produced that very calamity that he had striven for so long to avert. It had turned the United States, which could have been an ally, into a suspicious and possibly hostile power. The year 1824 was a gloomy year for Cobbett, but his fears of an outbreak of hostilities over the question of Spanish America were soon to be put at rest.

It was almost inevitable that with so much British capital invested in the new republics and with so many merchants profiting from the opening of new markets for their goods, Britain would eventually grant them recognition. Canning had a long fight to wage to convince the ultra-Tories and the King to take the final step. Fear of giving countenance to regimes which had overthrown their legitimate sovereign, and fear of offending the European powers, all of which stood out strongly against recognition, were not overcome until 1825 when Buenos Aires, Colombia and Mexico were formally recognised as independent states by Great Britain. A British representative in Colombia reported:

> All the people of Bagota are half mad with joy. Rockets are flying in all directions, bands of music parading the street, and the Colombians galloping about like madmen, exclaiming: "We are an independent nation".[31]

Spain, France, Russia, Austria and Prussia all ordered their ambassadors in London to make formal protests to the British government, but they took no further action.

In granting recognition to the republics, Britain had in effect aligned herself with the United States in interdicting any European intervention in Spanish America. Britain had

---
[31] Hinde, *op cit*, p 371.

reaffirmed her status as a great power by defying the rest of Europe and had come out unscathed. But even though Cobbett approved of the government's action in granting recognition, he poured scorn on Canning's famous boast that when France invaded Spain, he looked to other than military means to redress the balance of power in Europe. "I looked another way", Canning said. "I sought materials of compensation in another hemisphere. I resolved that if France had Spain, it should not be Spain 'with the Indies'. I called the New World into existence to redress the balance of the Old". Cobbett would have none of it.

> The frothy Canning said that he had called a new world into existence when he might have said that, as far as he had power to do it, he had really murdered that world.[32]

The reason why Cobbett thought that Canning had 'murdered' the New World was because he believed that the British government's actions had all along been motivated by a desire to support the interests of the British merchants and financiers who were exploiting the former provinces. He had long been engaged in a battle against city interests: against bankers and against paper money, against borrowing and loan-mongering. This was one of Cobbett's most passionately held of all his passionately held dogmas — his belief that the sufferings of his countrymen were due to successive British governments' reckless creation of a huge National Debt, and the intolerable burden this Debt laid on the nation.

---

[32] *Political Register* 65, 5 January 1828.

12

Banking, Paper Money and the National Debt

Throughout the course of the book, mention has been made from time to time of Cobbett's antipathy to banking, borrowing and the National Debt, and how it was Thomas Paine who had first alerted him to their significance. He summed up his debt to Paine by declaring that after reading his *Decline and Fall of the English System of Finance* he "saw the whole matter in its true light, and neither pamphleteers nor speech-makers were, after that able to raise even a momentary puzzle in my mind. PAINE not only told me what would come to pass, but shewed me, gave me convincing reasons *why it must come to pass*; and he convinced me also, that it was my duty to endeavour to open the eyes of my countrymen to the truths which I myself had learned from him".[1] That duty Cobbett conscientiously carried out, in season and out of season, from the early 1800's when he first read Paine's treatise, to the end of his life in 1835. Discussion of Cobbett's views on finance, so crucial to an understanding of his appraisal of the United States, has been postponed until now because it was not until some years after the War of 1812 that Cobbett began seriously to fear that America might fall prey to the evils which had arisen in England from the creation and augmentation of a National Debt and its funding by paper money. To follow his arguments, it is necessary first of all to look at

---

[1] *Paper Against Gold*, Letter XXV.

contemporary thinking on the subject of the National Debt itself, in order to set Paine's thesis and Cobbett's endorsement of it in its context.

England had been burdened with a National Debt from the end of the seventeenth century. Governments had borrowed, of course, almost ever since governments began, but the creation of a National Debt differed from previous transactions in that special taxes were levied on the whole nation to pay interest to the lenders until the debt could be discharged. Owing to a succession of wars in the eighteenth century, the Debt was not only never discharged, but after each war rose to higher and higher figures. As fresh money was needed for new wars, the government was forced to offer ever more attractive terms to its lenders. Life annuities were offered yielding as much as 10% to 14% per annum of the sums lent, and these annuities could sometimes be bequeathed to two or three named successors of the original lenders after his death. So, as the Debt rose, it came about that successive governments found themselves burdened with ever increasing demands on the exchequer and future generations found themselves taxed to pay dividends, life annuities and discharges of debts incurred long before they were born.

Almost from the start of this 'funding system', voices were raised protesting at the heavy burden on posterity, and efforts were made to create Sinking Funds to pay off the Debt. But good as these intentions were, the Sinking Funds were constantly raided by governments in power for more immediate needs. The cost of the American War of Independence, 1776-1783, alone raised the National Debt in England from around £76 million to over £227 million, and the anti-Jacobin and Napoleonic Wars had by 1810 raised it to over £800 million. The heavy burden of taxation the National Debt brought in its train was not the only ill of which the nation complained. The high returns paid to the lenders created a growing class of idle rentiers and pensioners who lived on the dividends and annuities. Furthermore, as the government's demands for further loans mounted, fortunes could be made by middlemen negotiating such loans, and a new class of financiers, fattening themselves on the government's need for money, arose in the City of London.

From about the middle of the eighteenth century, political economists such as David Hume, Adam Smith and David Ricardo all deplored the fact that the industrious members of society had to maintain the idle creditor. Hume spoke of "seventeen thousand creditors tyrannising over the mass of the people"; Adam Smith devoted a whole section of his *Wealth of Nations* to analysing the National Debt and forecast the eventual bankruptcy of the nation if the system continued; and Ricardo wrote that "the National Debt was an evil which almost any sacrifice would not be too great to get rid of".

In order to pay interest, dividends and annuities to its creditors, the government in 1694 chartered a national bank, the Bank of England. Lacking hard currency, which it had to expend to maintain its armies abroad, to subsidise foreign armies, and to pay for supplies from overseas, the government paid its interest and dividends to its fundholders in treasury notes issued on the Bank of England, and any note presented to the Bank could always be exchanged for gold or silver coins on demand. The legend on the notes, "The Bank of England promises to pay £..." was literally true. However the convenience of notes (which were issued only in large denominations of £20 or more) against weighty coin, and their general acceptance in business transactions within the country, backed as they were by the government itself, resulted in only a comparatively small number of notes actually being presented for payment in coin, and there was enough gold and silver in the Bank to meet demand.

Such then was the position in England when Paine published his *Decline and Fall of the English System of Finance* in 1796. The National Debt was (except by the fundholders themselves) considered as something to be extinguished as soon as possible, and strenuous efforts were being made at the time by the government under Pitt to create an inviolate Sinking Fund to pay off the Debt. But although the Debt was enormous, the stability of the government's finances was not questioned, because bank notes could always be exchanged into specie. It was this stability that Paine questioned in his paper. He was convinced that, in spite of the government's and the Bank of England's assurances to the contrary, the amount of gold and silver in the deposits was only a very small fraction of the amount issued by the Bank in notes, and the only reason why the government could continue to be so profligate in its borrowing (with the resultant heavy burden of taxation) was that it had deluded the public into the false assumption that the paper money in circulation could be converted into 'real' money. In his famous phrase "Public Credit is Suspicion Asleep", Paine prophesied that within about twenty years the whole system would collapse.

Cobbett did not read Paine's thesis until some years after it had been published. He had long been suspicious of banking and bankers, and these suspicions were fuelled by his discovery after he returned to England in 1800 of the huge fortunes being made by stock jobbers and speculators in the City of London. When he found that Paine considered that the whole fabric of the City was founded on fraud and delusion, he embraced Paine's theories with enthusiasm. Right up to the time of his death in 1835, he remained convinced that the time would soon come when the fraud would be exposed, when all the speculators, pensioners, fundholders and other 'tax-eaters' would meet their just deserts, and the nation at last be freed from the intolerable burden their existence imposed.

There was every reason for Cobbett to accept Paine's diagnosis of the precarious state of the nation's finances, because events moved rapidly and dramatically to confirm it after Paine's pamphlet was published. In the very next year, 1797, and possibly due to fears that the pamphlet might precipitate a great rush for conversion of notes into gold, the government began to pass a series of Bank Restriction Acts which forbade the Bank of England to discount its notes in gold, and made it illegal for any creditor to insist on his debts being repaid to him in hard currency. Bank notes, in consequence, became the legal tender of the country, whereas before that time any creditor could refuse bank notes and insist on his debts being paid back to him in coin.

The first of these Bank Restriction Acts, that of May 1797, suspended payment in specie for a mere fifty-two days, and gave as an excuse the fear of an invasion of England by French revolutionary armies. Even this short suspension, though, needed a lot of explanation from a government which had always maintained that the Bank of England had adequate gold and silver in its deposits. In his *Paper Against Gold* written in 1810 and 1811 while he was serving his sentence in Newgate Gaol, Cobbett traced the whole history of the Bank Restriction Acts, and in the extract below he described the scene in the House of Commons in May 1797 when the first Bank Restriction Act was laid before it.

Mr PITT, who was, in the House of Commons, *boldness*

personified, does, however, seem to have, for a while at least, felt himself humbled upon this occasion, and to have been as the vulgar saying is, completely *chop-fallen*. To come to the House of Commons, that scene of his long-enjoyed triumph; to come to that same bench, and thence to deliver a Message from the King, *announcing the Stoppage of Gold and Silver payments at the Bank of England*; to do this seemed to be too much even for Mr PITT; to come down to the House, and say that *necessity* had compelled him to issue an Order of the King's Council to forbid the Bank of England *from paying the just demands of its creditors*, was more than he was able to do without faultering, and it is, perhaps, more than any other man upon earth under similar circumstances would have been able to do at all. See him who only *four months* before had boasted that our "*resources were untouched*" and that there was "nothing *hollow* or *delusive* in our finances". Look at him now, not able to *say*; nay, not able to give an opinion, whether he shall propose Bank-notes to be made a legal tender or not! Even if the minister had made his mind up to go to that length. Even if he had screwed up his courage to the contemplation of such a measure, how was he to find face to propose it *all at once*? It required time for him to discover how his adherents felt and whether they were still to be depended upon. It also required time to break the matter to the public, and to afford the opportunity for the press, and for the minister's monied friends out of doors to exert their influence. To obtain this time, the scheme of a Committee of Inquiry was resorted to, the result of which inquiry and an account of the measures adopted, we shall see in the next Letter.[2]

In the Letters that followed, Cobbett described the measures adopted which were gradually to postpone the

---

[2] *Paper Against Gold*, Letter XII.

return to payment in specie. After further Bank Restrictions extending the period little by little, in November 1797 Pitt persuaded Parliament to agree to the suspension remaining in force until one month after the ending of the war with France. When the war did end with the Peace of Amiens in 1801, this one month was first extended to one year and then for another nine months. Before these nine months expired, the war with France was resumed, and the resumption of cash payments postponed until the war was over. Yet throughout the whole period, the government continued to assert that there was a sufficient supply of gold and silver to resume cash payments at any time.

The refusal of the government to divulge the amount of gold and silver in the deposits, the appointment of Secret Committees to look into the financial situation, and the extraordinary and often contradictory explanations the government gave to the Commons when presenting its successive Bank Restriction Acts, all seemed to confirm Paine's thesis. For Cobbett, writing in 1810, everything seemed to confirm Paine's assumption about the lack of gold and silver in the deposits, and he believed that Paine was equally correct in foreseeing the collapse of the system when the whole truth could no longer be concealed. Cobbett agreed with Paine that suspicion could not forever remain asleep. It was this belief that the whole system of paper money was based on a delusion, combined with his belief that it was his duty to hasten its end, that lay behind much of Cobbett's eulogies of the United States. For there he saw a vision of what England might become when the monstrous Debt was extinguished, and the tax eaters and tax gatherers it had spawned were extinguished with it.

The position in the United States when Cobbett was writing his *Paper Against Gold* was very different. In marked contrast to the British National Debt of £800 million, that of the United States stood at a mere $4.5 million, roughly equivalent to £9 million sterling. When the first government of the United States was established under the administration of George Washington in 1789, it found itself burdened with debts incurred during the War of Independence. From Washington's administration until the War of 1812 it had been the aim of every government to pay off the debts incurred in that war, and revenues were raised chiefly from import duties, excise levies and the sale of public lands. Particularly under the guidance of Albert Gallatin, Jefferson's Secretary of the Treasury, government expenditure was kept to a minimum and in spite of the $15 million which had to be raised for the Louisiana Purchase and the catastrophic fall in import duties during the years of the Embargo and the non-importation Acts, the Debt had been so reduced that it was confidently expected that it could be liquidated in the near future.

The War of 1812, however, necessarily entailed a great increase in government expenditure combined with a fall in import revenues, and Madison's government was obliged to purchase its supplies and pay its soldiers and sailors by issuing bank notes, at first promising to redeem them in specie within one year, but later it followed the British practice of suspending specie payments until the war was over. When peace came, the government, needing loans to tide it over until it could obtain enough revenue to repay its debts, proposed to establish a Second Bank of the United States. (After the War of Independence a charter was granted to the First Bank of the United States to run for twenty years, but when the charter expired it was not renewed.) Fearful of the consequences to the people of America, Cobbett published in his *Political Register* an Open Letter addressed to Mr Secretary Dallas, the Secretary of the Treasury, warning him of the dangers

I have read with great care, and uncommon interest, your proposition to Congress for the establishment of a *National Bank*: and as a part of the reasons which you urge in support of that proposition appear to be founded on the experience of a similar institution in England, I cannot refrain from endeavouring to show you what some of those effects really have been, and what is, at present, the situation of this country, owing, in a great measure, to the existence of a great Banking establishment, closely connected with the government.[3]

The Letter then proceeded to explain the enormous power the British government, through the Bank of England, was able to exert over the nation and how it had created a class of rich idlers who wrung from the people the fruit of their earnings until it had "at last brought misery home to the door of every man not paid out of the taxes"; how "it corrupts public morals", "creates a fallacious appearance of wealth" and "induces men to look for trick and speculation rather than industry for the means of rising in the world".[4]

Many Americans echoed Cobbett's condemnation of a National Bank. John Randolph, the outspoken and somewhat eccentric representative from Virginia said: "It was as much swindling to issue notes with the intent not to pay as it was burglary to break open a house",[5] and during the Debate on the establishment of a Second Bank of the United States, Daniel Webster of Massachusetts declared: "The government is to grow rich because it is to borrow without the obligation of repaying and is to borrow of a Bank which issues paper without liability to

---

[3] *Political Register* 30, 13 January 1816.
[4] *Ibid.*
[5] Quoted in David Rich Dewey *Financial History of the United States*, p 149, Longman, Green & Co, 1903.

redeem it... It *(the Bank)* is to issue its bills to the amount of $30 million when everybody knows it cannot pay them. It is to commence its existence in dishonor. It is to draw its first breath in disgrace".[6] However in spite of these strictures within the United States, and Cobbett's warnings from outside, a Second Bank of the United States was chartered by the narrow margin of 80 votes in favour and 71 against.

Before following the fortunes of this Second Bank, we must return to Cobbett's treatise, *Paper Against Gold*. So far attention has been concentrated on his finding that the Bank Restriction Acts confirmed Paine's thesis that there was insufficient specie in the Bank of England to cover the notes it issued. But *Paper Against Gold* was far more than a history of those Acts as its full title shows.

> PAPER AGAINST GOLD: Containing the History and Mystery of the Bank of England, the Funds, the Debt, the Sinking Fund, the Bank Stoppage, the lowering and the raising of the value of Paper Money; and shewing that Taxation, Pauperism, Poverty, Misery, and Crimes have all increased, and ever must increase, with a Funding System.

Cobbett's aim, as stated in his Introduction to the series of Letters, was "to render a subject, which has always been considered as intricate and abstruse, so simple as to be understood by every reader of common capacity", and he began by dealing with the subject of money itself. To summarise his arguments very briefly, Cobbett explained that if money circulated in the form of gold and silver, the relative scarcity of such precious metals ensured that there was always a finite, limited amount of money in circulation. If banks issued notes (paper money) redeemable in

---

[6] Quoted in Bray Hammond, *Banks and Politics in America*, Princeton University Press, 1957.

precious metals, the amount of such notes was also limited, though to a lesser extent. Although banks might count on a large number of people remaining content with bank notes in place of coin, they had always to be ready to pay in specie some proportion of the notes they issued, and so the number of notes issued was also limited. If, however, a government suspended a bank's obligation to redeem their notes in specie, as the British government did in 1797, banks were free to issue notes in any quantity they chose, and as lending is in itself a profitable venture, the quantity of bank notes in circulation will rise.

Cobbett explained all this to his readers in what he hoped were simple terms. Using the analogy that when apples are plenty apples are cheap, he said this was equally true of money. A large amount of money circulating in a country, purchasing a given quantity of goods, will tend to raise prices.

> Money, of whatever sort, is, like everything else, lowered in value in proportion as it becomes *abundant* or *plenty*. It is *plenty* or *scarce*, in proportion as its quantity is great or small compared with the quantity of things purchased and sold in the community; and whenever it becomes, from any cause, plenty, it depreciates, or sinks in value.

> We talk about *dearness*; we talk of *high prices*; we talk of things *rising in value*; but the fact is that the change has been in the *money* and not in the articles bought and sold; the articles remain the same in value, but the money, from its abundance, has fallen in *value*.[7]

The corollary to this, of course, is that just as an increase in the amount of money in circulation will lead to a rise in prices, so will a lessening of the money in circulation lead to a fall in prices.

---
[7] *Paper Against Gold*, Letter XXV.

When Cobbett was explaining all this to his readers from Newgate Gaol in 1810 and 1811, he was writing at a time when paper money and prices in England were both increasing. The effects of a diminution in the amount of money had yet to be experienced. The course of events which followed the creation of a Second Bank of the United States and a return to specie payment were to prove that Cobbett's diagnosis about the amount of money in circulation affecting prices was correct.

Although there had been no central bank in the United States since the First Bank was closed in 1811, there were many State and private banks throughout the country, whose function was to lend, at interest, to farmers and merchants awaiting payments for the produce they shipped to other parts of the country and overseas; to settlers who needed stock and equipment for their new lands; to buyers and developers of real estate; to manufacturers setting up workshops, etc. The amount these banks could lend was limited by the amount of specie in their deposits, for their notes were convertible on demand just as English notes had been before the passing of the Bank Restriction Acts. But when, during the War of 1812, the American government suspended specie payments, the banks were no longer so restricted. Peace brought with it a great wave of optimism: ships could now safely sail the seas; markets in Europe were at last fully open to American traders; the American continent could be exploited — new lands settled, roads and canals built. Banks free to lend found eager borrowers and there followed a period of boom and expansion. Paper money flooded the country, issued in all sorts of denominations and by a multitude of banks. But this very variety caused confusion and unease, and notes issued by banks in one State, or even within a single State were not always acceptable elsewhere.

The post-war monetary situation was generally considered intolerable. Banks continued to expand in number and note issue, without the obligation of redeeming in specie, and their notes continued to depreciate and fluctuate from bank to bank and from place to place. The number of banks increased from 208 to 246 during 1815 alone, while the estimated number of bank notes in circulation increased from $46 million to $68 million.[8]

The intention of Congress in establishing a National Bank was to bring back a uniform currency based on gold. With the vast lands of the United States waiting to be exploited, a national Bank backed by the government, would, it was hoped, attract investors both at home and overseas, to deposit gold to fund the bank and to profit from the interest which the Bank would charge those to whom it lent. But once established, the Second Bank of the United States was allowed great latitude in its operations. It failed to attract as much capital in the form of specie as was hoped; some of its own officers were guilty of embezzlement; and it itself indulged in lending in excess of its gold reserves, thus encouraging more borrowers and further expanding the note issue.

It was inevitable, then, that when a return to specie payments was introduced by the American government in accordance with its intention to create a sound currency based on gold, the effect was far from what the government had anticipated.

When payment in specie was resumed, it did not at first result in a great rush for gold. Because so many holders of bank notes had borrowed from banks, they were easily intimidated from demanding specie in exchange for the bank notes they held, by the threats of the banks to

---

[8] Rothbard, Murray N, *The Panic of 1819*, p 7, Columbia University Press, 1962.

withdraw their loans and demand immediate repayment if they insisted on redemption. But such intimidation signalled to the holders of bank notes that the banks had overstretched their resources and lacked specie. Loss of confidence in the banks and fear of their collapse increased the demand for specie, and as the demand rose, the Bank of the United States was forced to call in its loans and to demand specie from those to whom it had lent. The amount of notes issued by the Bank of the United States fell by half between 1818 and 1819 alone, and the smaller banks which had borrowed from the central bank were forced to call in their loans in order to repay the Bank of the United States. There ensued the so-called Panic of 1819.

It was now some nine years since Cobbett had published his *Paper Against Gold*, and his prediction in that book was now to be put to the test. Just as he had warned, as the number of notes in circulation in the United States decreased, so did prices.

> Economic distress was suffered by all groups in the community... The distress of the farmers, occasioned by the fall in agricultural and real estate prices, was aggravated by the mass of private and bank debts that they had contracted during the boom period... Speculators and others who had bought public lands during the boom were now confronted with heavy debt burdens. Merchants suffered from the decline in prices and demand for their produce and from heavy debts. So low were prices, and so scarce was the monetary medium in the frontier areas that there was a considerable return to barter conditions among farmers and other local inhabitants.[9]

So the Panic of 1819 confirmed what Cobbett had written

---

[9] Rothbard, *op cit*, p 14.

in 1810. But it is important to bear in mind that although Cobbett deplored the paper money system because it allowed fortunes to be made by bankers, stock-jobbers and fund-holders — the unproductive section of the community — he was always fully alert to the fact that a return to specie payments would cause enormous upheavals. Among other consequences, he foresaw that it would favour the creditors and cripple those had borrowed. In his *Paper Against Gold* he had made it clear that if, for instance, a farmer had borrowed money to extend his land when prices were high and had had to pay, say, £100 a year interest on his loan, he would, if prices fell by half, have to produce twice as much corn to obtain that £100 than he had had to produce when prices were high. His creditor, on the other hand, would find that his £100 interest would purchase twice as many goods as it had done when he first lent the money, and he would, in consequence, benefit.

Cobbett was an eye witness of the Panic of 1819 because it occurred while he was living on Long Island. He explained its causes to his readers

> Immense quantities of paper money got on float, or rather, were kept on float after the termination of the war. But in the month of May (1819) the bubble began to burst, and before the middle of July, a very considerable portion of the paper money was totally annihilated.[10]

And he described the consequences. Shortage of money led to a dramatic decline in prices; merchants and manufacturers unable to sell their goods at a profit, laid off workers; lack of demand exacerbated the situation; bank failures, bankruptcies and still higher unemployment were the result.

---

[10] *Political Register* 35, 14 August 1819.

In an Open Letter to his fellow reformer in England, Henry Hunt, Cobbett told how thousands of men in New York were now wandering the streets in search of work. Whereas only a few months previously it had been difficult to find a labourer, now, in August 1819, they were offering to work for board and lodging only. Prices had fallen by one half and traders owing money were ruined.

> Thus does an infernal paper money produce misery to the people and danger to the government even here. The man who first invented a national Debt ought to be *broiled in effigy* in every city, town and village in the whole world.[11]

When Cobbett left America three months later in November, the worst effects of the panic in the area around New York City had abated. So when in December the Prime Minister, the Earl of Liverpool, stated in Parliament that in no country was distress so severely felt as in the United States of America, Cobbett at once took pains to disabuse him of such a notion. In a long Open Letter to Lord Liverpool he wrote:

> I do not accuse your Lordship of wilful falsehood; but I can assure you that this report will do great discredit to your Lordship in that country. In the United States of America there is nothing of that description. The city of New York contains, they say, a population of about a hundred and thirty thousand souls. And I take it upon me to say that it does not contain one single creature, black or white, so much in distress as the average of our common labourers and working manufacturers at this day.[12] (The term manufacturers was in Cobbett's time used to denote factory hands.)

He went on to say that the lightness of taxes in America,

---

[11] *Political Register* 35, 6 August 1819.
[12] *Political Register* 35, 11 December 1819.

the various benevolent societies in existence, and the kindness of the numerous small farmers to their poor relations who "go without any ceremony and ask for what they want. Or go and take up their quarters with a mere 'how d'ye do' as an introduction and generally stay as long as they please, and generally without giving rise even to black looks", made the period of distress short-lived. There had indeed, Cobbett informed Lord Liverpool, been great distress and widespread bankruptcies in July of that year

> But, (and I beg your Lordship to mark it well) the embarrassment, as far as it affected labour, did not last two months. Wages came down, though not at the same rate as provisions had come down; great numbers of labourers and working tradesmen went forth into the country in all directions, and all the apprehensions that had been entertained in the month of July, had totally vanished before the last day in October. House rent in New York had fallen in price one half; food had fallen in price in the same proportion, and it was impossible to perceive in the state of the people any alteration as to dress or content.
>
> The cause of the derangement of the paper-money affair not having produced any lasting distress was that there was no tax gatherer to come and demand great sums from the people. There were no sinecure placemen to come and take two hundred bushels of wheat where he had before taken but one hundred. Thus then, my Lord, though a great Doctor in politics, and of very long experience, you have clearly misunderstood the case of your Transatlantic patient, whom you have supposed to be in a consumption, while she has really been troubled only with a fit of the colic.[13]

It was above all the conditions of the ordinary people, the labouring classes, which Cobbett considered to be the

---

[13] *Ibid.*

touchstone of the prosperity or distress of any country. In another Open Letter to the Prime Minister, Cobbett again emphasised the happy state of the ordinary citizens of America. There were no paupers in the English sense of the word: instead of, as in England, their being sent to the workhouse, orphans there were lodged with persons "of considerable wealth" from about the age of 6 to 10, worked in their houses, were given good food and education and treated like members of the family. "The name of servant is never given to them, and they themselves call their employers by name, and never call them master or mistress". And later, in the same Letter: "Even the poor, (so called) have meat three times a day, and as much fine bread as they can eat. And the mass of what are called poor, consists of newly-arrived emigrants, and by no means of the natives of that country either black or white".[14]

In his desire to disabuse Lord Liverpool of the idea that the distress in America could be compared in any way with the terrible and continuing distress in England, Cobbett was somewhat over sanguine in describing the Panic of 1819 as a mere "fit of the colic". The older financial centres in the East had been far more cautious in their lending during the boom period than those in the South and West, so that in the New York area the return to specie payment affected fewer people and was less severe than in areas where little check had been exercised on those wishing to take out large loans. It was particularly in the newer lands, in Kentucky, Tennessee, Indiana and Illinois that the calling in of loans was most keenly felt. Banks failed and those holding their notes found themselves penniless; it was there that farmers found themselves, with the sudden fall in prices for their products, unable even to pay the interest on the mortgages they had obtained, let alone the capital

---

[14] *Political Register* 35, 18 December 1819.

repayments, and saw their lands being repossessed by the banks from whom they had borrowed. Back in England, Cobbett watched with the keenest interest the state of finances in America now that it had established a National Bank and returned to payment in specie. He praised Monroe's speech to Congress on the state of the nation in December 1819 in which he frankly acknowledged that there were currency difficulties and some depression in the manufacturing sections of the community, so different from the empty phrases of the British government which in the midst of distress, spoke of the flourishing state of the country's finances.

> He fairly describes the embarrassments of commerce; acknowledges the falling of revenue. He does not jostle, shuffle and twist and evade. He does not boast of flourishing finances in order to delude, cajole, and lead by the nose.[15]

He praised the American government too for stopping "the career of paper money in time; not, indeed, before it had produced mischief; but before it produced ruin, misery and slavery".

At the end of the year 1820, Cobbett was more critical. This time Monroe's speech to Congress rejoiced "in the felicity of our situation" and though again acknowledging that difficulties were still being felt by certain interests attributed them to the sudden transition from war to peace. This shuffling off of government responsibility for the ills in the country, Cobbett felt smacked of English excuses, and the President's speech was, he wrote

> so much like something I have frequently read in our King's speeches, that I really thought at first that I was getting amongst the documents of St Stephen's, (a term

---

[15] *Political Register* 35, 15 January 1820.

used for the Houses of Parliament). Come, Come, Mr President! This is being a *little tricky*, as you call it in your country. It amounts to the full our doctrine that the King can do no wrong. Here is all the old empty stuff that has long been worn out here.[16]

The continuing bankruptcies and foreclosures of mortgaged estates to which the President was referring in talking of the difficulties being felt by certain interests in the country, Cobbect correctly attributed to the fact that those who had borrowed during the boom period were now having to repay their debts in much appreciated money. As prices were now lowered by as much as one half, a man who had borrowed $1000 in paper money had now to repay his debt in specie which was worth twice as much as the sum he had originally borrowed. Cobbett's remedy to this problem was to advocate what he called an "equitable adjustment": borrowers should pay back not the actual sum borrowed, but a sum which would purchase the same quantity of goods as it did at the time the loan was made. Or, in other words, if a man had borrowed $1000 to purchase a plot of land which now, with prices halved, was worth only $500, his debt to his creditor should be reduced accordingly. His creditor, in receiving $500, would be repaid in full for he would receive the *value* of what he had lent. What prevented such a just solution was the fact that the American government had established a National Bank in 1816 and allowed it to take over the financial management of the country. It was, of course, in the interests of the bank to receive the repayment of its loans in full, for it could thereby reap great profits. Cobbett believed President Monroe understood the situation, but feared the consequences of such a radical solution for the country's ills, for once established, national banks wield

---

[16] *Political Register* 37, 23 December 1820.

great power.

> The truth is that he is a very honest man; much too honest ever to have approved of a funding system; but that he is fairly entangled in it; and that meaning to be a President a second time, he dares not speak of it in the terms which it merits.[17]

However, Cobbett continued, so great was the injustice being done to borrowers by their being forced to repay loans at what was equivalent to double the price of the sum first borrowed, that he warned the result might be a dissolution of the Union. He foresaw a rising up of the impoverished and ruined farmers and traders in the West against the moneyed interests in the East. His warning was uttered in 1820. Eight years later, discontent among the impoverished debtors found expression in the election of a Senator from the State of Tennessee as President of the United States who was to institute a programme not dissimilar to Cobbett's — a President who was to wage war against what he termed the 'Monster Bank' and to support the debtor against the creditor. He had already earned praise from Cobbett for the part he had played in the War of 1812. He was to earn even more fulsome praise later. That President was General Andrew Jackson, the hero of the battle of New Orleans.

---

[17] *Political Register* 37, 23 December 1820.

13

America in the 1820s: a Reappraisal

Andrew Jackson was elected President in 1828, but it was not until some years later that he put into action his programme to reform the nation's finances and began to wage his war with the Bank of the United States. Until then, Cobbett's writings on America were devoted to other matters, and prominent among them was the question of emigration.

It will be remembered that Cobbett had advised small farmers and labourers to be wary of leaving their native land. He was particularly critical of plans being put forward by various Emigration Committees in Britain to ship paupers overseas in order to relieve the heavy burden of the poor rates.

> Listen to nobody that would advise you to emigrate. You have a right to a maintenance out of the land, unless there be labour for you of another sort elsewhere. You are willing to work. It is not you who caused any part of the distress that now prevails.[1]

But during the 1820s the post-war depression caused distress to spread to the middle classes as well as among the labourers. As early as January 1820 Cobbett replied in his *Political Register* to a "gentleman asking his advice about emigration" not to be tempted to go out to the newer

---
[1] *Political Register* 41, 26 January 1822.

lands but to settle on the Atlantic coast, "having myself enjoyed such perfect health there; never having witnessed misery of any kind; having been surrounded with good and kind neighbours; and having known so many persons in Long Island, in particular, healthy and active and even vigorous at a very, very old age".[2] To another gentleman with capital of £20,000 asking his advice a year later, he wrote: "if, to a negro woman with cap the colour of a devil and smell like that of an unfortunate butcher's shop late of a Saturday night in the dog days, he greatly prefer having all these things done by a servant-maid with a white apron and dry and clean skin",[3] he should remain in England. Cobbett had no desire to aid the rich to better themselves even further.

In all his writings on the subject of emigration to the United States Cobbett recommended Englishmen to settle in the Eastern States. In 1818 in a postscript to his *Journal of a Year's Residence in the United States*, he had appended a letter addressed to Morris Birkbeck who had recently published a book *Letters from Illinois* in which Birkbeck had encouraged English farmers with two or three thousand pounds capital to try their fortunes in the West. Though warning of the hardships, the petty miseries and the "every day evils of life", Birkbeck held out the prospect that they could acquire in the new lands a fine freehold domain. But, Cobbett wrote, for a man with only a modest sum to invest (unlike Birkbeck who had large sums behind him):

> For an English Farmer, and more especially an English Farmer's wife, after crossing the sea and travelling to Illinois, with the consciousness of having expended a third of their substance, to purchase, as yet, nothing but sufferings; for such persons to boil their pot in the

---

[2] *Political Register* 35, 15 January 1820.
[3] *Political Register* 40, 4 August 1821

gipsy-fashion, to have a mere board to eat on, to sit and sleep under a shed far inferior to their English cow-pens, to have a mill at twenty miles distance, an apothecary's shop at a hundred, and a doctor nowhere: these, my dear Sir, are not to such people "every day evils of life".

If English Farmers must emigrate, why should they encounter unnecessary difficulties? Why should they, at an expence amounting to a large part of what they possess, prowl two thousand miles at the hazard of their limbs and lives, take women and children through scenes of hardship and distress not easily described, and that, too, to live like gipsies at the end of their journey, for at least a year or two, and, as I think I shall show, without the smallest chance of their finally doing so well as they may do in the Atlantic States? And what is his wife to do; she who has been torn — from all her relations and neighbours, and from every thing that she liked in the world, and who, perhaps, has never, in all her life before, been *ten miles* from the cradle in which she was nursed? An American farmer mends his plough, his waggon, his tackle of all sorts, his household goods, his shoes; and if need be he *makes* them all. Can our people do all this, or any part of it?[4]

During the depression Cobbett's advice was constantly sought about the prospects in the United States and he decided to collect his thoughts together into a book on the subject. *The Emigrant's Guide*, published in 1829, like all Cobbett's expository works, is written in an easy and colloquial style. In it he accompanies the emigrant step by step on his journey, warning him of the many difficulties he is likely to encounter, and advising him how best to overcome them. He opened the book by saying that although he had previously written against emigration, taxation had now reached such heights that he had revised

---

[4] A Journal of a Year's Residence, paras 976 and 985.

his opinions: "in short, things have now taken that turn, and they present such a prospect for the future, that I not only think it advisable for many good people to emigrate, but I think it my duty to give them all the information I can to serve them as a guide in that very important enterprise".[5]

His first advice to the would-be emigrant was to stress the necessity for the husband to prepare his wife for what was to come; to assure her that mishaps at sea were of rare occurrence, and that there was probably more danger in the journey from London to Exeter than from Exeter to New York; to explain that sea-sickness is usually overcome within ten days; and — a truly unique touch — to support her in the unusual circumstances surrounding the use of lavatories on board ship. These, he explained, are on the deck and in full view of everybody.

> Use every argument in your power to get over this difficulty with your wife; be very attentive to her in every circumstance and point attending to this matter; and if she be in a state, from her seasickness, not to admit of removal from her bed, you must be prepared not only with the utensil suitable to the case, but you must yourself perform the office of chambermaid.

And later, in a different context, but still speaking of the wife:

> The howling of the wind through the shrouds of the ship; the sudden calling up of hands on the deck in a dark night, the bawling of the speaking trumpet to overcome the roaring of the wind, and the doleful answer of the sailor in the shrouds...in times like these, be you very watchful, very attentive; tell her it is nothing.

On the choice of ship, Cobbett strongly recommended

---

[5] Cobbett, *The Emigrant's Guide*.

an American one on the grounds that they were faster, carried more sail, and that American captains were, in his opinion, more conscientious than others in carrying out their duties. Here again Cobbett gave prominence to those everyday matters that can make or mar the success of the voyage. He advised the emigrant not to criticise the ship or pester the captain with silly questions about the expected time of arrival. The captain and his mate, he explained, looked upon the ship as their home and "will not like you for seeming to be in such indescribable haste to get out of their company. They like the ship; they can see no reason for disliking her; they know her to be the best piece of stuff that ever swam upon the water".

After listing the provisions to be taken on board if the emigrant was travelling steerage — flour, rice, candles, salt, pepper, potatoes, sugar, tea and coffee etc, — he suggested also the taking of brandy "to be judiciously administered in bribes to the black cook. He would bid you toss your money into the sea, but he will suck down your brandy; and you will get many a nice thing prepared by him which you would never get, if it were not for that brandy". For those who might be tempted to take servants with them, Cobbett warned of the consequences. Apart from the expense, there was every likelihood that they will quit service once they landed: "liberty and equality are in the atmosphere; the English catch them, the moment they land; and, like all converts, they surpass their teachers".

In considering what to do on arrival in the United States, Cobbett once again referred to the need to keep up the spirits of the womenfolk. His own wife, it will be recalled, stayed only a short time with him in Long Island, and it is not fanciful to suppose that Cobbett, hurt as he must have been by his failure to keep his own family with him, attributed that failure to the fact that they had come over some months after him, and he had been unable properly to prepare them for the change. Be that as it may, his first advice to the emigrant on landing was to indulge his wife and children by buying them new clothing which could be purchased in New York at a trifling expense compared with the price in England. Then, he wrote, they will bless God for coming to the United States, and every time the wife "looks at the American dress, she will not fail to whisper to herself the fact that she must have lived and died in England, and never possessed such things".

The remainder of *The Emigrant's Guide* is less personal in its approach. Cobbett recommended farmers, artisans and shopkeepers to seek work under an employer before attempting to set up on their own. For those who came out with some capital, he again advised a cautious approach. As interest rates were high in the United States, he believed it wise to begin by investing the money and using the interest to rent a property a little outside New York. From there they could travel to the city to visit "the museums, picture galleries, great booksellers shops, public libraries and playhouses", and get to know the country by attending horse racing events and enjoying the abundant opportunities for shooting woodcock, quail, partridge, plover and water fowl before deciding to purchase a place of their own.

In the general comments with which Cobbett ended *The Emigrant's Guide*, he strove to help the newcomer to settle into society and advised him not to give too poor an impression of England. Many Americans, he maintained, believed England to be a fine country and would not welcome an Englishman who extolled America to the detriment of his own country. "It is unnatural", he wrote, "to rave in general terms against your country". Although it was right to speak of the misrule and misery in England, it was unwise to rail against England "in the lump". Nor, on the other hand, should one criticise what may seem unattractive — the rail and post fences in place of England's fine hedgerows, the stumps of trees which littered the ground, the slovenliness of the fields, or the curse of the innumerable flies and mosquitoes. These last, he said, "are inseparable from the heat that will give you orchards of peaches and melons and apples and cherries and plums, and you cannot have all these unaccompanied with flies".

Last of all, Cobbett touched on the subject which he had referred to in his *Journal of a Year's Residence in the United States* some ten years earlier — the danger of over indulgence in intoxicating liquor which could be obtained so cheaply in America. He believed it to be the great destroyer of health among American men. "Oh, how many men — how many bright men — how many strong men, have I seen sink into mere nothings in consequence of this detestable vice". Yet, even so, he thought it wisest not to condemn what was accepted as normal in the country, and to offer drink to those one employed.

> The best way is to take things as you find them and make the best of the blessings you enjoy. You cannot alter the customs and the manners, you cannot teach morality to a nation: but you can be the monitor, both by example and by precept, to your own family.

Cobbett's writings on America were not confined to helping his countrymen to settle there. Another subject to which he frequently referred at this time was his hope that some trees and plants native to America might be cultivated with profit in England. In April 1823 he announced in his *Political Register* that some apple grafts he had ordered from the States had now arrived in London "just as fresh as if they were this moment cut from the tree". Some months later he proudly told his readers that several buyers of his American apple grafts had written to him to say how successful they had been: one purchaser had made 119 plants out of the 32 grafts he had bought. By July of that year he wrote.

> I look upon this importation of grafts to be a matter of great consequence. Every body allows that our orchards need renovation. The regular and rapid decay of our apples is a matter of general complaint in the cyder countries.[6]

Apples were not the only American trees that Cobbett introduced. In the same year he advertised for sale the seed of hickory, black walnut, persimmon, occidental plane, the tulip tree, white oak, sweet chestnut, paper birch, and the two shrubs, catalpa and althea frutex, all with instructions for planting. But in Cobbett's opinion the very tree of trees was the American locust or false acacia (*robinia pseudo acacia*), at this time only occasionally planted in England for ornamental purposes. "The durability of this wood", he wrote, "is such that no man in America will pretend to say that he ever saw a bit of it in a decayed state. It is absolutely indestructible by the power of earth, air or water".[7] For proof of this Cobbett had brought back to England some posts of a fence made of locust wood which had stood in Long Island some twenty-eight years from 1791 to 1819, and he invited his readers to inspect these posts at his office in Fleet Street where they were on display with signed certificates guaranteeing their authenticity. So great was Cobbett's enthusiasm for this tree that he said he hoped the time was not far distant when the American locust would be more common in England than the oak, and would be used for window-sills, posts and gates, axle

---

[6] *Political Register* 47, 12 July 1823.
[7] *Political Register* 48, 29 November 1823.

trees and hop poles, and in shipyards for stanchions, tillers and trammels.

Cobbett had imported seeds of the locust and planted them in his grounds at Botley in the early 1800s shortly after his return from his first sojourn in America. These, he told his readers, had achieved heights of forty feet and girths of forty or more inches at the base, in the seventeen years since they were planted. Having had to abandon these trees with the loss of Botley after his bankruptcy, he had planted new seed imported from the United States in his garden at Kensington in 1822, and had sold a large number of two-year-old plants to an old friend, Lord Folkestone of Coleshill in Wiltshire in 1824. Two years later, during one of his Rural Rides, he visited Lord Folkestone's estate and found that these locust seedlings had grown to an average height of sixteen feet in the two years since they were transplanted, whilst the chestnuts, elms, oaks and ash planted at the same time were less than half their height. He was

> for many reasons, more delighted with the sight than with any that I have beheld for a long time. They are the most beautiful clumps of trees that I ever saw in my life. What a difference in the value of Wiltshire if all its elms were locusts! As fuel, a foot of locust-wood is worth four or five of any English wood. It will burn better green than almost any other wood will dry. If men want woods, beautiful woods, and in a hurry, let them go and see the clumps at Coleshill. Think of a wood 16 feet high, and I may say 20 feet high, in twenty-nine months from the day of planting; and the plants, on an average, not more than two feet high when planted: Think of that: and any one may see it at Coleshill.[8]

In his enthusiasm for American hardwoods, Cobbett

---

[8] *Rural Rides*, 6 September 1826.

declared his intention to have one or two stage coaches built entirely from American locust, hickory and white oak which, he maintained, would cost no more, would be lighter in structure, and yet would last five or six times longer than a similar coach built of English wood. The project does not appear to have been carried out.

Best known of all Cobbett's introductions into England is Indian corn or maize, although, strictly speaking, it was not he himself who introduced it, and the plant did not come from the United States. When farming in Long Island, Cobbett had been greatly impressed with the utility of this cereal where it was fed to pigs, poultry, sheep, cattle and horses, and also used in making bread and puddings. He experimented with growing Indian corn from seed imported from America after his return from Long Island, but found that unless the summer was exceptionally hot, it would not ripen in England. Some few years later, his eldest son, William, who had been with his father in Long Island, brought back from France some seeds of a dwarf variety he had seen growing in Artois (Pas de Calais), believing it might be suited to the English climate. This was found to ripen in England even in cool summers, and Cobbett devoted some acres of his nursery garden to growing this French seed and advertised seed for sale in his *Political Register*. He called this strain "Cobbett's Corn" to distinguish it from other dwarf varieties, and in 1828 published a book entitled *A Treatise on Cobbett's Corn* in which he acknowledged his indebtedness to his son, gave instructions for preparing the ground, planting and tending it, and detailed the many uses to which it could be put.

Such then were Cobbett's views on the transplanting of British people to American soil and of American plants to British soil. Of Anglo-American relations he had less to say. After Britain's recognition of the Spanish American

States relations between the two countries sailed into somewhat calmer waters. During John Quincy Adams' administration friction arose over tariffs, but Cobbett, believing that it was the duty of governments to protect the interests of their own nationals, defended each from accusations by the other.

In 1824 Monroe's second term of office expired and he was succeeded by his Secretary of State, John Quincy Adams, the son of the second President of the United States, the Federalist John Adams of Massachusetts. With his election the so-called Virginia Dynasty of Jefferson, Madison and Monroe came to an end. These Virginian Democrats were all men who had applauded the French Revolution and whose sympathies lay with their sister republic, France, in her war with Britain. After the election of 1800 in which Jefferson only narrowly defeated his predecessor, John Adams, all the subsequent elections — those of 1804, 1808, 1812, 1816 and 1820 — swept Jefferson and his followers to power. The election of 1824 was different. Once again the incumbent Secretary of State for Foreign Affairs succeeded to the Presidency but there the similarity ended. The unity the nation had displayed during the run up to and the War of 1812 had begun to disintegrate. There were differences between the free States in the north and the slave States in the South, and Cobbett had correctly diagnosed the antagonism which existed between the moneyed interests in the East and their debtors in the West.

In the election of 1824, therefore, there was no smooth transition from one President to the next, and five candidates from five different States — Massachusetts, Kentucky and Tennessee, South Carolina and Georgia — put themselves forward for the Presidency. Following precedent, the most obvious candidate was John Quincy

Adams, the Secretary of State. He had responded to Jefferson's call for unity after he had defeated John Adams, "We are all Republicans — all Federalists", and had served with distinction in Madison's administration as the American Minister to Russia and Great Britain; had played a crucial role as one of the Commissioners appointed to the peace convention at Ghent; and, when Monroe vacated the office on being elected President in 1816, had succeeded him as Secretary of State for Foreign Affairs. It was not from the Old Federalist party that Adams faced opposition in the election of 1824. Founded on a distrust of French republicanism and sympathy for Britain in her war with France, the main plank of the Federalist party's platform ceased to exist when the European war ended. When both countries were monarchies, the distinction between Francophile and Anglophile became meaningless. Furthermore, the attempt by the Federalists during the War of 1812 to withdraw the North Eastern States from the Union if the war with Britain were prolonged, plunged the party into ignominy when the British were so signally defeated at New Orleans.

John Quincy Adams' most formidable rival for the Presidency was General Andrew Jackson from Tennessee. In the first poll Jackson received 99 votes to Adams 84, and it was only because neither candidate had an overall majority among the five candidates that the election had to be decided by the House of Representatives voting by States. Adams won by a very narrow margin. The issues on which the election was fought and which were to lead to Jackson defeating Adams four years later, will be referred to in the next chapter. Suffice it to say here, though the issues are grossly oversimplified, that Adams visualised the future of the United States as a powerful nation united under a strong federal government. He wished federal revenues to be expended on creating a navy strong enough to deter any nation from interfering in American affairs, on fostering and protecting industry and agriculture, on a programme of public works such as road and canal building, on founding national universities and technical institutions, and on making the city of Washington the cultural centre of the nation, equal to any capital city in Europe.

Jackson, on the other hand, represented the views of those adventurous souls who had left the settled areas in the East and South to tame and cultivate the great empty lands in the West. Men who had endured the hardships of journeying through untracked land, who had with their own hands cleared the forests, built their rude log cabins, made virgin soil fertile, improvised the making of the tools and equipment for the task, and defended their new settlements from hostile Indians — such men mistrusted a powerful and distant government which they feared was likely to pursue policies favourable to the interests of the established East to the neglect of their own.

Cobbett, although so keen an observer of affairs in the United States, allowed the contest for the Presidency of 1824 to pass without comment. Both during and after his residence in Long Island, he had, except for his intervention on the question of the recognition of the Spanish American republics, kept himself aloof from any involvement in internal American politics. His first mention of Monroe's successor is in his review of the new President's inaugural speech of January 1825. Again he drew attention to the fact that Adams, like Monroe some years earlier, boasted of the nation's prosperity and glossed over financial problems.

> He forgot to tell the world that his country was again inundated with rascally paper-money. He forgot to tell us that Bank Notes, issuing from, perhaps, a couple of

thousand banks, are in numerous instances at an open discount; ' and, in some cases, at a discount of more than 50%.[9]

Cobbett also took exception to Adams' condemnation of the continuing traffic in slaves from Africa to the New World. Two years after Wilberforce's Bill outlawing slave traffic in British ships had passed Parliament in 1807, Congress, following Britain's example, made it illegal for any American ship to traffic in slaves, but the law was widely flouted. In an effort to tighten the law, Congress passed another Act in 1820 making trafficking in slaves punishable by death, and sent an American squadron to the coast of Africa to intercept and bring to trial illegal traders. Britain then suggested that the two navies might collaborate (the Royal Navy was already active in intercepting British slavers), and proposed that both nations should allow their own merchant ships to be searched by the other's navy if suspected of carrying slaves. This at once aroused memories of the former British practice of impressment, and John Quincy Adams, when Secretary of State, had been adamant in refusing the British proposal. In his inaugural speech as President, Adams regretted that the slave trade in American ships had not been completely repressed, but re-iterated his adherence to the principle that in no circumstances should the United States allow foreign warships to search her vessels. Referring to that part of the President's speech deploring the inhumanity of the slave trade, Cobbett wrote: "I dislike this exceedingly on account of its hypocrisy", pointing out that it was well known that free negroes were seized in the northern States of America to be sold to the slave States in the south, and that ships were fitted out in Baltimore to carry slaves from Africa to French and Spanish colonies; yet Congress appeared

---

[9] *Political Register* 53, 15 January 1825.

to be taking no action to stop these practices. Nor did Cobbett welcome the new President's refusal ever to allow British men-of-war to search American ships, believing it imperative for a trading nation like Britain to maintain its right of search in wartime.

> The late war against America was unjust on our part; for we exercised the right of taking their own native subjects out of their ships and making them serve us. This forms no part of our rights; but we have a right to take the enemy's goods from out of the ship of a friend; and if we do not exercise this right, we are the weakest nation of Europe, in war.[10]

In Cobbett's criticisms of Adams he never referred to his narrow victory over Jackson or to the charges levelled against Adams by Jackson's supporters that he had "bought" votes to gain the Presidency. It is more than probable that Cobbett regretted the outcome of the election, for his admiration of Jackson for the part he played in the war of 1812 is well known as is his sympathy for the debtor farmers in West; but he adhered to his determination not to meddle in internal dissensions in the United States.

There were two more general aspects of American politics which caused Cobbett concern during the 1820s. The first was that he feared that the United States with its fast growing population and almost unlimited resources might succumb to the temptations of aggrandisement as France had under Napoleon. It is crucial to remember that much as Cobbett admired the American republic and its institutions, he never wished it to become a great power. He believed it to be, and wished it to remain, a great nation, but it must be remembered that his criterion for 'greatness' in this context was the well-being of all

---

[10] *Political Register* 64, 8 December 1827.

its citizens. This, he was convinced, was best promoted by simple unostentatious government, husbanding the nation's resources for its own people and those who chose to find refuge there from persecution or penury, and by keeping itself free from foreign entanglements. The second was that he discerned in the post-war administrations the beginnings of some of that arrogance and hypocrisy that characterised the ruling classes in England. As early as 1820 Cobbett had criticised Monroe's speech to Congress as smacking too much of the twists and evasions of speeches at Westminster. Adams inaugural speech of 1825 seemed only to confirm his suspicions, and by 1827 Cobbett attacked the administration even more severely, this time over its support of the cause of Greek independence.

The Greek's uprising against their Turkish overlords had aroused great sympathy in the United States (though in words, not deeds), and both President Monroe and President Adams had, in addresses to Congress, spoken of the heroic struggle being waged by the Greeks for their independence. It was not until after Adams' election that Cobbett began viciously to attack both Monroe and Adams for hypocrisy — an indication, perhaps, that Adams' election had confirmed his growing suspicions that the United States was beginning to meddle in international affairs. For the Greek uprising had repercussions among the great powers of Europe. Russia, with designs on parts of the Ottoman Empire, strongly supported the Greeks in the hope that if they were successful, their revolt might spark off further revolts in Turkish domains and so weaken her powerful neighbour. Britain, fearing Russian hegemony in the near east, had no desire to see the Turkish empire dismembered, for its existence acted as a brake on Russian expansionism.

In an article written after Adams' election, discussing the

Greek question. Cobbett referred to a speech made by Monroe when he was President, in which he had expressed great sympathy for the Greeks, and accused him of playing power politics.

> He had been set to work by Russia; and did not care one millionth part so much about the restoring of the Greeks to liberty, as he cared about keeping his own negroes in slavery in Virginia; and it was curious enough, to be sure, to hear a man who had left about fifteen hundred negro slaves at home, working upon his estate, begin, the moment he got to the Capitol, prattling away about its being the duty of all Christian nations to assist the Greeks, that is to say, to assist the Russians to get into the Mediterranean to be there ready to assist the Americans and France to curb the maritime power of England.[11]

Cobbett could not attack John Quincy Adams of Massachusetts on quite the same lines, but he found another in which he could also denounce the fortunes being made by land speculators in the United States. Two months after his attack on Monroe, he referred to the subject again in comments on recent speeches in Congress advocating active support for the Greeks.

> One would think they had enough to do, in their constant invasions upon the territories of the Indians, in their incessant works of extermination of all these original owners of the land, which land, the just and liberal Congress is continually selling to adventurers from all parts of the world; one would think that there was enough for any government of common enterprize to have upon their hands. They want, forsooth, to free the Greeks because their country was the cradle of liberty. The truth is that Mr Adams and his Congress have no desire to cause liberty to exist in Greece any

---

[11] *Political Register* 64, 17 November 1827.

more than they have to free the abject slaves of their own country. There is not perhaps a single week, during the session of the Congress, when troops of slaves, fastened together with a long chain, may not be seen within a few yards of the famous Capitol. Such people cannot be sincere. It is the extreme of folly to suppose it possible for them to be sincere.[12]

It was during this same period that Cobbett criticised republicanism itself as a form of government. The first time, in 1822, he chose the form of an Open Letter to a fellow reformer, Richard Carlile, the editor of a radical newspaper *The Republican*. Carlile, a fearless promoter of reform, and an ardent admirer of Thomas Paine, had in defiance of the law published Paine's *Age of Reason* and was at the time serving a six year prison sentence for seditious writing. Like Cobbett before him, he continued to publish his paper from prison, and in it he stated his conviction that there could be no real reform in Britain without the adoption of a republican form of government. In this Letter Cobbett distanced himself from such ultra-radical proposals, and attempted to demonstrate that republican governments were no guarantee of freedom. Selecting Paine himself as an example, he traced the shabby treatment meted out to him after his return to America from France in the early 1800s. Paine had been denied the right to vote ostensibly on the grounds that he was not a citizen, but in reality because he was the author of the *Age of Reason*. He was constantly derided and insulted; and a man who had shot at Paine through the window of his farmhouse and "who had no hesitation in *acknowledging* and *boasting* of the deed, was held to bail, tried, and acquitted amidst a *cheering audience*".[13] It was under a republican government, Cobbett

---

[12] *Political Register* 65, 5 January 1828.
[13] *Political Register* 41, 2 February 1822.

continued, that a man had been tried and imprisoned in New Jersey in 1819 for impugning the Holy Trinity; and if one were to use phrases such as Carlile had used — "in the year 1822 of the Carpenter's wife's son" — one would soon find oneself tarred, feathered and ridden on a rail in the United States. Neither were republican governments necessarily free from corruption: during his residence in Long Island, Cobbett had learned of open trafficking in places in the State of Pennsylvania.

In a speech to the Radical Reform Society in London some years later, Cobbett enlarged on the shortcomings of a republican system of government. He explained to his audience that the American government did not consist only of a President and Congress, but each of the twenty States had its own Senate and House of Representatives. In Pennsylvania the Governor, initially elected for three years, could be twice re-elected and so serve nine years in office. Because the Governor depended on votes for his office, the system produced "partialities of the worst description". He cited an instance where a robber who had been active in securing the election of a certain Governor, had been pardoned even before he came to trial. In another case in the same State, Cobbett stated that opponents of a recently elected Governor accused the new incumbent of murder and successfully convicted him to ten years solitary confinement, but when the appeal was heard in a higher court, the man was found to be innocent of the charge and freed. Although, Cobbett continued, he knew from personal experience that Pennsylvania was inhabited by kind and virtuous people, "such have been the effects of an elective chief magistrate".[14]

This startling volte-face in his writings on the American

---

[14] *Political Register* 68, 12 September 1829.

government and on the republican system on which it was founded, seems to give substance to Hazlitt's view of Cobbett as a man who

> takes both sides of a question, and maintains one as sturdily as the other... He is not like a man in danger of being *bed-rid* in his faculties: he tosses and tumbles about his unwieldy bulk, and when he is tired of lying on one side, relieves himself by turning on the other.[15]

Yet considered in their context they appear in a somewhat different light. The leaders in the movement for a Reform of Parliament did not all speak with one voice. Some, like Cobbett, advocated constitutional measures, some pressed for more overt defiance of the government, and yet others called for full scale revolution in the manner of the French and the overthrow of established institutions. It was not difficult, therefore, for the enemies of Reform to seize upon the more revolutionary sentiments and depict the movement as threatening the whole fabric of society. But when peace failed to bring with it the hoped for prosperity: when prices fell and farmers, merchants and manufacturers found themselves ruined; when the burden of taxation and rates showed no signs of diminishing; then many of the middle classes began to see the reform movement in a new light. The glaring anomalies of the franchise, the virtual exclusion of the new industrial towns from any representation in Parliament, the endemic corruption in high places, and the stonewalling by the government of even very modest proposals for a reform of the franchise, brought more and more people to view what they had previously perceived as dangerously 'jacobinical' demands to be perhaps both necessary and acceptable. Cobbett realised that to win these people fully to his side, it was imperative to allay their fears that Reform was necessarily

---

[15] Hazlitt, W, *Spirit of the Age*, 1825.

associated with the overthrow of the monarchy, or with atheism, or with the destruction of private property. "It is of the greatest importance", he said at a meeting of Reformers, "that we, who are taking the lead in this affair, should neglect nothing within our power to convince the people at large that our efforts do not tend to the producing of that confusion which would put property and life in danger". He believed that those who opposed reform because they would lose the many privileges and places they enjoyed under the present system were far less formidable than

> those who range themselves amongst Radical Reform, but who tell you at the same time that they themselves wish to go much further; that they wish for a total change in the form of government; the substance of the laws: that, in short, they are *republicans*. They cause our motives and intentions to be called in question, and be you well assured gentlemen, I beseech you to take this solemn assurance from me, that if we leave in the minds of the middle- classes of this country, that we have lurking in our minds motives and intentions of this description, we shall never, by our exertions, at all promote, but shall retard and perhaps ruin, the cause of radical reform.[16]

It seems, then, that Cobbett's criticisms of republicanism were due less to anti-American sentiments than to the need to dissociate himself and the Reform movement from the ultra-radicals. If he is to be condemned it should be for opportunism rather than inconsistency. Though he mistrusted some of the actions of Monroe and Adams and believed that corruption was creeping into American society, he continued to maintain that the American system was vastly superior to the unreformed system in Britain and

---

[16] *Political Register* 68, 12 September 1829.

was forthright in expressing his opinions on the subject. In 1828 he praised the Presidents past and present in these words.

> Whoever has been the observer of the character and conduct of Washington, Adams, Jefferson, Madison, Monroe, and lastly of the son of Adams, have observed in them men of spotless life, of the strictest decorum in manners, of the most perfect dignity in language and deportment, and have seen them treated with respect the most profound by all the people under their control, and by every foreign nation on the face of the earth. During the fifty-two years that these men have succeeded each other in their chief rulership of that country, *the whole of them have, in the whole of the fifty-two years, received only the sum of two hundred and ninety-nine thousand pounds*: that is to say, less than a *quarter part* of the sum which the King of England and his family have received in *every one of those fifty-two years*. It is not money or trappings that give dignity. Jefferson was so poor as to be in actual need of selling his paternal estate before his death; and yet whoever maintained his dignity and the dignity of his country in a more admirable manner than that celebrated man?[17]

A year later, we find him defending his advocacy of universal suffrage and the ballot by referring to the United States. In a Parliamentary debate the Marquis of Blandford attacked these demands of the reformers, saying that they would result in 'universal confusion'.

> And, my Lord, is there universal confusion in that country which has been FIFTY-THREE YEARS independent, the population of which has increased in that time from three millions to twelve, in which country has grown up a navy able to contend with ours single-handed? In the course of the fifty-three years

---

[17] *Political Register* 64, 9 August 1828.

there has been but one single commotion; and that was in consequence of an excise law which was soon after repealed. That commotion was put down upon the bare appearance of the Chief Magistrate surrounded by not a soul but volunteer citizens.[18]

(The reference here was to the Whiskey Rebellion of 1796.) The article went on to compare the peaceful state of America with that of England where whole districts were in a state of disturbance, where soldiers were sent to fire upon the people, where men were sent to prison for unlawful assembly, and where the scaffolds were "streaming with the blood of innumerable persons executed for treason". And the reason for the difference? Cobbett had no difficulty in finding the answer: in the United States, he asserted, the people were well-fed, well-clad, and very lightly taxed.

The decade from 1820 to 1830 was not an easy one for Cobbett. It was during this period that he became the foremost and most influential leader in the movement for Parliamentary Reform. Growing opinion in favour of reform throughout the country made the prospect of success tantalisingly close to realisation, and fully aware of the influence he wielded, Cobbett needed to be circumspect in his utterances. If he alienated his supporters among the middle classes by appearing to harbour 'jacobinical' designs on established institutions, the cause would founder. Only if one realises the difficulties under which he laboured in having to reconcile what he considered to be his prime duty — to better the lot of the destitute labourers in Britain — with his admiration and warm affection for the United States, can one understand how he could at one and the same time attack and defend, praise and censure, that country in which he freely acknowledged he had spent some of the happiest years of his life. Nor should it be

---
[18] *Political Register* 68, 25 July 1829.

overlooked that the *Political Register* was widely read in the United States as well as in Britain. In criticising certain aspects of American policies, Cobbett may well have had in mind not only the need to allay the fears of his English readers, but also the need to alert his American readers to what he perceived as signs of the beginnings of a betrayal of the noble principles upon which their nation was founded. That his suspicions were not without foundation will be seen in the course of the chapter to follow.

Cobbett was destined to live only five and a half years into the next decade (he died in June 1835) and in that period this clash of loyalties was resolved. For then Andrew Jackson was firmly established in the Presidency; a Reform Bill passed Parliament; and Cobbett, profiting from the extension of the franchise, was elected as Member of Parliament by the "sensible and virtuous and spirited people" of the town of Oldham in Lancashire.

14

Member of Parliament

In repudiating the republican ultra-radicals and insisting that a reform of the franchise was possible without overthrowing established institutions, Cobbett could justly claim that it was in no small measure due to his efforts that the Reform Bill of 1832 was enacted. Yet the extension of the franchise resulted in only a tiny number of radicals being elected to Parliament, and Cobbett found himself treading an ever lonelier path in the last years of his life. In his isolation he found a source of inspiration and hope in the actions of Andrew Jackson, the President of the United States. Cobbett's enthusiasm and mounting excitement as he followed the struggle between the pro-Bank and anti-Bank forces led him to devote many pages of the *Political Register* to praising Jackson for putting into practice in America what he had been advocating for the past thirty years as the essential first step towards radical reform in England — the liquidation of the National Debt and the destruction of the paper-money system. His admiration for Jackson needs to be set in the context of his own position in England at this time.

The so-called Great Reform Bill of 1832 was great only in one respect. By abolishing the rotten boroughs (those with only a handful of voters), enfranchising many of the new towns and increasing the number of county members, it went a long way towards making the representation in Parliament reflect the distribution of the population. But it fell far short of the demands of the radicals. Suffrage was confined to £10 freeholders in the towns and £50 copyholders and leaseholders in the country, thus excluding almost the whole of the labouring classes. Voting continued to be in public and bribery and intimidation were as rife at elections after 1832 as they were before the Bill was passed.

The Bill took nearly two years of debate from its first introduction to Parliament to its receiving the Royal Assent. During the furore which accompanied its chequered passage through the two Houses, Cobbett found himself differing from other reformers on a number of issues. Although he strongly advocated universal male suffrage and the ballot box, he was convinced that neither of these measures would ever be countenanced by the existing Parliament and believed it better to support the Bill than to have no extension of the franchise at all. Once the door was opened, he believed further reforms would follow: on this issue the more ultra-radicals condemned him for deserting the cause. On another issue the position was reversed, for here it was Cobbett who condemned many of those who supported the Bill for losing sight of the objectives. He had long insisted that the evils and abuses of the present system would never be overcome until Parliamentary representation had been extended, but that an extension of the franchise was, in itself, nothing. It was necessary only because without it there could be no change. But in the excitement engendered during the two years when Parliament was debating the Bill clause by clause and the issue hung precariously in the balance, Cobbett felt that attention seemed to be centred solely on getting the Bill passed and the reasons why it was necessary were being ignored. The movement for reform had by now been largely taken over by the middle classes, i.e. those who would benefit by the extended franchise. They, posing as the champions of the rights and liberties of the people, organised mass meetings up and down the country calling for "The Bill, the whole Bill, and nothing but the Bill". These meetings were, in Cobbett's opinion, distracting men's minds from the real issues at stake — the appalling distress in the country. In an Open Letter addressed "To the Working People" he wrote:

> What good will a reform of Parliament do you? The words rights, liberty, freedom and the like; the mere words are not worth a straw, and very frequently they serve as a cheat. What is the sound of liberty to a man who is compelled to work constantly and who is still, in spite of his toil, his vigilance, his frugality, half naked and half starved? To vote is a political right but it is of no real value unless men are BETTER OFF in consequence of possessing it.[1]

Cobbett had, as was seen in the last chapter, been moderate in his utterances in order to woo the middle classes to his side, but once he had forged the tool which would, he hoped, enable some radicals to be elected to the House of Commons, he directed all his energy to the task in hand. He put himself forward as a candidate in the General Election which followed the passing of the Bill on Fourteen Propositions and now with the Bill passed he no longer needed to be circumspect in quoting examples from the United States as models for Britain to follow. The Propositions included one to abolish the standing army and replace it by a militia on the lines of the militia raised in America; another to scrutinise all government pensions and sinecure posts and to reduce all salaries to the far more modest American standards. He called for the expropriation of all Crown and Church lands except for churches, churchyards and parsonage lands. Though

---

[1] *Political Register* 72, 7 May 1831.

Cobbett's description of the voters of Oldham as "sensible and virtuous" might be called into question, they surely richly deserved his epithet of "spirited".

In the context of his writings on America, the Propositions which most concern us here were those numbered 6 and 7 which dealt with the National Debt. The interest paid by the government to those who had lent it money amounted at this time to as much as one half of all the taxes raised, and many of these taxes were on essentials, such as sugar, soap, candles, beer, etc, and so fell heavily on the labouring classes. These two Propositions read as follows:

> 6. To cease during the first 6 months after June 1832, to pay interest on a fourth part of the debt; second 6 months, to cease to pay interest on another fourth; and so on for the other two-fourths; so that no more interest on any part of the debt would be paid after the end of two years.
>
> 7. To divide the proceeds of all the property mentioned in Para 5 (which dealt with the selling of Crown and Church lands) and also in Para 2 (which dealt with the selling of army establishments) in due proportion, on principles of equity, amongst the owners of what is called *stock*, or, in other words, the *fund holders*, or persons who lent their money; and to give to the fund holders, out of the taxes, nothing beyond these proceeds.[2]

Almost immediately after taking his seat in the Commons in January 1833, Cobbett began to act in accordance with the Propositions set forth in his manifesto. He submitted a long and detailed Amendment to the Address which set forth the new government's proposals for the coming session, putting forward in its place his own views on what needed to be done. But it was apparent from the start that he was fighting a battle against all odds. Apart from

---

[2] Cobbett's *Manchester Lectures*, 1831.

the twenty-three Irish Catholic members led by Daniel O'Connell who often supported Cobbett as he, in turn, supported them, such radical reforms as Cobbett proposed found almost no support. His Amendment to the Address was defeated by 323 votes to 23. Undeterred he launched his first specific attack on the government's financial policies by proposing a petition to the King asking him to remove Robert Peel from the Privy Council.

Peel had been appointed Home Secretary and a member of the Privy Council under the previous Tory government of 1828, and when the Whigs came to power in 1830 he became the Leader of the Opposition in the Commons. Privy Councillors, once appointed, retained their positions whether in or out of office, and Cobbett's proposal to strike him off the list, coming as it did from a newly elected Member of Parliament and attacking a former Secretary of State and leader of his party was almost unprecedented in audacity. The motion of censure Cobbett justified because Peel had been responsible for the measures adopted for Britain's return to specie payments. In spite of the fact that during the twenty-two years of war with France the government had suspended cash payments, there was never any question in the minds of leading economists, politicians and the public at large that the suspension was temporary and a return to a metallic currency based on gold, or gold and silver, would follow the ending of the war. Indeed, it will be remembered that the British government tried to maintain the fiction, and perhaps in some cases actually believed, that the paper currency in circulation was backed by an adequate supply of gold in the deposits throughout the period of suspension. Shortly after the war ended, the government stated that cash payments would be resumed in 1819, and, anticipating the resumption, the Bank of England had from 1816 onwards begun to redeem some of its notes in gold. As the date for full resumption drew near, the government made preparations for a complete return to cash payments, and appointed Committees to devise how best it should be done. "The question, in its various branches" wrote a contemporary historian, "gave rise to about fifty debates and conversations in the two Houses, the reports of which cover between four and five hundred columns of Hansard".[3]

Early in 1819, while Cobbett was in America, Robert Peel, the Chairman of the House of Commons Committee appointed to make preparations for the return to specie payments, laid his report before Parliament. Although full of assurances that the Bank had adequate resources, it admitted that some of the gold had been drained away partly because the Bank had resumed making some of its payments in gold coin. To ensure that there would be an adequate supply on resumption, Peel proposed a Bill which forbade the Bank to cash any more of its notes in coin for a further four years, but allowed sums exceeding £230 to be redeemed in gold ingots. Peel's Bill effectively prevented any run on gold: the small notes remained in circulation, and the demand for bars of gold worth £230 or more, hardly a convenient form of currency, was slight. At this time, Cobbett was living on Long Island, and the reader can readily imagine the scorn with which he received the news that yet another Bank Restriction Act had been enacted preventing redemption of Bank notes in cash.

The four year suspension of cash payments was later reduced to three, and in 1822 cash payments were at last resumed in Britain. Unlike the situation in the United States where cash payments had been suspended only during the War of 1812, and a return to specie resumed shortly

---

[3] Martineau, Harriet, *op cit,* Vol I, Ch XV.

afterwards, Britain had by 1822 experienced a suspension for nearly thirty years. So that whereas in America the Bank of the United States deemed it imperative to retract its note issues when there was a return to gold, knowing that those who held its notes would prefer specie in their pockets to the somewhat suspect and unfamiliar notes they were holding, the Bank of England was in a very different position. The partial resumption of cash payments between 1816 and 1819, the bland assurances of the government that there was an adequate supply of gold in the deposits, added to the fact that gold was available, albeit only in large sums and in ingots, not coin, lulled suspicion. Prices fell and had indeed been falling ever since the government had set a date for a return to specie, but the Panic of 1819 in America was not re-enacted in Britain when it returned to gold in 1822.

Another important reason why the return to specie in England had far less dramatic repercussions than in the United States was the unexpected opening of the Spanish Republics to British exporters in the early 1820s. Having suffered severely from the transition from a wartime to a peacetime economy and from competition from overseas once the seas were open again, the opportunities for investing in and exporting to the new republics was seized upon almost as a divine gift. Britain's return to specie occurred therefore in the midst of an almost unprecedented period of optimism. Harriet Martineau, the English historian of the period, describes the scene.

> As for what the speculation was like, it can hardly be recorded, even at this day, in the open pages of history, without a blush. Companies were formed to obtain gold and silver from mountain tops and clefts, where there were no workmen or tools to do the work, no fuel for the fires, and no roads or carriages to bring away the

> produce. There were to be pearls from the coast of Columbia; gems and pearls were to abound to such a degree that the jewels of ancient families were soon to be shamed. It is on record that a single share of the Real del Monte mine, on which £70 had been paid, yielded £2000 per cent, having risen speedily to a premium of £14.00 per share.
>
> People who declined the grosser kind of gambling — by Stock Exchange speculations — attached themselves to the idea of growing rich by trading with the new markets opened on the other side of the Atlantic. At Rio de Janeiro more Manchester goods arrived in a few weeks than had been before required for twenty years: and merchandise, (much of it perishable) was left exposed on the beach, among thieves and under variable weather, till the overcrowded warehouses could afford no room for its stowage. It is positively declared, that warming-pans from Birmingham were among the articles exposed under the burning sun of that sky; and that skates from Sheffield were offered for sale to a people who had never heard of ice.[4]

As the projects failed, so did the banks, and towards the end of 1825 a panic, far worse than that in America in 1819 ensued. "Here, a man passed with a gloomy face, and a bank-note clutched in his hand; there a woman wrung her hands and wept" continued Harriet Martineau and told how even now (she was writing in 1849 some twenty or more years later) middle class people "cannot think of that year without pain".

> They saw parents grow white-haired in a week's time; lovers parted on the eve of marriage, rural gentry quitting their lands; and whole families relinquishing every prospect in life, and standing as bare under the storm as Lear and his strange comrades on the heath.

---

[4] Martineau, Harriet, *op cit,* Vol II, Ch VIII.

They saw something even worse than all this. They saw the ties of family honour and harmony snapped by the strain of cupidity first, and discontent afterwards, and the members falling off from one another as enemies. They saw the guilty rewarded and the most virtuous involved as deeply as any in the retribution. But it would be an endless task to adduce the sorrows of that time; nor can their issue ever be recognised.[5]

Although the precipitating cause of the crash was not the return to specie payment, the fact that England had returned to cash in 1822 exacerbated the situation. For not only did the smaller banks fail, but the Bank of England, aware that in financial crises there is bound to be a great demand for gold, called in its loans, just as the Bank of the United States had done in 1819. Ever since 1819 when Peel's Bill providing for the return to gold in Britain in 1823 had passed Parliament, Cobbett had warned that the result would be a great fall in prices. In an Open Letter to the Middle Classes in England written from Long Island at the time, Cobbett compared the plight of the middle classes in America when prices plummeted after the return to specie there, with the very much worse consequences which would ensue in England because of the enormous weight of taxes. It would be the fund holders, the pensioners and all those on fixed salaries, he warned, who would benefit from the fall in prices, and those who paid taxes to support them who would be ruined. So certain was Cobbett that a return to specie without making provisions for reducing taxes by extinguishing the National Debt by what he called "an equitable adjustment" would plunge a large part of the country in ruin, that he issued at this time his famous challenge to the government. If, he wrote, he were to be proved wrong in his prediction, "I will give Castlereagh

---

[5] Martineau, Harriet, *op cit*, Vol II, Ch VIII.

leave to put me on a gridiron, while Sidmouth stirs the fire, and Canning stands by making a jest of my groans". From that time onward Cobbett often reproduced a picture of a gridiron on the mast-head of the *Political Register* and wrote of his intention to hold a great Feast of the Gridiron when his diagnosis should be proved to be correct. When the crash came in 1825 and 1826 he printed underneath the gridiron, not as formerly his challenge to the government, but these two extracts from recent speeches made in the House Commons.

> "He was sorry to see the day arrived, that SHOWED MR. COBBETT'S PROPHECIES TO BE REALIZED, and when, in fact, they were threatened with the FEAST OF THE GRIDIRON". Mr Hume's Speech in the House of Commons, 27th February, 1826.

> "He was persuaded that without an amicable, or, if he might use the words in that House, an 'Equitable Adjustment', they could not resort to a metallic, but must continue a paper currency". Mr Palmer's Speech in the House of Commons, 28th February 1826.[6]

The Feast was held, and thereafter the gridiron appeared on nearly every subsequent issue of the *Political Register* until Cobbett's death in 1835.

When Cobbett entered Parliament some seven years later in 1833, although there had been a partial recovery of the economy, the plight of the labouring classes had shown no improvement. The fall in prices had been accompanied by a fall in wages, there was widespread unemployment, and outbreaks of rioting and rick-burning by the distressed labourers were occurring throughout the country. Convinced that unless his radical financial policies as set out in his Propositions were followed there

---

[6] *Political Register* 57, 4 March 1826.

could be no relief for the near-starving working people, Cobbett chose to publicise his views by the startling motion of censure against Peel, the author of the policy for the return to gold. In his Address on the motion, Cobbett illustrated the effects of Peel's measures by quoting prices of various articles before the Bill was passed, then in 1822 when specie payment was resumed, and then in 1826 after the crash. For instance wool, selling at 2/11d a lb. in 1819, fell to 11d in 1822 and to 9d in 1826; wheat in those years from 11/8d a bushel in 1819 to 5/1d in 1822, and so on. Yet, and this was the crux of Cobbet's motion of censure, throughout the period of falling prices, no provision had been made to lower the interest rates paid to fund holders, so that their incomes effectually almost doubled; salaries of government officials, judges, army officers, etc, which had been increased during the time of high war-time prices were not reduced when prices fell; and farmers, manufacturers and merchants who had borrowed during the time of high prices now found themselves unable to repay their debts because of the huge fall in the prices they now obtained for their products. Furthermore, because no provision had been made to extinguish the National Debt, taxes were as high as ever. Peel's failure to make the necessary adjustments which a return to specie demanded had resulted, Cobbett said in his speech, "in setting landlords and tenants, creditors and debtors, brothers and sisters, parents and children, to tear each other to pieces, bringing down thousands of families from a state of competence and ease and many from a state of opulence, to a state of utter ruin and beggary" while those living on taxes received double pay and "were rolling in wealth and lording it over the rest of the community".[7] It is interesting to note how closely Cobbett's description of the crash follows that of

---

[7] *Political Register* 80, 18 May 1833.

Harriet Martineau written some fifteen years later, even though Martineau had a very high opinion of Robert Peel and a very low opinion of Cobbett.

This motion of Cobbett's, embracing as it did, his long held conviction that the measures he proposed were absolutely essential if the working people were ever to receive a fair share in the nation's wealth, received a stormy reception in the House of Commons. When he rose to speak a Scottish paper reported:

> The yells, groans and hootings which prevailed in the honourable House appear to have been louder than any that ever took place at an election. (*Glasgow Evening Post*, May 25th 1833)

Peel's speech in reply which unlike Cobbett's was loudly cheered, avoided any direct references to Cobbett's accusations and dwelt mainly on the fact that all his measures had had the full approval of the House. When Cobbett got up to question Peel's evasive and inadequate reply, the same Scottish paper continued:

> Another remarkable feature of the debate was the unparalleled clamour with which Mr COBBETT's voice was drowned when he rose to reply.

A description confirmed by *The Times* in its report of the debate.

> Mr Cobbett rose to reply amidst groans and murmurs from all parts of the House, during the continuance of which, throughout the hon Member's address, little or nothing of what he said could be heard in the Gallery. (*The Times* May 16th 1833)

The number of those who voted in support of Cobbett's motion was six; those against, two hundred and ninety-eight, and the Commons then voted to expunge Cobbett's motion from the Proceedings of the House.

Unable to obtain any hearing for his views, Cobbett found consolation in a very different reception given to him by his fellow-countrymen across the Atlantic. Two months after this débacle in the Commons, he reprinted in the *Political Register* a report in the *Philadelphia Gazette* of a meeting of Englishmen in that city held to celebrate his return to Parliament. Unaware at the time of the reception he had received in the House of Commons, they had met to celebrate the election of the man who had had the courage to stand for the truly radical programme of his Fourteen Propositions. The meeting resolved:

> That having witnessed the astonishing efforts of mind that have been made by our illustrious countryman, William Cobbett, to produce the change of public feeling which has destroyed the rotten borough system, and having the fullest confidence in his integrities and abilities, we highly approve of his introduction to the House of Commons.
>
> That the people of Oldham, having done themselves the honor of returning Mr Cobbett to Parliament, are entitled to our warmest thanks, and that an address expressive of our feelings be sent to the truly honest and independent electors of that borough.

The meeting was then addressed by a Thomas Brothers who expressed the hope that the British people would rally round and support "that great champion of the rights of Englishmen in carrying into effect his "wise propositions". Then addressing the people of Oldham he went on:

> be the result what it may, your children's children will have cause to be proud of their ancestors for having been the first to send to Parliament a man who has, for thirty years, been ably contending for the ancient institutions of his country: disputing, inch by inch, the encroachments of a faction that has scarcely left a vestige of right to the poor man.

Toasts were drunk to "the health of William Cobbett, the able, uncompromising, and invincible champion of a radical reformation in both church and state" and to the "patriotic, disinterested, and public-spirited electors of the borough of Oldham: may the beacon they have raised throw its powerful light over the entire nation".[8]

The high esteem in which Cobbet was held in the United States, by many Americans as well as Englishmen, was due to the fact that his writings on banking, paper-money and the National Debt were widely known and appreciated. In particular, they validated the financial measures currently being undertaken by President Jackson in order, as he put it, "to protect the poor and humble from the Tyranny of wealth and power".

Although the economic and social problems facing the United States in the 1820s and 1830s differed in very many respects from those in Britain, in America, too, there was a movement for reform. Her National Debt, miniscule compared to Britain's, was nevertheless considered a burden, particularly because revenue had to be raised to pay interest to her fund holders who, like their English counterparts, were among the richest section of the population and a sizeable proportion of whom were foreigners. The salaries paid to government officials were comparatively modest, and the United States had no sinecure posts in the English sense to give to its supporters. However, there were many Federal and State appointments where opportunities existed for kickbacks, bribes or outright embezzlement, and only too often these opportunities were eagerly seized upon by the incumbents, not a few of whom obtained their positions by offering to share the illicit proceeds with those who appointed them. Crown and church lands yielding

---

[8] *Political Register* 81, 13 July 1833.

huge revenues and influence to aristocratic families and the princes of the Church did not exist in America, but in the sale of public lands, it appeared that the interests of land speculators rather than the needs of the poorer sections of the people governed their allocation. Most pressing of all the needs for reform, was the plight of debtors forced to pay the interest on their loans in appreciated currency from incomes greatly diminished by the fall in prices after the return to gold and the Panic of 1819.

It was because Andrew Jackson had specifically pledged himself to tackle these problems and was adopting measures to eradicate the abuses that Cobbett, crying out in vain against much worse but very similar abuses in his own country, went to such lengths to publicize in England what was happening across the Atlantic. After Jackson became President, Cobbett's faith in the American Republic was restored, and he was able once again to hold up to his English readers a picture of the United States as an example which Britain would do well to follow.

Jackson held the office of President for two terms, from 1828 to 1836 — his second term expired eighteen months after Cobbett's death. Reference was made in the preceding chapter to his defeat by John Quincy Adams in the election of 1824, when Jackson polled the highest number of votes in the first ballot, but failed to obtain a majority over all so that the election had to be referred to the House of Representatives voting by States. Adams won by the narrowest of margins and was almost immediately accused by the Jackson party of having used bribery to obtain his victory. Throughout his four years in office charges of profligacy and corruption — nearly all of them unsubstantiated — were heaped upon him, and the subsequent election of 1828 swept Jackson to office with his promises of "reform, retrenchment and economy".

As in the previous election of 1824, Cobbett allowed the election of 1828 to pass without comment. His first reference to the Jackson administration occurred in the course of an Open Letter he published in the *Political Register* in July 1830 which he addressed to the new King, William IV who had recently succeeded to the throne after the death of his brother, George IV, the former Prince Regent. In this Letter he reminded the new King of how he had warned his brother, then the Prince Regent, of the folly of going to war with America.

> The first instance in which I offered advice to the late King was that relating to the war against the United States of America, than which, on our part, no war was ever more unjust in its grounds, insolent in its pretensions and avowed objects, more disgraceful in its result, and more fatal in its distant consequences.

England, he went on to say, had engaged in that war because of her hatred and fear of a republic prospering without titles or Lords and enjoying the blessings of cheap government.

> However, freedom defeated the undertaking; England suffered disgrace in attempting to crush it. She has a Debt of 70 million owing to that attempt; but the seat of freedom was preserved.

After the war was over, Cobbett explained, he had warned the Prince Regent in the Petition he had addressed to him from Long Island in 1817, of the necessity of curbing the power of the United States by securing Mexico from annexation. Here again his warnings had been ignored. Both John Quincy Adams and Jackson had passed measures to increase the American navy and it was now not at all improbable that she might soon extend her territory into Mexico and the Caribbean. "A few more years of the boroughmongering system, and an English sail will not dare to see the sun in the Gulf of Mexico, or in the West Indian Sea".

It was after having thus, as it were, presented his credentials to the new King, that Cobbett turned to the subject of the evils attendant on banking and paper-money and first mentioned the new American administration's determination to eradicate those evils.

> Upon this subject, your Majesty ought to be informed of the conduct of the Government of the United States with regard to that infamous thing called *paper-money*. The House of Representatives have very recently passed the following resolutions:
>
> "That paper-money, or the system of banking, is in its tendency ruinous to the interest of industry and dangerous to the liberties of the people"

and

> "that the House will not consent to the renewal of the charter of the bank of the United States".[9]

Six months later, in January 1831, Cobbett published in the *Political Register* the full text of Jackson's message to Congress of December 1830 which reviewed the actions of the government since he took office. It told of the progress made in adjusting differences with France and England; the successful beginning of his measures to remove the Indians from their reservations in the eastern States to areas west of the Mississippi; and how his policy of retrenchment in public spending was leading to the steady liquidation of the National Debt. The message ended with this warning shot aimed at the Bank of the United States.

The importance of the principles involved in the

---

[9] *Political Register* 70, 17 July 1830.

inquiry whether it will be proper to recharter the Bank of the United States requires that I should again call the attention of Congress to the subject. Nothing has occurred to lessen in any degree the dangers which many of our citizens apprehend from this institution as at present organised.

Jackson's message to Congress was published in the *Political Register* without any introduction or comment. One is tempted to speculate why Cobbett kept silent first when the great hero of New Orleans assumed the Presidency in 1828 and now, when his policies of retrenchment and economy were bearing fruit in the liquidation of the National Debt, a topic so dear to Cobbett's heart. The Reform Bill had not yet been passed and as was seen earlier, Cobbett was circumspect in all his utterances at this time. But there may have been other reasons. Did he, perhaps, find his Indian policy difficult to justify? Was he alarmed at his attempts to readjust America's boundaries with Mexico and feared the United States acquiring hegemony throughout the New World? Or was he uncertain whether Jackson was in earnest in threatening to abolish the Bank of the United States? All these issues may have influenced him, but overriding them was his complete dedication to the great issue of Parliamentary Reform in his own country. Everything was subordinated to this and it was not until the Bill was passed at the end of 1832 that Cobbett began to comment fully on affairs across the Atlantic.

There was, however, one occasion during the passage of the Reform Bill through Parliament when Cobbett used the example of the United States as an argument for reform. Of all those opposing the Bill, the Duke of Wellington was the most uncompromising. In a speech in the Lords opposing the Bill, he went so far as to say that the present system of representation in Parliament "possessed the full and entire confidence of the country" and that "no better system could ever be devised by the wit of man", a speech which shocked even some of his strongest supporters. Cobbett could not let such statements, so completely out of touch with the mood of so many of his countrymen, pass without comment and in the course of an article rebutting the Duke's remarks, he listed all his titles — Duke of Wellington, Marquess of Douro, Knight of the most Noble Order of the Garter, Knight Grand Gross of the most Honourable Order of the Bath, Prince of Waterloo, Duke of Cuidad Roderigo, Marquess of Torras Vedras, Count of Vimeira, etc and then compared the mass of honours given to Wellington to the way the heroes and statesmen in America were treated.

> Alas! how flat, after this, would appear the plain names of George Washington, John Adams, Thomas Jefferson, James Madison, James Monroe, John Quincy Adams and Andrew Jackson. How vapid! yet when one reflects that the people of whom they have been the chief magistrates, EAT MEAT THREE TIMES A DAY, while those who live in the country where these fine titles abound live upon potatoes from the 1st of January to the 31st of December; when one reflects on this, and when one knows at the same time that the jails of America are empty; that not ten men have been hanged out of twelve millions, in forty years; that such a thing as a special commission was never heard of in that land; that, under that mild and gentle government, no standing army has been required, though it has carried on a triumphant war, by sea as well as by land, against the undivided power of this great country itself; when one reflects on these things, one is almost tempted to believe that the plain names of George Washington and Andrew Jackson are worth all the titles, all the coronets, all the ribbons, stars and garters in the world.[10]

---
[10] *Political Register* 71, 12 February 1831.

And some months later, Cobbett found another opportunity to compare the two governments when reporting the death of James Monroe. He reprinted an article from a New York paper describing the funeral and the crowd of mourners who followed him to his grave, and told his readers how "this able and upright statesman" had, after retiring from office, lived quietly with his son-in-law in New York State without honours or fortune.

> Here, in our squandering system, he would have had pension, or sinecure, or grant; would have been living upon the sweat of the labourer; but then his death would have excited joy instead of mourning, and he would have gone to his grave either covered with curses, or wholly unobserved.[11]

A somewhat different issue regarding America caught Cobbett's attention towards the end of 1831. In one of the seemingly endless debates on the Reform Bill, mention was made of an article in the *North American Review* published in Boston which, in discussing the controversy raging in Britain, reported that many American politicians and professional men strongly supported those opposed to the Bill. After all that Cobbett had written on the United States, it was imperative for him to provide some explanation of how it could come about that men enjoying the blessings of a freely elected President and legislature should be in favour of England retaining her present system of aristocratic privilege and power. He rose magnificently to the challenge. Try to imagine, he told his readers, what England would be like if it got rid of its Boroughmongers and "this little tight and truss country", with its divisions healed, with its people happy and well fed — how powerful it would then become. Compare, he said, this vision of a reformed England with the situation in the United States:

---

[11] *Political Register* 73, 13 August 1831.

see more than one half of the country cursed for ever with dangers arising from Negro slavery; look at the country cut asunder cross-ways, from the sea to the Alleghany mountains, each inhabited by a people whose very interests make them more than half the enemy of the other; look at the division length-ways of the Western from the Atlantic states, and see the former much more the enemy of the latter than Spain can ever be of France.[12]

Cobbett then told his readers how when he was in America he used to tell the people there how quickly England would regain her old power when it had reformed its system: "it would do America no harm but my duty to my own country would forbid me to suffer you to indulge in ambitious views injurious to her greatness". Was it surprising, then, that some Americans saw a reformed Britain as a threat to their ambitions? Why was it that the Americans had rejoiced at the revolutions in France and Belgium in 1830 and had celebrated the overthrow of Charles X with public processions, but had received the news of Britain's proposals for reform with "dark doubts and glum silence or abuse and ridicule"? England's unhappy circumstances had led many people to emigrate to the States, bringing money and skills with them, but all this would cease if the country were to become prosperous under a new reformed system of government. "Amongst all the people that are enemies of reform, the land-jobbers of America are the very greatest", Cobbett declared. It was to their interest to see England slowly growing more and more feeble "while they were swaggering about all over the world 'purchasing' half Mexico and all Cuba" while England stood impotently by. Small wonder, then, that they were enemies of any movement for reform which might result in restoring

---

[12] *Political Register* 74, 29 October 1831.

England to her former position of one of the greatest of European powers.

Embroiled in the great battle to get the Reform Bill passed, Cobbett did not refer to the United States until more than a year later and after the Bill was passed. Interestingly his first articles on America dealt with those very divisions within the country which he had described in the article just quoted.

Towards the end of 1832 South Carolina threatened rebellion against the Federal government. Very briefly, the disaffection arose from the imposition of high tariffs on imported manufactured goods by the previous administrations in 1824 and 1828. South Carolina, whose prosperity was based on revenues received from exporting raw cotton suffered severely from the tariffs on two counts: firstly manufactured goods rose in price, and secondly, because Britain, shut out from many of its outlets for its exports to the United States by the high duties imposed, had less purchasing power to pay for imports from America, and began to look to other sources to supply its needs. Already suffering from competition from the new cotton plantations established further west on the rich lands around the Mississippi basin, South Carolina defied the Federal government by an Exposition questioning the power of the central government to pass laws detrimental to the interests of any of the States of the Union. In November 1832, the State legislature declared the tariff acts to be "unauthorised by the constitution of the United States, null, void and no law nor binding upon this State, its officers and citizens". It refused to collect the import duties and threatened to use force if Federal officers were sent to collect them. Jackson firmly upheld the right of the Federal government, and in March 1833 succeeded in getting Congress to pass a Bill authorising him to use force, if necessary, to ensure the customs duties were collected in the State. This measure, combined with a new tariff bill gradually reducing the duties, was successful in quashing the threatened insurrection, and South Carolina repealed its nullification law.

Cobbett's articles on this subject were written while South Carolina was still resisting the Federal government. The anti-reformers in Britain, still a powerful body even after the Reform Bill was passed, had seized upon the secessionist movement in South Carolina as an example of the weakness of a republican government, but Cobbett saw the movement as a "practical illustration of the rights which in every free country reside *somewhere* to resist oppressive taxation. It is unequal burdens, unequal taxation, of which these States complain, and they are now showing us that a free and spirited people will not feel this injustice without open resistance".[13] He explained to his readers how the heavy tariffs on imported goods had favoured the industrial States — New England, New York, New Jersey, Pennsylvania and Delaware — at the expense of the rest of the Union, where the absence of industrial centres forced them to buy manufactures from their northern neighbours now that British goods were excluded.

> The effects of the unjust boon (to the northern States) show themselves in lofty chimneys with thick smoke going out of their tops in immense buildings with endless windows, in power looms, and particularly in the establishment of those deadly instruments of usury and monopoly, banks, paper-money and accommodation notes.[14]

He was confident, however, that the American system

---

[13] *Political Register* 79, 26 January 1833.
[14] *Political Register* 79, 19 January 1833.

of government would be able to resolve the problem by obtaining "a seeming obedience" and that the Federal government would then "repeal the unjust taxes which caused the resistance" — a confidence confirmed two months later when Jackson's threat to use force and his subsequent measure to reduce the tariffs led South Carolina to repeal its nullification law.

These articles on South Carolina were written after Cobbett had taken his seat in Parliament but before he had had the opportunity to present his proposals for economic reform. Once it became apparent to him that his propositions were to find no support in Britain, he turned eagerly to watch and report on measures currently being adopted in the United States which, like his own proposals, sought to destroy "the deadly instruments of usury and monopoly, banks, paper-money and accommodation notes."

Cobbett's detestation of these deadly instruments was shared to the full and perhaps even exceeded by Andrew Jackson. Just as Cobbett looked back to the old days in his country before the Bank of England and the paper-money it spawned as a golden age when the labouring man had meat on his table and good clothes on his back, so did Jackson hark back to the ideals of the Founding Fathers of his country. "I weep for the Liberty of my country", he wrote shortly after he had been defeated by Adams in the Presidential election of 1824, "when I see at this early day of its 'successful experiment' that corruption has been imputed to many members of the House of Representatives, and the rights of the people have been bartered for promises of office". When elected President four years later, one of his first acts was to expose and punish the perpetrators of gross fraud and embezzlement in the Treasury Department, the Naval Department and the Customs Houses. Indeed, so widespread and accepted had corruption become under the previous administrations of Monroe and John Quincy Adams, that even one of Jackson's own appointees, a Samuel Swartwout, was found to have absconded with over a million dollars after a few years in office as Collector of Taxes in the Port of New York.

In his Message to Congress of December 1829 at the close of his first year in office, Jackson had spoken of the need to liquidate the National Debt and to scrutinise the necessity of continuing the existence of the Bank of the United States which, he maintained "had failed in the great end of establishing a uniform and sound currency". In the next year, 1830, he vetoed a number of Bills passed by Congress allocating revenues to internal improvements such as the building of roads, canals, lighthouses, dredging harbours, etc, on the grounds that the money should be used for paying off the National Debt, and as early as May 1830 he was able to declare that with the Debt now being reduced at the rate of $12 million a year, the remaining $36 million could be liquidated in three years time. The last instalment was, in fact, paid off in January 1835.

Having successfully put in train measures for eliminating the Debt, Jackson could turn his guns on the deadliest instrument of all — the Bank of the United States. It is almost impossible to exaggerate the hatred which the Bank inspired amongst a large section of the American people, particularly those living in the Western States. It stood, in their eyes, for the dominance of the old north-eastern States of the Union over the rest of the nation. Whereas the southern States, exemplified by South Carolina's defiance of the Federal government over tariffs, saw the great manufacturing interests in the north-east as the primary enemy, the farmers and merchants in the west directed their fire against bankers and financiers, and Jackson's exposure of widespread corruption deepened their hatred.

> The simpler forms of cheating and stealing were well enough known, but the more complicated dishonesty of distinguished-looking persons who sat at their desks month after month in plain view while appropriating other people's funds to their own use through bookkeeping entries, false reports or no reports, substitutions and euphemisms — all this was beyond the simplicities of common law.[15]

We saw in Cobbett's description of the Panic of 1819 the effects of the creation of the Second Bank of the United States and the return to specie in the area around New York City. In the newer lands in the west the effects were far more serious because so large a proportion of the population were farmers with mortgages on their lands. Nearly all westerners depended on credit. The long distances their produce had to travel to reach the markets meant long delays before payment was received, and loans were needed to tide farmers and merchants over the period between shipment and payment. The dependence of westerners on banks for mortgages and loans aroused the antagonism which naturally exists between the man toiling by the sweat of his brow and the man sitting comfortably at his desk. When the activities of the newly created Second Bank of the United States centred thousands of miles away resulted in loans becoming more difficult to obtain; when local banks failed and their notes became worthless; and when all this was accompanied by a devastating fall in prices for their produce, it was understandable why the westerners came to look upon the Bank as a Monster, and to rally behind the man who had pledged himself to destroy

---

[15] Bray Hammond *Banks and Politics in America*, p 269, Princeton University Press, 1957.

it. In the extracts that follow, Marvin Myers, discussing the phenomenon of what he terms "The Jacksonian Persuasion", conjures up the passionate feelings that lay behind the war with the Bank of the United States.

> The great specific mission of Jacksonian Democracy was against the Monster Bank. A monster is an unnatural thing, its acts are out of reason, and its threat cannot be estimated in popular practical terms.[16]
>
> * * *
>
> To the Bank's influence, Jacksonians traced constitutional impiety, consolidated national power, aristocratic privilege and plutocratic corruption.[17]
>
> * * *
>
> The Monster thrives in a medium of paper money, the mere specter of palpable values......to knock down the institution, then, and with it a false, rotten, unsubstantial world becomes the compelling object.[18]

A westerner himself, owning and farming land in Tennessee, Andrew Jackson was able to articulate the prevailing sentiments in his denunciations of the Bank. The charter of the Second Bank was not due to expire until 1836, but faced with Jackson's threat to destroy it, the Bank presented a memorial to Congress in 1832 for its continued existence. A Committee was appointed to examine the activities of the Bank, and after considering its report, Congress voted for the Bank's recharter. Jackson refused to sign the Bill on the grounds that only a few owned its shares and they alone reaped the profits from the funds invested in it by the government; that £8 million of its stock was owned by foreigners living outside the United States; and that its

---

[16] Myers Marvin, *The Jacksonian Persuasion*, Stanford University Press, 1957.
[17] *Ibid*, p 11.
[18] *Ibid*, p 26.

control was in the hands of the wealthy who violated the charter by using the vast funds at its disposal to bribe and corrupt Congressmen to support measures which would increase their power and influence over the nation's affairs. In his message to Congress justifying his veto of the Bill, Jackson said:

> It is to be regretted that the rich and powerful too often bend the acts of government to their selfish purposes. Distinctions in society will always exist under every just government. Equality of talents, of education, or of wealth cannot be produced by human institutions. In the full enjoyment of the gifts of Heaven and the fruits of superior industry, economy, and virtue, every man is equally entitled to protection by law; but when the laws undertake to add to these natural and just advantages artificial distinctions, to grant titles, gratuities, and exclusive privileges, to make the rich richer and the potent more powerful, the humbler members of society — the farmers, mechanics and labourers — who have neither the time nor the means of securing like favors to themselves, have a right to complain of the injustice of their Government.[19]

In his recent biography of Jackson, Robert Rimini confirms the President's belief that the Bank exerted undue influence.

> The Bank of the United States was indeed something of a monster just as Jackson said. It enjoyed enormous financial and political power... It corrupted Congressmen with loans and regular retainer's fees. It intruded into the political process to assist particular candidates for office over its possible enemies. It was the single institution that most represented the concentration of power within the nation and as such was seen by Jackson as a threat to the liberty of the American people.

---

[19] Quoted in Rimini, R, *Andrew Jackson and the Cause of American Freedom*, Vol II, p 368, Harper & Row, 1981.

Congress had the power to override a Presidential veto but needed a two-thirds majority to do so. The debate on the veto aroused intense interest with the pro-Bank faction depicting Jackson as a tyrant and dictator seeking to divest Congress of its authority, and succeeded in obtaining a small majority in favour of overriding the veto, but it fell far short of the two-thirds necessary. Jackson's stand was confirmed by the American people in the Presidential election held six months later at the end of 1832 in which Jackson was re-elected for a second term by 219 votes as against his main rival Henry Clay's total of 49.

> What must not be forgotten in any analysis is what this election demonstrated about Jackson's relation to the American people. Clay insisted on the Bank recharter as an issue with which to fight Old Hickory at the polls and it was as potent an issue as anyone could have desired. Still the issue and the Bank's money were not powerful enough to unseat the General — or come anywhere near it.

Secure in the knowledge that the nation supported him, Jackson felt free in his second term to open the war with the Monster in earnest. In order to destroy the Bank, Jackson wished to remove the deposits entrusted to it by the Treasury and to distribute them among a number of State banks, thus smashing its monopoly and diffusing its power throughout the nation. Many members of his cabinet, and Duane, the Secretary of the Treasury in particular, were against precipitate action and wished Congress to be consulted first. Jackson compromised and agreed not to remove the deposits existing in the Bank, but to draw on them gradually to meet current expenditure until they were exhausted. But he insisted that all future revenues received by the government were to be deposited in specially selected State Banks (the original number was seven but in the course of his Presidency the number was increased to nearly ninety) whose directors were known to be friendly to the present administration. This proposal Duane felt unable to accept without Congressional approval. Jackson dismissed him and appointed in his place a man willing to carry out his proposal, and in September 1833 an official announcement was made that as from October 1st all future deposits would be distributed among selected State banks, and those remaining in the Bank of the United States would be withdrawn until none were left. Jackson justified his action on the grounds that his election for a second term showed that the people were firmly behind him in desiring to root out the "sinister aspirations of wealth and to check the growth of an authority so unfriendly to liberal government and the just rights of the people".[20]

What Jackson had done by taking into his own hands the fiscal management of the nation's resources was to defy Congress and to initiate a hitherto unprecedented extension of Presidential power. Major cabinet appointments had to be approved by Congress: yet, without consulting Congress, Jackson had dismissed the approved Secretary of the Treasury, appointed another to carry out his programme and had himself decided which banks were to receive and administer the government's revenues. Congress, like Parliament in England, jealously upheld its right to control the nation's purse-strings, and the Bank, with powerful support in and out of Congress, prepared itself to fight back. In the war which followed there was no more staunch supporter of General Jackson than the Englishman, William Cobbett.

---

[20] Quoted in Rimini, R, *op cit* Vol III, p 98.

15

Andrew Jackson, the Greatest Benefactor of Mankind

Jackson's war with the Bank, begun in the middle of 1833, came at an opportune time in Cobbett's career for by then he had realised that, hard as he had worked for an extension of the franchise, the result was worthless. The new ministry under Lord Grey was no less severe than its predecessors in repressing discontent in the country, and measures were afoot to deter the growing number of paupers from asking for relief by incarcerating them in large Union workhouses far from their homes where they were to be subjected to a harsh regime of degrading work and just the minimum of nourishment to keep them alive. As for the reformed Parliament adopting any of the measures Cobbett had set forth in his Fourteen Propositions, all hopes were dashed.

When Cobbett heard of Jackson's letter justifying his veto of the Bill for a recharter of the Bank of the United States, he began to publish a series of Open Letters addressed to the President of the United States. In the first, written at the end of October 1833, he said he had read Jackson's letter justifying his veto "with the greatest possible attention and with the greatest possible delight".

> This letter is the first great blow; and indeed the first blow which by a man in great power, has been levelled

at that infernal system of paper-money, in a combat against which I have spent a very considerable part of my pretty long life.[1]

But even in his enthusiasm, Cobbett thought it right to explain that his first duty lay always with the welfare of his own country. Much as he regarded many of the Americans he had known with affection and gratitude, he must, he said, "love his country first, just as Americans showed how bravely they loved theirs in the 1812 war". It was because he saw in Jackson's measures a hope for his own country that he wished the President to succeed, and, if he did, "I shall rejoice for the sake of your country; but rejoice much more heartily for the sake of my own".

Having praised the President for the steps he was taking to eliminate the National Debt and for his action in removing the deposits from the Bank of the United States and distributing them among the state banks, he then warned him that this, in itself, was not enough.

> You certainly break up a great body of enemies, but although you do not create others so immediately formidable to you, you create a great body of influence in each of those states to which you transfer the money. Be assured that these bodies will combine against any government that could possibly be created, unless that government favour their views of pillaging the people.

All banks that issue paper-money, Cobbett insisted, have great influence.

> But though you have no debt, and scarcely any internal taxes, the paper-money of itself is sufficient to ruin the nation and destroy its liberties. You have undertaken to check the progress of this damnable scourge; and if you destroy this monster, your glorious victory of

---

[1] *Political Register* 82, 2 November 1833.

NEW ORLEANS will be forgotten, or will pass for very little, in the describing of your merits. But, sir, you will not do this by merely changing the seat of corruption. You must destroy the thing itself. You must put an end to the circulation of banknotes. Then your country will be what it formerly was, inhabited by virtuous and hospitable people content with the fair fruits of their labour. Already you are entitled to greater admiration and to more gratitude than any man living; and that you may consummate the glory of a life so useful, and which must be so renowned; that you will do this, by extirpating from your country this monster of all monsters, is the ardent prayer of him who has the honour to be, your most obedient and most humble servant, Wm. Cobbett.[2]

Cobbett followed up this letter with two more written shortly afterwards. In the first of these he referred to the fears being expressed in the United States that credit and commerce were being greatly injured by the President's action against the Bank. There was bound to be, Cobbett said, some disruption and hardship but he suggested that those opposed to the measures should consider "whether anything can happen to America so fatal as that of a gradual taking away of the farms from their virtuous farmers and their families, and giving them, for nothing, to scoundrels with pens stuck behind their ears, and the far greater part of whom never earned a pound of bread from the day of their birth to the present hour",[3] and he urged Jackson to stay firm for the longer the delay in carrying out the measures, the greater would be the suffering.

One cannot but be somewhat amused at Cobbett's third letter in which he showered Jackson with no less than eight books and pamphlets on the subject of usury and

---

[2] *Political Register* 82, 2 November 1833.
[3] *Political Register* 82, 30 November 1833.

paper-money and the evils they generated. They included a report of the Committee of the House of Commons on agricultural distress in Britain; a report on the spy system created in England to detect signs of rebellion; a book *The Curse of Paper Money and Banking* written by an American, William Gouge, with an introduction by himself; his own book *Paper Against Gold*, and a long article also by himself entitled "A Flash in the Pan" which gave a detailed exposition of his motion of censure on Peel, the reasons why he had condemned his policies, and the subsequent debate on his motion in the House of Commons. In all these Letters to the President Cobbett took pains to inform him of the present dreadful state of England: how the accumulation of wealth into fewer and fewer hands which banking and paper-money had made possible, had led to gross extravagance by the government, crippling taxation, the ruin of small farmers, to the reduction of the standard of living of many of the labouring classes to near starvation, to increasing crime and to outbreaks of serious rioting throughout the country.

Early in the next year, 1834, Cobbett wrote an article praising Jackson's great success in reducing America's National Debt, and compared his actions with the abortive attempts which Britain had made in trying to reduce her own. Ever since Pitt's days at the turn of the century, Britain had embarked on various schemes to create Sinking Funds to pay off her debt, but invariably the funds accumulated had been raided for other purposes and the debt had continued to augment. The American President, Cobbett explained, had acted in a very different way. He had, as Cobbett had long been urging his own government to do, reduced government expenditure, used the money saved to buy up the stocks owned by the fund holders and "burned it, as a man would burn a mortgage deed when he pays off a mortgage. Ours was a borrowing with one hand and paying with the other: it was taking money out of the waistcoat pocket and putting it into the breeches pocket".[4]

Cobbett followed up this article by an Open Letter addressed to the People of the United States of America.

> You remember PAINE, baptised "Tom"; for our aristocracy and money-men are so frugal that they cannot afford so long a word as Thomas. Our old friend "Tom" who gave tyranny harder knocks than any man who ever lived, concluded his dedication (which he addressed to Washington) to that thunderbolt, the first part of The Rights of Man, in these words: "That the new world may regenerate the old, is the fervent prayer of your most obedient servant, THOMAS PAINE".

He praised the people of America for continuing the work of regeneration ever since, and now, with their attack on the evils of the paper-money system, "seem to have set about finishing the good work". He ended the Letter with his own prayer.

> That your President may stand firmly to his resolution, that you may stand firmly by him; and that the pillaging, plundering, thieving, desolating monster of paper-money may be destroyed in your country, flesh, blood, sinews, veins, bone, skin, hair and all; is the sincere prayer of your faithful friend and most obedient servant, Wm. Cobbett.[5]

At this time the President needed the support of the people in his war with the Bank. Although many of the accusations Jackson levelled against the Second Bank of the United States for exerting pressure on and bribing

---

[4] *Political Register* 83, 11 January 1834.
[5] *Political Register* 83, 1 February 1834.

Congressmen and the press to advance policies favourable to its interests were justified, the Bank was well organised under its Director, Nicholas Biddle. It was cautious in its policies and kept the ratio of specie in its deposits to the amount it lent well under control. Hence, even when it no longer received government revenues, it was in a powerful position to fight back. Its first major action was to call in loans and demand repayment in specie, hoping in this way to cause panic among debtors which would lead them to demand a reversal of Jackson's policies. Economic circumstances were favourable to the Bank, for this was a time of boom and expansion created both by the growth of manufacturing and the opening up of internal markets by improved methods of transport and especially by the building of the great Erie Canal. The sudden calling in of loans when funds were urgently needed for carrying out large enterprises resulted, as the Bank intended, in a slump in many of the major cities. Prices fell, unemployment rose, banks failed, and deputations were sent to the White House urging the President to restore government revenues to the Bank of the United States so that loans would again be available. Matters came to a head in March 1834 when the Senate passed a motion of censure on the President for acting outside the powers granted him by the Constitution and declaring that the reasons he had given for removing the deposits were "unsatisfactory and insufficient".

Jackson, not called Old Hickory for nothing, refused to bend to the storm. To all the deputations he gave the same answer: ask the Bank, ask Biddle; he it is who has the specie, it is to him and not to me that you should apply for loans. To the Senate's motion of censure, Jackson replied with a Protest emphasising that he had been elected by the people to fight the Bank, and it was in consequence his solemn duty to take action against its "exposed abuses and corruptions". Jackson's firmness, buttressed by powerful articles in the pro-Jackson press accusing the Bank of deliberately engineering a panic had the desired effect. In April, a month after the Senate's motion of censure, the House of Representatives voted for no recharter of the Bank, for a continuance of the policy of depositing revenues in state banks, and, even more importantly, voted for a committee to be set up to enquire into the accusation that the Bank had instigated the panic for its own purposes. Biddle capitulated; the Bank of the United States eased its policies regarding loans, and the government granted extra money to state banks to enable them to extend their lending to overcome the crisis.

In his *Political Register* Cobbett kept his readers fully informed of these happenings across the Atlantic and their significance. How was it, he asked, that in the United States there had been a great increase in crime and pauperism in recent times? They had hardly any taxes, no great army, no great lords. They know nothing "of gateways costing seventy-five thousand pounds" and "have no half pay people to look through panes of glass costing five pounds a piece".[6] The answer, of course, was that they had created the Second Bank of the United States in 1816 and were now afflicted with the curse of paper-money. But in an article headed "Good News", Cobbett was able to reassure his readers:

> That that brave, skilful, resolute and inflexible man, who laid more than two thousand British troops dead on the plains before New Orleans and drove the survivors back helter-skelter into the sea; that brave man, who sprang from poor Irish emigrant parents; who engrafted the common soldier upon the plough boy during the war of the revolution; who engrafted the lawyer upon the

---

[6] *Political Register* 83, 1 March 1834.

common soldier; then the General upon the lawyer; and who has now engrafted the President upon the General; that this excellent man has now set resolutely to work to destroy that paper-money system.[7]

A week later, he followed this article by another called "Good News Indeed" in which he was able to report not only that the President was standing firm, but that his own contributions to the Bank war were not without effect. He quoted an extract from a letter published in the *New York Journal of Commerce*:

> It is reported that General Jackson has received a letter from William Cobbett encouraging him to persist in his hostility to monied monopolies, and informing him that the eyes of Europe are upon him and that the hopes of the peoples of Europe will be disappointed if he yields to the Bank in the present conflict.[8]

And another from a correspondent from New York who wrote to Cobbett to tell him that:

> Your Letters to the President have been published all over the country; and the frightful state to which the paper money has reduced England, does not a little, I can assure you, in support of the President's resolution.[9]

Emboldened by this praise, Cobbett wrote the introduction to his next Letter to the President in his own hand "for the purpose of giving you this mark of my respect" and because of "the boundless gratitude that I feel for the services which you have rendered to the cause of justice and freedom".[10] He told Jackson how his admiration for him had increased since he had read Eaton's *Life of Andrew*

---

[7] *Political Register* 83, 15 March 1834.
[8] *Political Register* 83, 22 March 1834.
[9] *Political Register* 83, 29 March 1834.
[10] *Political Register* 84, 5 April 1834.

Jackson and how he intended to publish this biography in England adding a further chapter covering the years from 1815 (where Eaton's biography ended) to the present day.

It is unlikely that when Cobbett wrote his Open Letters, he either expected or intended the person to whom he addressed the letters to take notice or act upon them: he used the form because by presenting his views to a named individual closely and actively involved in the subject he was discussing he could formulate them more pointedly than in an impersonal article. The Letters to Jackson, however, strike a somewhat different note. Ever since he had read Paine's *Decline and Fall of the English System of Finance* in the early 1800's, Cobbett held passionately to his conviction that the hideous and ever widening gap between the rich and the poor could never be closed until the deadly instruments of banking and paper-money had been destroyed. Of the many books he wrote, *Paper Against Gold* was the one he was most proud of, yet it was on the issues he raised in that book that he found the least support even among his fellow reformers, many of whom were frightened off by the drastic measures he proposed for eliminating the National Debt and returning to hard currency. Even when his hopes were buoyed up by his election to Parliament on Propositions based on the opinions he had expressed in *Paper Against Gold*, they were quickly dashed by the ignominious defeat he suffered at the hands of the House of Commons when he tried to present his views. Yet now, at what must have seemed to him the nadir of his political life, rejected and insulted in Parliament, and only too palpably proved to have been wrong in believing that the moderate extension of the franchise he had espoused would lead to the election of a significant body of reformers to the House of Commons, there arose from the ashes of his disappointment the phoenix of Andrew Jackson.

It is this that makes his Letters to the President different from any of the Open Letters he had written before. Even so, the possibility should not be discounted that Cobbett neither sent the books he listed in his third Letter nor wrote in his own hand the introduction to the fourth. He was an exceptionally able journalist, knowing to a nicety how to attract and keep his readers' attention. By listing the books and articles he said he had sent to Jackson, he was able to remind his readers of all he had written on the subject and prove to them that his ideas, scorned in his own country, were being taken seriously in the United States. By stating that he had written a letter to the President of the United States in his own hand, he suggested a certain intimacy between himself and the Chief Magistrate of the most powerful nation in the New World. Yet, given all the circumstances, it seems likely that the books and the handwritten introduction were indeed sent to the White House. Cobbett knew that his writings were widely read in America and his name well known there. Some months earlier he had reported in the *Political Register* a meeting which had been held in Brooklyn, New York, (by Americans, not Englishmen this time) to celebrate "Mr Cobbett's Birthday" at which toasts had been drunk to "The Author of Paper Against Gold" and to "The Surrey Ploughboy: may he clear the political fields of pensioner's docks, sinecure thistles, clerical and other obnoxious weeds, that have been planted in it by the odious boroughmongers",[11] a sure sign, from its phraseology that his writings on the evils that existed in England had been read with due attention.

Might he not, then, seeing how closely Jackson appeared to be following his prescriptions for ridding the country

---

[11] *Political Register* 80, 4 May, 1833.

of its National Debt, breaking the power of its national bank and returning to honest money based on gold, have believed that Jackson was in truth indebted to him and would welcome his advice and encouragement? Of advice and encouragement, Cobbett was not sparing in the body of the printed Letter that followed the handwritten introduction. He reminded the President that paper-money was invented in Britain "for the sole purpose of upholding a foreigner upon the throne (referring here to the creation of the Bank of England after William III from Holland was called to the throne to replace the exiled James II); that immediately after its invention the taxes raised upon the people became ten times as great as they had been before", and that through its agency the British government had been enabled to make wars which had plunged the country into ruin and its people into misery. Cobbett reiterated his belief that if Jackson succeeded in breaking his country free from the stranglehold of banking and paper-money, it would sound the death knell of similar institutions in the Old World. He believed, too, that the moneyed interests in Britain were fully alive to this threat to their continuing existence and were actively engaged in doing all they could to ensure that Jackson's experiment failed. He warned the President that the recent emancipation of British slaves in the West Indies was partly due to the British government's desire to create disturbances in the slave states in America, and that 'miscreants' in England were even now collecting money to preach emancipation in America with the purpose of injuring the United States by fostering rebellion and anarchy there.[12]

In the same month, Cobbett completed his book the *Life of Andrew Jackson*. He described in his *Political Register* the frontispiece which he had had specially designed for the

---

[12] See *Political Register* 84, 5 April 1834.

book which depicted the ramparts at New Orleans and Packenham's armies strewn about the plain below, and, he told his readers, "I have by no means forgotten to exhibit Packenham himself tumbling from his horse, shot dead by the Tennessee riflemen". In the background could be seen Lord Cochrane, the British admiral, "making off with his 200 ships and boats to go home and tell John Bull of the success of his enterprise in pursuit of 'booty and beauty'". Not content with all this, he had two gibbets drawn — on one hung a Creek Indian "one of the tens of thousands hired (by the British) to shed the blood of the American people" and on the other hung a "paper-money maker" as a tribute to the hero of the battle.

> But have I no feeling for the honour of my country? Yes; but not for its dishonour: not for contributing, either by silence or by word, to cause that to be believed of it which is false.

Then, castigating the army and navy for their never-ending pretensions that they had saved their country, Cobbett continued:

> Did they, then, save us at New Orleans? Did they save us at Chippewa? Did they save us at Sandusky? Did they save us at Plattsburgh? Did they save us at Fort Erie? Did they save us on the seas, where they got knocked to pieces, smashed, pummelled to morsels? Did the hectoring navy save us when, with 534 ships, of which 72 ships were of the line, and with 75,000 men, they were beaten like stock-fish by an American navy of 30 ships and vessels of war, and not one of the line? Is it for this that the heroes of this service now come and demand of us two millions a year in half-pay and retired allowances and pensions for their wives and children?[13]

---

[13] *Political Register* 84, 12 April 1834.

After such a frontispiece and such an introduction, the book itself comes as something of an anticlimax. The first five chapters were taken from Eaton's biography, with some passages left out which Cobbett thought "would not have been so interesting here, and which were not necessary to the furthering of my object". In these chapters, Eaton related how Andrew Jackson had been born in 1767 (he was four years younger than Cobbett) of recent immigrants from Ireland, and had been told from an early age stories of British oppression in Ireland. He joined the American armies at the age of fourteen in the War of Independence, studied and practised law in the State of Tennessee, and his "patriotism, firmness and talents" won him such respect that he was elected to Congress as Senator for Tennessee at the age of thirty. His career as Major General of the Tennessee volunteers, his skill and bravery in the encounters with Indians, his fortitude when wounded, his concern for the welfare of his men, his promotion to full General in the War of 1812 and his great victory at New Orleans, bring the story up to the beginning of 1815. Cobbett inserted occasional comments on the way, and added a sentence at the end of Eaton's description of the battle of New Orleans which read; "This battle broke the heart of European despotism; and the man who won it did in that one act, more for the good and the honour of the human race than ever yet was done by any man besides himself".

Cobbett's own chapter, covering the period from March 1815 to February 1834 began by describing Jackson's defeat by John Quincy Adams in the Presidential election of 1824 and his victory over Adams in that of 1828.

> The people wanted a man of tried fidelity and resolution; and, above all things, a man hostile to the frauds of paper-money; they knew they had a hydra to destroy

and they wanted a Hercules for a President. Now it was, and now it is, that he had, and has, to overcome a more deadly enemy of his country than either the British or the savages, namely the *monster* of paper-money.

Cobbett discussed in some detail the opposition Jackson faced from Henry Clay when he stood for a second term in the election of 1832. Although, Cobbett wrote, Clay spoke with great eloquence against the 'tyranny' of the 'dictator' Jackson, his speeches seemed "to have produced no more effect on the American people, than is produced on them by the squeaking of frogs, the clamour of the kiddadids, or the whistling of the whipper-wills". His account of Jackson's second term of office, his removal of the deposits and the Bank's efforts to thwart him is little different from the articles he wrote in the *Political Register* on the subject, and his chapter ends on an optimistic note, even though at the time of his writing some of the adverse effects of Jackson's measures were still being felt:

> the consequences have been bankruptcies all over the country, and a tremendous bursting of the bubble, a return, in great part already, to hard money; a sweeping away of banks, bankers and clerks, a cessation of the robbery of the industrious and of sustaining innumerable idlers upon the fruits of their toil.

And, Cobbett ended, when one has read the story of Jackson's life:

> not a shadow of doubt can be entertained that the President will never cease his efforts till he has totally suppressed that fraudulent, that robbing, that accursed paper money which has steeped England in her present troubles and her more than half revolution.

An interesting side-line on Cobbett's last chapter comes from his telling his readers some months later how he wrote it.

> The LIFE OF JACKSON was written one Saturday, during the last session of Parliament, I lying in bed having been up in the House till one o'clock in the morning, and my secretary taking down the words for the press. At the conclusion I remembered that I said to him: "There! that's a nice handful of hot lime, that will make the vagabonds curl up and foam and sputter and spew till they expire.[14]

Peter Porcupine was still alive and kicking at the age of seventy-one.

The 'handful of hot lime' Cobbett spoke of to his secretary probably referred not to the body of the book, but to the long Post-Script which he added at the end of the book. In this he related how when he had written the final chapter to Eaton's biography, he decided to look into the antecedents of that Earl, Packenham, who had led his large army, assembled and armed at such cost in the West Indies, to death and defeat on the plains of New Orleans, and to compare Packenham's ancestry with the humble pedigree of Andrew Jackson.

> Until I saw the peerage of the antagonist whom he laid sprawling upon the ground; until I saw this peerage; this bragging, this boasting peerage, I had not the means of making the contrast so striking as it ought to have been made.

He then quoted at length from the peerage book the entry for Packenham, which began with a William of Packenham of the time of Edward I (1272-1307), detailed all the marriages and all the lands and titles the family had accumulated over the centuries, down to the Earl, Thomas Packenham "killed in action near New Orleans, in America, January 8th 1815, to whose memory a monument is erected in the cathedral of St. Paul's, at the public expense".

---
[14] *Political Register* 86, 15 November 1834.

> Here is a pretty story: here is a rigmarole: this is the sort of way in which the base part of mankind is held in subjection. Why, it must give me pleasure; it must fill me with delight to see such contemptible rubbish brought to the test and to be proved to be worth not a straw. Mark, too, the curious way in which his death is mentioned: "killed in action near New Orleans in America.......". Now observe, first that you do not know whether he was a commander or not; second, whether those on his side were victors or not; third, whether it was a battle fought for the purpose of taking New Orleans or for defending it; but taking into view the fact immediately following, that he had a monument erected to his memory at St Paul's at the public expense; and is there one single man in this world who, being unacquainted with the facts, would not believe that he lost his life in the arms of victory in a battle which happened to take place near the city of New Orleans in America? Thus it is that the people of England have been basely betrayed and insulted and cheated.

Cobbett then went on to belittle the noble Earl for his stupidity in attacking Jackson's army without first using his artillery to destroy the parapet behind which Jackson's small handful of men were assembled, comparing his action with Jackson's masterly and courageous action in waiting until the last moment before opening fire.

> He (Packenham) could see with his glasses the cotton-bales, as plainly as I can see this paper; he knew that rifles were behind them; and he had the stupidity to believe that the Yankees would run away at the approach of his glittering army, and leave that army to vault over the cotton bags.
>
> This was something to make the nation pay for a monument to this man, and in St. Paul's too. But it is no matter: if a commander belongs to any of these people, beaten or not beaten, so that he die he is sure

to have a monument to his memory at the people's expense in order to keep up the blaze of these families. But, not to waste any more words upon the subject, here we have all this swaggering nobility, this hunting down from "William de Packenham" in the time of Edward the First to the present time; and only think of their publishing their mottoes: "Gloria virtutis umbra", that is to say "Glory is the shadow of virtue": a saying we can hardly understand the meaning of; but the more senseless, the more it excites the cogitating wonderment of stupid and base people.

Always aware of the accusations of inconsistency hurled against him by his detractors, Cobbett once again defended himself for having in the past extolled the British system of King, Lords and Commons. The Dukes and Earls and so forth that England has now, he explained,

> are no more like those in former times than a French crab (apple) is like a Newton pippin; or than a Catherine Peach (many degrees baser than a white turnip) is like a French *mignon* or an early *Montauban*. *Then* the lords called out their people, found them arms and clothing and provisions and money out of their own pockets. What do we behold now? Every great family, as it is called, *not* paying for warriors to come forth to defend their country, but *making the people pay for them*, men, women and children, to the amount of thousands and thousands upon thousands. In short it is a prodigious band of spungers living upon the labour of the industrious part of the community. If the people of England think nothing of these things, if this be their taste, if they throw away the substance to amuse themselves with the shadow, and will elect *Captain Swallow Pension*, and reject a man that scorns to deceive them, then let them suffer; and my consolation is, that *I will not suffer along with them.*

It was at the time that Cobbett was writing his *Life of*

Andrew Jackson that preparations were being made in the United States to abolish small bank notes and to replace them with gold and silver coin. In June 1832 a Coinage Act was passed and gold and silver coins newly minted. "The drops of sweat which fall from the farmer's brow will be turned into silver... His bushels of corn, wheat, etc will not be resolved into a dirty rag in the corner of pocket promising to pay what the insurers do not have the means of paying",[15] Jackson declared. So only a month after Cobbett had vented his spleen on the base fools in England who allowed themselves to be duped and deceived by high-sounding titles, he had the gratification of knowing that all the advice he had given the President was being followed. Even more gratifying to him was the fact that this was known in America. Spleen gave way to triumph when Cobbett was able to publish in the *Political Register* the following report from the *New York Commercial Advertiser* on an interview Jackson had had with a Committee from Delaware protesting at his removal of the deposits from the Bank of the United States.

> It will be seen from the interview between General Jackson and the Delaware committee, that he had adopted the opinions of the notorious Cobbett, and had determined to apply them to the commerce and institutions of the United States. We have in our possession two letters addressed by the arch-radical to General Jackson in October and November last, in which he extols to the skies the measure of removing the deposits, and recommends the very course which the President expressed his determination to the Committee to follow.[16]

Cobbett, composing this article in his office in London

---

[15] Quoted in Rimini, *op cit,* Vol II, p 169.
[16] *Political Register* 84, 10 May 1834.

in Bolt Court, could hardly find words to express his delight.

> Oh! my God!, how great is the pleasure which I derive from the thought of having been able to disturb this band of robbers. That I, sitting at Bolt Court, should be able to trouble these robbers; these plunderers of the working classes; these bands of miscreants who have brought the happy Government of America into jeopardy, and who have stripped thousands and hundreds of thousands of farmers of their farms, and made misery reign in a country which I knew so abounding in happiness! What pleasure, what pride, do I feel, what a guarantee for immortality; what a disregard for what becomes of this body when I witness the effect of the emanations of my mind.

He reminded his readers how he had in 1816 when the Second Bank of the United States was created, questioned its legality and warned that it would destroy "the happy mediocrity of fortune and of means" that existed in the nation, would create an aristocracy of wealth which would destroy the freedom of elections and lead finally to the destruction of the republican form of government in America. All this he had set out at length in an Open Letter to A.J. Dallas, the Secretary of the Treasury at the time of the creation of the Second Bank of the United States, and his predictions had been proved true.

> Look at the country at this moment and see the monster struggling to stifle industry and hold its ill-gotten power; behold neighbour against neighbour, employer against workman: look at a hundred and twenty banks actually broken, and the note-holders in part ruined; look at the nineteen banks broken in Pennsylvania: judge of the ruin that has taken place and the greater ruin that is yet to come. Look at all this, and say whether my opinions be not worthy of the attention of even this greatest of

men, the President of the United States.[17]

Confirmation that Cobbett's writings exerted influence in America came when his *Life of Andrew Jackson* was republished in the States, and the booksellers in Philadelphia met and voted that none of them would sell it. This, Cobbett believed, would only make it sell the more.

> Oh what a glory to me that I am able to drop the hot lime upon those devouring slugs, even from such a distance; that, sitting quietly at my farm, amused with the chirping of the birds in the day, and lulled to sleep by the carolling of the nightingale, I am able to drive to distraction the bands of fraudulent scoundrels, who are plundering my kind and hospitable friends, the farmers of America![18]

Further confirmation came a little later when it was reported that in

> newspapers opposed to Jackson's measures "strong and indignant execrations are being hurled against the celebrated William Cobbett whose recent "Life of Andrew Jackson" appears to have excited the most bitter hatred in the breasts of those persons opposed to the policy of that statesman. The long vocabulary of hard names appears to have been literally exhausted in describing what are termed his atrocities.[19]

Towards the close of 1834, during the Parliamentary recess, Cobbett toured Ireland. Although he had been aware for many years that distress in Ireland was even worse than in England, his association with the Irish Members of Parliament, and his admiration for their efforts to alleviate the misery, determined him to see the country himself

---

[17] *Ibid.*
[18] *Political Register* 86, 8 November 1834.
[19] *Political Register* 86, 15 November 1834.

so that he could more convincingly support them in the House of Commons. Shortly after he landed he addressed a short Letter to the President of the United States. "Here I am in this country which has the honour to be the birthplace of your father and mother, and which was very near to having the honour of being the birthplace of yourself"[20] and he went on to congratulate him yet again on his success in defeating the Bank of the United States which, he said, was causing great alarm among the moneyed interests in England.

In Ireland Cobbett found scenes such as he had never imagined to be possible: men women and children sleeping on wisps of straw in the streets of Dublin; miserable leaking cabins in the countryside with naked and starving children lying in filth. Yet all around he saw the land yielding abundant crops, and cattle, sheep and pigs well fed and well housed. Worse still, he saw the produce loaded into wagons and taken under armed escort to the docks and knew that, when it was sold in England, all the proceeds would go, not to the starving people who raised it, but to rich absentee landlords who would squander it in luxurious living.

In his many writings on Ireland over the years, Cobbett had always defended the Irish people against the accusations of barbarity, brutality and lawlessness levelled against them in Parliament and the press. He was convinced that if the atrocities of which they were accused were true, they could have been committed only by a people made desperate by ill-usage and hunger. In an issue of the *Political Register* many years previously he wrote an Open Letter addressed to the American People in which he compared the picture of the Irish people drawn in the British press with the Irishmen who had left their native country to settle in America.

---

[20] *Political Register* 86, 18 October 1834.

"Do you ever hear", he asked, addressing his American audience, but in reality speaking to his English readers,

> of any of this depravity, any of this untameable ferocity, any of these 'combinations against all law' on the part of these people? You want no army, no extraordinary police, no suspension of ordinary laws to keep them in order. Considering the low class of life, of which the great mass of Irish emigrants consist, my belief is, that they have surpassed in success the emigrants from any other nation. Does the salt air change their nature while they are crossing the seas? What is there in Pennsylvania or New York to subdue and keep down this ferocious disposition: this disposition to combine against 'all law'? Not a single bayonet! Nothing but, the constable's staff![21]

Having from the early 1800s stoutly defended the Irish people, it was a matter of very special interest to Cobbett that the President of the United States was the son of poor Irish emigrants, and he had dedicated his *Life of Andrew Jackson* to The Working People of Ireland from whom he had sprung. In a long introduction he expressed his feelings.

> My Friends. Ever since I became acquainted with the nature and extent of the ill-treatment of the people of Ireland, I have availed myself of every opportunity to endeavour to show that I held their persecutors in abhorrence. I now dedicate to you a history of the life of the bravest and greatest man now living in this world, or that ever has lived in this world, as far as my knowledge extends. It has given me pleasure, which I cannot describe, to find that this famous man sprang from poor emigrant Irish parents and that he was born in the United States of America two years after the landing of his parents. You will read, with uncommon

---

[21] *Political Register* 30, 4 May 1816.

interest, the clear proof of his having been urged on to perform the wonderful acts of his life by his recollection of the ill-treatment of his parents in their native land. For more than two hundred years, the laborious Irish people were scourged because, and only because, they would not apostatize from the religion of their fathers; and even to this day, every effort is made to keep them down and represent them as an inferior race of man. It is, therefore, in the name of truth and justice, that I send this book forth amongst the people of this whole kingdom to prove to them, that this ill-treated Ireland, this trampled-upon Ireland, has produced the greatest soldier and the greatest statesman whose name has ever yet appeared upon the records of valour and of wisdom. According to all the laws of all nations a man, though born in a foreign country, if born of parents native of another country, is a native of the country to which his parents belong. Thus this famous man is an *Irishman*; and I beseech you to look at his deeds and to applaud that just Providence, which has made him an instrument, though in a manner so indirect, of assisting to avenge the manifold wrongs of ill-treated Ireland.[22]

After he had witnessed the terrible scenes of distress in Ireland, any reservations Cobbett might have had in the past in expressing truly revolutionary sentiments were thrown to the winds. Since the Irish Parliament had been abolished by the Act of Union of 1800, Ireland had been ruled directly from Westminster. It was his own government that was responsible for the appalling conditions across the Irish Sea, and almost immediately after he returned to England at the end of 1834, Cobbett wrote a book *Legacy to Labourers*, as forthright in its questioning of authority as had been Paine's 'thunderbolt' *The Rights of Man* published in 1791. *Legacy to Labourers* set out to answer the questions: What

---

[22] *Life of Andrew Jackson*, 1834.

right have landlords to their lands? Can they do what they like with their lands? Can they use them so as to drive the natives from them? Can they use them so as to cause the natives to perish of hunger or of cold? This book, which Cobbett completed in December 1834, he dedicated to Sir Robert Peel who had just been appointed Prime Minister "A nation", he wrote in the dedication, "may exist without landlords; but without labourers, not only its political, but its physical existence is impossible; and therefore it is that the Apostle says that 'The husbandman that laboureth must be the first partaker of the fruits'".[23]

In February 1835, with the last Open Letter he was to write to Andrew Jackson, Cobbett sent the President a copy of the book.

> I do myself the honour; and I well consider the meaning of these words before I use them: I do myself the *very great honour* to send you for your acceptance, a copy of a little book which I have just written and published, called "A Legacy to Labourers". To you, sir, who are a lawyer, as well as the greatest statesman and the greatest military commander of this age, I need say nothing in explanation of the principles, of the facts, and of the arguments contained in this little book. But it may not be unuseful to inform you, that of all the things that I ever published, this, in point of effect, appears to be the greatest. An edition of five thousand copies has been able to stand the demand for only about twenty days; and I have not the smallest doubt that, before twelve months are over our heads, this work will have been read, and its principles adopted, by one million of Englishmen and Scotchmen; I having great doubt whether any effort of mine or of any body else, can cause it to be read by any considerable portion of the people of Ireland, whose lot I have just beheld

---

[23] *Legacy to Labourers*, 1834.

> with my own eyes; and with regard to whom, the only consolation I have is, that the oppressions of Ireland sent you forth to do the famous things which you have done, and the still more famous things which are in reserve for you to do.
>
> I pray you to receive this little book, Sir, as the fruit of the best talents, the most sedulous industry, and the most ardent zeal which I ever possessed: I beg you to receive it as the thing which I possess the most worthy of being presented to you, as the greatest benefactor of mankind whom I have ever known.[24]

Four months later, Cobbett was dead. He had been suffering for some time from periodic inflammations of the throat, and after staying up late for consecutive nights to vote in the House of Commons, he went down to his farm in Surrey seriously ill. His faculties remained with him to the end and in describing his last hours, one of his sons wrote:

> He continued to answer, with perfect clearness, every question that was put to him. In the last half hour his eyes became dim; and at ten minutes past one p.m. he leaned back, closed them as if to sleep, and died without a gasp.[25]

---

[24] *Political Register* 87, 14 February 1835.
[25] *Political Register* 87, 20 June, 1835.

Retrospect

Looking back over the years when Cobbett strove to promote good relations between England and America, one striking feature is his antipathy to Thomas Jefferson who was to become the third President of the United States, and on whom posterity has bestowed such high praise. By a strange quirk of fate it was to Jefferson that Cobbett first applied for employment when he arrived in Philadelphia from France in 1792. He had brought with him a letter of Introduction to Jefferson, then Secretary of State for Foreign Affairs under Washington's Presidency, from the American Minister at the Hague, William Short, recommending Cobbett to him as a man of worth and talent. How Cobbett came by this letter of introduction is not known for there exist almost no records of his activities during the six months he spent in France. On receiving Cobbett's letter offering his services to the government and enclosing Short's letter, Jefferson wrote Cobbett a courteous reply regretting that "public offices in our government are so few and of so little value, as to offer no resource to talent. When you shall have been here some small time, you will be able to judge in what way you can set out with the best prospects of success, and if I can serve you in it, I shall be very ready to do it". As Cobbett soon found employment as translator and teacher in Wilmington, he had no need to take up Jefferson's offer, and by the time he left Wilmington for Philadelphia in 1794, Jefferson had retired from office, and Cobbett was well on his way to becoming an impassioned francophobe, fanatically opposed to Jefferson and his party.

That Cobbett should have been antipathetic to Jefferson

while he was in the United States needs no explanation, utterly absorbed as he then was in denouncing the French Republic and all those who supported or defended it. In England during Jefferson's two terms as President from 1800 to 1808, Cobbett was almost fully engaged in inspiring his countrymen to defend themselves against the possibility of invasion by the bloodthirsty troops of France. Although the threat receded after Nelson's defeat of the French fleet at Trafalgar in 1804, it was not until his incarceration in Newgate in 1810, two years after Jefferson's terms of office had expired, that Cobbett began to see American affairs from a different and more informed viewpoint.

Was Cobbett, who read so widely, ever aware of the many aspects of Jefferson's opinions which coincided so closely with his own? No one could have agreed more strongly than Cobbett with Jefferson's statement in a letter he wrote to John Jay that "Cultivators of the earth are the most valuable citizens. They are the most vigorous, the most independent, and the most virtuous". Both Jefferson and Cobbett deplored the growth of cities and the herding together of labourers in manufactories. It was Jefferson who, in Washington's first administration., most vigorously (though unsuccessfully) opposed the creation of the First National Bank of the United States in 1791 using much the same arguments against banking and paper money that Cobbett was to use some twenty years later in his book *Paper Against Gold* which he wrote and published while in Newgate.

Cobbett, a cultivator of the earth for the first twenty years of his life, brought with him to the United States just those valuable qualities of vigour and independence that Jefferson had praised, but with them he also brought unlettered prejudice. He attacked Jefferson not only because of his support of the "blasphemous and anarchical" principles of the French Revolution: the Sage of Monticello was in Cobbett's eyes a dilettante philosopher who speculated on such futile questions as the origins of bones, the language of American Indians and the native endowments of the black races. There exists always a gulf between the cultured aristocrat and the self-taught commoner. Paradoxically in this case it was the American leader of the Democrat Party who was the aristocrat, and the defender of the British monarchy who was the commoner. The man who had moved in the intellectual salons of late eighteenth century France was always to speak a language unintelligible to the man who began his education in a barracks and completed it in a prison. Jefferson could write of Cobbett in 1798:

> Though I have made up my mind not to suffer calumny to disturb my tranquillity, yet I retain all my sensibilities for the approbation of the good and just. That is, indeed, the chief consolation for the hatred of so many, who, without the least personal knowledge, and on the sacred evidence of Porcupine and Fenno alone, cover me with their implacable hatred. The only return I will ever make them will be to do them all the good I can, in spite of their teeth.

Cobbett could never have written in those terms; his invariable response to calumnies heaped upon himself was to give a kick for a bite. It is this lack of what might be called nobility of sentiments in Cobbett's make up that blinded him to Jefferson's qualities. Nowhere is this better illustrated than in his reactions to Jefferson's efforts to avert the horrors of war by calling on his countrymen to endure the hardships of an Embargo. Cobbett knew instinctively that what he crudely called 'the back and the belly' were more powerful motivators of men's actions than appeals to their higher instincts. He wrote as a man utterly without pretensions, belittling titles, honours, rank and education, believing the common man to be the equal of his so-called superiors. Indeed he went further than this: he believed that men and women far from becoming more enlightened and humane as they rose in society and distanced themselves from those whose labours sustained their privileged positions, became more selfish, more greedy and more divorced from the simple virtues which mankind holds in common with the animal kingdom. When he was living on Long Island he wrote this entry in his journal where he compared the sow's attachment to her young with the common practice among the upper classes to hire wet nurses for their babies.

> March 16th 1818, Very cold wind. We try to get the sow and pigs into the buildings. But the pigs do not follow, and we cannot, with all our temptations of corn and all our caresses, get the sow to move without them by her side. She must remain 'till they choose to travel. How does nature, through the conduct of this animal, reproach those mothers who cast off their new-born infants to depend on a hireling's breast.

Cobbett's identification with the aspirations and sentiments of the common people from whom he sprang and with whom he had lived during the formative years of his life, was one source of his wide appeal as a journalist. This, combined with the clarity of his style, the felicity of his comparisons and illustrations, and the freshness and vigour with which he expressed his opinions, challenging his readers to find any arguments which could refute them, led William Hazlitt, one of the foremost literary critics in England of the time, to say of Cobbett. "He is not only unquestionably the most powerful political writer of the present day, but one of the best writers in the language. He speaks and thinks plain, broad, downright English".

Cobbett was not a popular journalist in the modern sense of the word which implies that the writer panders to the lowest taste (though in his early days as Peter Porcupine he could be accused of doing so in his "delightfully disgusting" pictures of French atrocities). His popularity stemmed from his addressing his readers as men like himself who would, once they became aware of the true facts, see through the hypocrisy and machinations of those who tried to delude them. It was because of this deeply held belief in the ordinary man's good sense and good judgement that he never despaired in spite of the long series of disillusions and disappointments that punctuated his life. The high expectations which the Abbe Raynal's writings had aroused in him when he first came to America were shattered when he left Wilmington for Philadelphia and found so many of its citizens rejoicing in the cruelties of the French Revolution. His high hopes that his writings would be influential in bringing Britain and the United States into an alliance against France faded when President Adams "tacked about" and sent a conciliatory mission to France. Far worse, for him, was the revelation that Britain, far from being the bulwark of liberty and justice he had imagined it to be, was a country where men lived in "want, hideous want" under a corrupt and repressive legislature callously indifferent to their plight.

It could be said that Cobbett owed America a great debt for showing him his true vocation as a writer. The debt deepened as the years progressed. America came to his rescue during the War of 1812 by vindicating his belief in the strength of a free people. What he found in his second visit to the United States in 1817 seemed to confirm all he had written of that country across the Atlantic "without a king, without lords, without knights and squires, and without any established church, without tythes and without priests paid from compulsory levies of money, and where the press is unrestrained and the government chosen by the people". And when he had to face the devastating realisation that his efforts in the cause of Reform had resulted in a Parliament little different from its predecessors, and that his own election to it found him impotent to better the lot of the working people, he was able once again to look across the Atlantic for inspiration. There, President Andrew Jackson was engaged in what he called his War with the Monster Bank, and beginning to put into effect measures curtailing the power and influence of the bankers and financiers in the United States; measures which Cobbett had advocated in his book *Paper Against Gold* which he wrote and published while serving his sentence in Newgate and continued to advocate on the floor of the House of Commons after he took his seat as a Member of Parliament.

In his last years Cobbett devoted very many pages of his *Political Register* to praising President Jackson, and perhaps it is as well that he died before it became apparent that Jackson's War with the Monster Bank was to be as unsuccessful in its outcome as had been his own attempts to reform the British Parliamentary system. As it was, he was able to end his life on a note of high optimism. In April 1835 just two months before he died; he wrote from his farm in Surrey an article for his *Political Register* in which he compared the cuckoo's ruthless use of other birds to bring up its young with "the at once lazy and greedy and ungrateful and cruel vagabonds who devour the fruit of our labour".

> This morning, long before four o'clock. I heard the blackbirds making the fields echo with their whistles; and a few minutes after four, I, for the first time this year, heard the cuckoo which I never before heard earlier than May-day. But, my .friends, I do verily believe that, before we shall hear this harbinger of summer again, the

vagabonds, of whom it is the type, will have received a souse, such as they never received before.

One wonders whether, had it not been for the existence of the republic of the United States of America, Cobbett would have kept intact to the end his belief that his efforts had not been in vain and his faith that better times lay ahead for the people of the United Kingdom.

Cobbett's writings referred to in the book

Periodicals:
    The Political Censor, 1796-7, Philadelphia
    Porcupine's Gazette, 1797-1800, Philadelphia
    The Rushlight, 1800, New York
    The Political Register, 1802-1835, London
    The American Political Register, 1816, New York

Books and Pamphlets:
    A Bone to Gnaw for the Democrats, 1795
    A Little Plain English Address to the People of the United States, 1795
    The Bloody Buoy, 1796
    The Life and Adventures of Peter Porcupine, 1796
    The Cannibal's Progress, 1798
    Letters to Thornton 1795-1800 (edited by G D H Cole 1937)
    The Court Martial, 1809
    Paper Against Gold, 1815
    A History of the Protestant Reformation, 1819
    The Emigrant's Guide, 1829
    Rural Rides, 1830
    Manchester Lectures, 1830
    History of the Regency and Reign of George IV, 1830
    Legacy to Labourers, 1834
    Life of Andrew Jackson, 1834

Bibliography

BAILEY, Thomas. *A Diplomatic History of the American People*, Appleton Century Crofts, New York, 1964.
BEARD, C A and M R, *The Rise of American Civilisation*, Macmillan Co, New York, 1930.
BOWERS Claude G, *Jefferson & Hamilton*, Houghton Mifflin Co, 1925.
BRIGGS, Asa, *The Age of Improvement*, Longmans 1959.
BRISSOT de Warville, J P, *New Travels in the United States of America*, performed in 1788, J S Jordan, 1792.
BROWN, Roger H, *The Republic in Peril*, Columbia University Press, 1964.

CHESTERTON, G K, *Cobbett*, Hodder & Stoughton, 1926.
CLARK, M E, *Peter Porcupine in America, The Career of William Cobbett 1792-1800*, Philadelphia, 1939.
CAFFREY, Kat, *The Anglo-American War 1812-1815*, Andre Deutsch, 1978.
COBBETT, William, see separate sheet.
COLE, G D H, *The Life of William Cobbett*, Collins & Co, 1924.
COLE, G D H (ed.) *Cobbett's Letters to Thornton 1797-1800*, 1937.
COLES, Harry L, *The War of 1812*, University of Chicago Press, 1965.

DANGERFIELD, George, *The Era of Good Feelings*, Methuen & Co, London 1953.
DEWEY, Davis Rich, *Financial History of the United States*,

Longman Green & Co, 1903.
DICKENS, Charles, *American Notes* 1842.
Martin Chuzzlewit, 1834.

FAY, Bernard *L'Esprit Revolutionnaire en France et aux Etats-Unis*, Paris, 1925.
FEARON, Henry, *Sketches of America*, Longman Hurst, Rees, Orme & Brown. 1819.
FISHER, H A L, *Napoleon*, Oxford University Press, 1967.
FOSTER, Sir Augustus, *Jeffersonian America*, Huntingdon Library, 1954.
FREEMAN, D S, *Washington,* Eyre & Spottiswoode, 1970.

GASKELL, Elizabeth, *Sylvia's Lovers*, Everyman Library, 1964.

HAMILTON, Thomas, *Men and Manners in America*, Wm. Blackwood & Sons, 1843.
HAMMOND, BRAY, *Banks & Politics in America*, Princeton University Press, 1957.
HAMPTON, Christopher (ed.) *A Radical Reader,* Penguin Books, 1984.
HAZLITT, William, *The Spirit of the Age*, London 1935.
HIBBERT, Christopher, *George IV Regent and King*, Allen Lane, 1973.
HINDE, Wendy, *George Canning,* Collins, 1973.
HOFSTADER, Richard, *The American Political Tradition*, J Cape, 1962.
HORSMAN, Reginald, *The Causes of the War of 1812*, University of Pennsylvania Press, 1962.

KOCH, Adriénne, *Jefferson and Madison: The Great Collaboration,* Oxford University Press, 1976.

MACKAY, Hitsman, *The Incredible War of 1812,* University of Toronto Press 1965.
MACKENZIE, Norman, *The Escape from Elba*, Oxford University Press, 1982.
McMASTER, J B, *A History of the People of the United States*, D Appleton & Co, New York, 1895.
MALONE, Dumas, *Jefferson and his Time,* volumes 4 and 5, Little, Brown & Co, 1970.
MARTINEAU, Harriet, *History of England During the Thirty Year's Peace*, Charles Knight, 1849.
Society in America, Saunders & Otley, 1839.
MELVILLE, Lewis, *The Life and Letters of William Cobbett*, Bodley Head, 1923.
MORISON, S E, *The Oxford History of the American People,* New York – Oxford University Press, 1965.
MYERS, Marvin, *The Jacksonian Persuasion: Politics and Belief,* Stanford University Press, 1957.

OLIVER, F S, *The Life of Alexander Hamilton: An Essay on the American Union,* Thomas Nelson & Sons, 1906.
OMAN, Carola, *Britain Against Napoleon*, Faber & Faber, 1942.

PENDLE, George, *A Huistory of Latin America*, Pelican, Penguin, 1963.
PERKINS, Bradford, *The First Rapprochement: England and the US 1795-1805*, University of Pennsylvania Press, 1955.
Prologue to War 1805-1812, University of California Press, 1961.
Castlereagh and Adams, 1812-1823, University of California Press, 1964.
PERKINS, Dexter, *A History of the Monroe Doctrine*, Longmans, 1960.

PHILLPOTTS, Eden, *The American Prisoner*, 1904.
The Farm of the Dagger, 1904.

RAYNAL, The Abbé, *The Revolution of America,* Translated, London 1781.
REILLEY, Robin, *The British at the Gates*, Cassell, 1974.
RIMINI, R V, *Andrew Jackson and the Cause of American Freedom 1822-1832*, Harper & Row, 1981.
ROTHBARD, Murray N, *The Panic of 1819*, Columbia University Press, 1962.
RUSH, Richard, *A Residence at the Court of London, 1819-1825*, Rich Bentley, 1845.

SEARS, L M, *Jefferson and the Embargo*, Duke University Press, 1927.
SMELSER, Marshall, *The Democratic Republic,* Harper & Row, 1968.
SMITH, Edward, *William Cobbett: a Biography*, Sampson, Low, Marston, Searle & Rivington, 1878.
SMITH, Sydney, *Works*, Vol 1, 1859.
SMITH, T C, *The Wars between England and America,* Williams and Norgate, 1914.
SPATER, George, *William Cobbett: The Poor Man's Friend*, Cambridge University Press, 1982.
STAGG, J C A, *Mr Madison's War,* Princeton University Press, 1983.
STOWE, Harriet Beecher, *Uncle Tom's Cabin*, 1852.
SUMNER, W G, *Andrew Jackson as a Public Man*, Houghton Mifflin & Co, 1890.

TOCQUEILLE, Alexis de, *Democracy in America,* Longmans Green & Co, 1875.
TROLLOPE, Frances, *Domestic Manners of the Americans,* Whittaker, Treacher & Co, 1832.

UPDYKE, Frank A, *The Diplomacy of the War of 1812*, John Hopkins Press, 1915.

Index

Adams, John, 2, 51, 189, 339
Adams, John Quincy, 40, 155, 275-87, 293, 328-32, 356, 357
Adams U.S.S, 146
Age of Reason, 256, 258, 263-8, 335
Alexandria, 146
American Packet letters, 188-90
American Political Register, 175-93
Amiens, peace of, 29
Apple Grafts, 324-5
Austria, 28, 61, 77, 288

Bainbridge, Captain, 132, 162
Baltimore, 142, 147, 158
Bank of England, 299, 305, 346, 350
Bank of the United States, 304-9, 330, 348, 359-69, 372-8, 390
Bank Restriction Acts, 301, 303, 306, 308
Banking, 297, 355
Bastille, 13
Bayard, James, 155, 156
Berkeley, Admiral, 40, 62, 101
Berlin Decrees, 47, 81
Biddle, Nicholas, 377-8
Birkbeck, Morris, 319
Birmingham, 86
Blacks (see Slaves)
Blockades, 65, 139, 141, 155-64
Bonaparte, Napoleon (see Napoleon)

Botley, 72, 73
Bourbon Dynasty, 136
Brighton Pavilion, 91
Brissot de Warville, 230, 235
Brock, Major-General, 125, 128
Broken Voyage, 43
Buenos Aires, 295
Burdett, Sir Francis, 74
Burke, Edmund, 24
Byron, Lord, 87

Canada, 18, 69, 76, 99, 110, 113, 123-9, 153-61
Canning, George, 40, 53, 55, 66-70, 271-9, 281-8
Capitol, 141
Carlile, Richard, 335
Carlton House, 91
Carolinas, 144
Cartwright, Major, 73, 170, 253, 266
Castlereagh, Viscount, 210, 214, 271, 274
Champlain, Lake, 125, 140, 147, 152, 184
Charlotte, Princess, 91, 191
Chesapeake, USS, 40-9, 52-6, 62-6, 89, 101
Chesterton, G K, 20, 258
Chile, 288
Churcher, Mrs, 228
Clark, Mary, 21
Clay, Henry, 69, 156, 248, 254, 285, 291, 370, 385
Cobbett, Anne (wife), 21, 22
Cobbett, James, 245
Cobbett, John, 212
Cobbett, William, boyhood 7, left home for London 7-8, joined army 8-9, sojourn in France 9-10, settled in Philadelphia 10-20, fined and returned to England 20, founded newspaper 29, imprisoned in Newgate 72, completed sentence 107, fled to Long Island 212,

returned home 262, elected MP 341, visited Ireland 392, died 396.
Cobbett, William, Jnr, 230, 245, 327
Collins, Charles, 261-2
Columbia, 295
Commissioners to Ghent, 155-9, 180, 248
Congress of the United States, 231
Congress of Vienna, 179
Connecticut, 119
Constitution, USS, 132
Contraband goods, 42
Convention of Hartford, 170
Cotton merchants, 65, 202, 291-2
Coventry Election, 270
Craig, Sir James, 112
Cuba, 273

Dearborn, General, 134
Decatur, Captain, 132, 133
Declaration of Independence, 11, 144, 145
Decrees, French, 61-5, 70-85, 95, 113
Democrat Party, 3, 16, 56, 78, 193, 196, 246
De Tocqueville, 236
Detroit, 134
Dickens, Charles, 228
Distress, 4, 86-7, 105, 144, 190, 209-12, 264, 291-2, 310, 312
Drunkenness, 232, 324
Duane, James, 370
Dublin, 392

Eaton, Daniel, 256
Elba, Island of, 136, 175, 199
Embargo, 51-5, 61-5, 86, 111-6, 122, 304, 399
Emigrants Guide, 320

Emigration, 318-324
Erie, Lake, 134, 184
Erskine, David, 66, 67, 68, 70, 101
Essex (merchantman), 43, 44

Fay, Bernard, 15
Fearon, Henry, 221, 235
Federal Army, 116-18
Federal Party, 3, 14, 31, 57, 108, 113, 163, 172, 187, 188, 329
Ferdinand VII, King of Spain, 272-88
Floridas, 100, 102, 123, 167, 168, 248, 286, 287
Folkestone, Lord, 326
Foster, Sir Augustus, 101, 102, 110, 112, 222, 234
Fourteen Propositions, 344-6, 351, 372
Fox, Charles, 92, 93
French Canadians, 9
French Decrees (see Decrees, French)

Gallatin, Albert, 155, 156, 159, 304
Garrison, William, 237
Gaskell, Elizabeth, 39
George III, 2, 51, 90, 145, 147
George IV (Prince Regent), 92-7, 123, 128, 147-9
Georgia, 144
Ghent, 151, 156, 161, 167, 170, 173, 246, 248
Gibbon, 266
Gordon Riots, 26
Grays Inn, 7
Great Lakes, 54, 159, 161
Greek Independence, 333
Grenville, Lord, 38
Gridiron, 351
Guelph, 205
Guerriere, HMS, 89, 132, 133

Habeas Corpus Act, 216, 245, 269
Halifax, 22, 40
Hamilton, Thomas, 222, 223, 236
Hammond, George, 22
Hampton, 141
Harper, Goodlee, 163
Hartford Convention, 165, 170, 186
Hazlitt, William, 400
Hempstead, North, 217
Henry, John, 115
Holland, 74, 75, 77
Honiton, 60
House of Commons, 18, 353
Hull, Isaac, 131, 132
Hull, William, 120, 124, 129, 132, 133, 134
Hume, David, 299
Hunt, Henry, 73, 312
Hunt, Leigh, 97
Hyde Park, 148

Important Considerations, 29-30, 122
Impressment, 2, 34, 49, 51, 62, 65, 88, 105, 107, 123-9, 134, 139, 155-60, 294, 331
Inconstant, brig,
Indefeasible Allegiance, 36-7, 134-5
Indian corn, 327
Indians, American, 98-9, 110, 121, 130, 134, 156, 160, 334, 358
Ireland, 391-4

Jackson, Andrew, 126, 168, 169, 231, 232, 248, 317, 329-30, 342, 355-7, 363, 372-402
Jackson, Francis, 68, 70, 80, 101
Jacobinism, 30, 33, 61, 108

Java, HMS, 132, 162
Jefferson, Thomas, 30-3, 45, 48, 53-7, 61, 108, 111, 163, 189, 234, 258, 339, 397-9
Jeffrey, Robert, 74, 77

Kent, Duke of, 23
Kingston (Canada), 121, 125

Law of Nations, 2
Le Havre, 10, 12
Leander, HMS, 44
Legacy to Labourers, 394, 395
Leopard, HMS, 41, 48
Liston, Sir Robert, 22
Little Belt, HMS, 89, 96
Livingston, Robert, 19
Liverpool, Lord, 163, 173, 214, 271, 312
Long Island, 5, 217-32, 245, 319
Louis XVI, 108
Louis XVII, 176, 177, 186
Louisiana, 29, 248, 286, 287
Louisiana Purchase, 100, 102, 304
Lowth Grammar, 8
Luddites, 87

Macedonia HMS, 132
Macon Act, 82, 85
Madison, James, 37, 55, 65-9, 82, 97, 102, 109-14, 122, 128, 130, 131, 138, 142-8, 155, 160, 170, 181, 246, 339
Maine, 146, 156, 159, 160
Maize, Indian corn, 327
Manumission, 237
Martineau, Harriet, 222, 230, 348, 353
Maryland, 144
Massachusetts, 54, 165-6

Merry, Anthony, 101
Mexico, 252, 275, 283, 289, 295, 357, 359, 362
Milan Decree, 81, 82
Militia, 119-20
Mississippi, 159
Mitchell, Colonel, 228-9
Mitford, Mary, 72
Monroe, James, 45, 97, 101-19, 159, 246, 284-90, 315-6, 328, 361
Monster Bank, 317, 367, 368, 369, 370
Montreal, 121, 125, 134
Morgan, John, 27

Napoleon, 3, 25, 28, 29, 38, 55, 61, 71, 74, 90, 95, 103, 109, 113, 136-143, 155, 156, 175-82, 185, 246
Napoleonic Wars, 2, 33, 139
National Debt, 297, 298, 342, 345, 350-9, 366, 373, 375, 380, 382
Naturalisation papers, 32, 37
Negro, (see blacks)
Neutrality, 33
New Brunswick, 8, 9, 121
New England, 3, 54, 108-13, 155, 160, 164, 364
New Jersey, 108, 364
New Orleans, 126, 141, 156, 158, 167, 168, 172, 246, 387
New Rochelle, 259
New York, 21, 108, 140, 158, 216, 364
Newgate Prison, 71, 74, 77, 105, 256
Niagara, 128
Nile, battle of, 26
Non-importation Act, 45, 50, 66, 67, 68, 70, 78, 80, 85, 93, 110, 111, 304
Nore, 35
Normandy, 10
North Hempstead, 217-9

Nova Scotia, 8, 121

O'Connell, Daniel, 346
Ontario, Lake, 128, 137
Orders in Council, 2, 47, 55, 61-7, 78-95, 102-12, 121-9, 139
Otis, Harrison Gray, 163

Paine, Thomas, 31, 255-68, 297-300, 335, 376, 380
Pakenham, General, 168-70, 383, 386, 387
Panic of 1819, 310, 311, 314, 348, 367
Paper Blockade, 65
Paper Against Gold, 301, 303, 306, 380
Paper money, 93, 342, 355, 358, 373-382
Parliament, 202-8
Passaquoddy Bay, 146
Peel, Robert, 271, 346, 347, 353
Peninsular War, 3, 111, 140
Pennsylvania, 57, 364
Perceval, Spencer, 87, 88, 91, 105, 112
Perry, Commander, 134, 162
Peterloo, 264
Philadelphia, 4, 7, 8, 9, 12, 16, 20, 22, 23, 150, 196
Pickering, Timothy, 97, 163, 164
Pinckney, Thomas, 45, 68, 69
Pinkney, William, 83, 102
Pitt, William, 28, 46, 59, 301, 302, 303
Plattsberg, 125-34, 140, 146, 152, 160, 184, 383
Political Register, 5, 29
Political Register, American edition, 193-208
Porcupine, Peter, 4, 122, 195
Porcupine, The newspaper, 27, 28, 29
Porcupine Works, 27
Portugal, 55
President, USS, 89

Press, English, 200-02
Press Gangs, 34, 35
Prevost, Sir George, 140, 146, 147, 152
Priestley, Joseph, 12, 13
Prince of Wales (see George IV)
Prince Regent (see George IV)
Prisoners of War, 134, 162, 199
Privateers, 42, 153
Proclamation of Hull, 127, 131
Prussia, 61, 77, 288

Quakers, 235
Quarterly Review, 201
Quasi-war, 32, 34
Quebec, 121

Randolph, John, 54
Raynal, Abbé, 10, 11, 60, 401
Reform Bill, 336-40, 342-4, 359, 361
Republican Party, 108, 109, 111, 112, 117, 119
Ricardo, David, 299
Rights of Man, 257, 376, 394
Rodgers, John, 89, 121, 133
Ross, General Robert, 141, 145, 146
Rousseau, Jean-Jacques, 11
Royal Family, 204-8
Rural Rides, 271
Rush, Dr Benjamin, 13, 15
Rush, Richard, 19, 20, 111, 281-4
Russell, John, 156
Russia, 28, 61, 136, 155, 288, 333, 334

San Domingo, 29
Sandwich, 127, 131
St Dominique, 12, 13

Index

St Petersburg, 155
Shelley, Percy Bysshe, 91, 185
Sidmouth, Lord, 210, 212, 214
Sinking Fund, 298, 375
Six Acts, 269
Slavery, 233-44, 331-2, 335, 362, 382
Smith, Adam, 299
Smith, Robert, 66, 80, 97
Smith, Sydney, 224, 241
South Carolina, 363, 366
Spain, 55, 272-294
Spanish America, 247-55, 271, 276, 280-3, 290-4
Spanish Minister, 19
Spithead, Mutiny of, 35
Stephens, James, 43
Stowe, Harriet Beecher, 237
Strong, Caleb, 164, 187
Sweden, 28, 75, 77

Taxes, 224
Tippicanoe, 99
Tithes, 226
Tobacco, 231-2
Toulon, 25
Trafalgar, battle of, 43
Treaty of Amiens, 29, 34
Treaty of Ghent, 167, 170-4
Treaty of Paris, 181
Trees, imported, 325
Trollope, Fanny, 231

Uncle Tom's Cabin, 237
United States, USS, 132, 133

Vermont, 152

Vittoria, battle of, 136

War of 1812, 113, 116-27, 128-51, 401
War of Independence, 1
War Hawks, 69, 98, 100, 110-2, 116, 124
Wars, anti-Jacobin, 2, 33, 41
Wars, Napoleonic (see Napoleonic Wars)
Wars, Peninsular (see Peninsular Wars)
Washington, DC, 138, 141-5, 158, 160, 183
Washington, George, 5, 17, 31, 118, 258, 359, 360
Waterloo, 4, 178, 184
Wealth of Nations, 299
Webster, Daniel, 305
Wellesley, Marquis, 37, 42
Wellington, Duke of, 69, 83-4, 102
West Indies, 37, 42, 129, 141, 153
Whigs, 59, 90
White House, 141
Wilberforce, William, 240-4
William IV, 357
Wilmington, 12
Windham, William, 27
Wood, Alderman, 73
Wordsworth, William, 10

Yellow Fever, 19-20
York (now Toronto), 121, 125, 134, 142
York, Duke of, 25